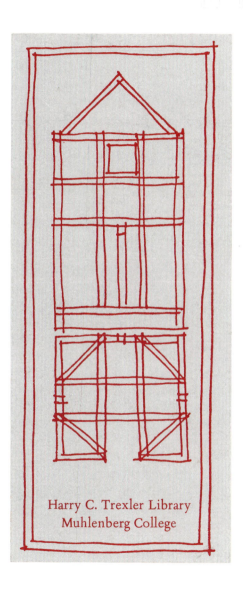

Harry C. Trexler Library
Muhlenberg College

Salah S. Hassan, PhD
Erdener Kaynak, PhD
Editors

Globalization of Consumer Markets: Structures and Strategies

Pre-publication REVIEWS, COMMENTARIES, EVALUATIONS . . .

"Two well-known international experts successfully managed to put together a volume on *Globalization of Consumer Markets*. THIS VOLUME IS LOADED WITH MOST UP-TO-DATE INFORMATION ON THIS MOST IMPORTANT AND, UP-TO-NOW, MOST NEGLECTED AREA OF INTERNATIONAL MARKETING. It is a must for academicians and practitioners alike."

A. Coskun Samli, PhD
Research Professor of Marketing and International Business, University of North Florida

Globalization of Consumer Markets
Structures and Strategies

INTERNATIONAL BUSINESS PRESS
Erdener Kaynak, PhD
Executive Editor

New, Recent, and Forthcoming Titles:

International Business Handbook edited by V. H. (Manek) Kirpalani

Sociopolitical Aspects of International Marketing edited by Erdener Kaynak

How to Manage for International Competitiveness edited by Abbas J. Ali

International Business Expansion into Less-Developed Countries: How to Use the International Finance Corporation Mechanism by James C. Baker

Product-Country Images: Impact and Role in International Marketing edited by Nicolas Papadopoulos and Louise A. Heslop

The Global Business: Four Key Marketing Strategies edited by Erdener Kaynak

Multinational Strategic Alliances edited by Refik Culpan

Market Evolution in Developing Countries: The Unfolding of the Indian Market by Subhash C. Jain

A Guide to Successful Business Relations with the Chinese by Huang Quanyu, Richard Andrulis, and Chen Tong

Industrial Products: A Guide to the International Marketing Economics Model by Hans Jansson

Euromarketing: Effective Strategies for International Trade and Export edited by Erdener Kaynak and Pervez N. Ghauri

Globalization of Consumer Markets: Structures and Strategies edited by Salah S. Hassan and Erdener Kaynak

Globalization
of Consumer Markets
Structures and Strategies

Salah S. Hassan, PhD
Erdener Kaynak, PhD
Editors

International Business Press
An Imprint of The Haworth Press, Inc.
New York • London • Norwood (Australia)

Published by

International Business Press, an imprint of The Haworth Press, Inc., 10 Alice Street, Binghamton, NY 13904-1580

Library of Congress Cataloging-in-Publication Data

Globalization of consumer markets : structures and strategies / Salah S. Hassan, Erdener Kaynak, editors.
    p.   cm.
    Includes bibliographical references and index.
    ISBN 1-56024-429-1 (acid-free paper).
    1. Export marketing–Management. 2. Advertising–Standards. 3. Consumer behavior. 4. International business enterprises–Management. I. Hassan, Salah S. II. Kaynak, Erdener.
HF1416.G58 1994
658.8'48–dc20
                                                    93-10607
                                                         CIP

ABOUT THE EDITORS

Salah S. Hassan, PhD, is an Associate Professor of Marketing at the School of Business and Public Management at The George Washington University. He is recognized for his research on global marketing, new product management, and market competitiveness. His work has been cited in leading publications such as *Advertising Age, AdWEEK,* and *Marketing News.* Dr. Hassan is widely published in trade and academic journals, and has two books on global marketing. He has consulted for marketing and research projects for several organizations in diverse industries such as travel and tourism, information services, packaged goods, and manufacturing. He has also conducted numerous executive training programs for international business managers under the auspices of the U.S. Agency for International Development, American University in Cairo, Westinghouse Electric Corporation, Price Waterhouse, and ARAMCO.

Erdener Kaynak, PhD, is a Professor of Marketing at the School of Business Administration at The Pennsylvania State University at Harrisburg. He has extensive teaching, research, consulting, and advising experiences in five continents in over 30 countries. A prolific author, Dr. Kaynak has published 18 books and over 150 articles in refereed scholarly and professional journals on international marketing and cross-national/cultural consumer behavior in a number of languages. One of his books was translated into Chinese and another one into Japanese. He has served on the Board of Governors of the Academy of Marketing Science and currently serves in the capacity of Director and Executive Vice President of International Management Development Association (IMDA). Dr. Kaynak also serves on a dozen U.S.- and European-based marketing and international business journal review boards and is Executive Editor for International Business Press (IBP) as well as being Senior Editor (International Business) for The Haworth Press, Inc., where he serves as Editor of *Journal of Global Marketing, Journal of International Consumer Marketing, Journal of Teaching in International Business, Journal of International Food and Agribusiness Marketing,* and *Journal of Euromarketing.* As a guest editor, he has prepared special issues for a number of leading U.S. and European journals. He was also the organizer and chair or co-chair of seven major international conferences. Dr. Kaynak is also listed in *Who is Who in America* and *Who is Who in Advertising.*

ABOUT THE CONTRIBUTORS

Riad Ajami is Professor of International Business in the College of Business at The Ohio State University, Columbus, OH.

Nizamettin Aydin is Associate Professor of International Business in the School of Business at Suffolk University, Boston, MA.

A. Tansu Barker is Professor of Marketing at Brock University, St. Catharines, Ontario, Canada.

Roger D. Blackwell is Professor of Marketing in the College of Business at The Ohio State University, Columbus, OH.

Michael R. Czinkota is Professor of Marketing and International Business in the School of Business Administration at Georgetown University, Washington, DC.

Lee D. Dahringer is Associate Professor of Marketing in the Emory Business School at Emory University, Atlanta, GA.

V. Mukunda Das is Professor of Rural Management at the Institute of Rural Management, Anand, Gujarat, India.

O. C. Ferrell is Distinguished Professor of Marketing and Business Ethics at Memphis State University, Memphis, TN.

John Paul Fraedrich is Assistant Professor in the Department of Marketing at Southern Illinois University at Carbondale, Carbondale, IL.

Charles D. Frame is Associate Professor of Marketing in the Emory Business School at Emory University, Atlanta, GA.

John H. Hallaq is Professor of Marketing in the College of Business and Economics at the University of Idaho, Moscow, ID.

Paul A. Herbig is affiliated with the Department of Management/Marketing in the College of Business Administration at Jacksonville State University, Jacksonville, AL.

Neil C. Herndon, Jr. is Assistant Professor in the Department of Marketing at Southwest Missouri State University, Springfield, MO.

John S. Hill is Associate Professor of International Business at the University of Alabama, Tuscaloosa, AL.

William L. James is Associate Professor and Chairperson of the Marketing Department at Hofstra University, Hempstead, NY.

Lea Prevel Katsanis is Assistant Professor of Marketing in the Faculty of Commerce and Administration at Concordia University, Montreal, Quebec H3G 1M8, Canada.

Hugh E. Kramer is affiliated with the Department of Marketing in the College of Business Administration at the University of Hawaii-Manoa, Honolulu, HI.

Janet McColl-Kennedy is Lecturer of Business in the Graduate School of Management at the University of Queensland, St. Lucia, Australia.

Jose F. Medina is Assistant Professor of Marketing in the College of Business at the University of Texas at San Antonio, San Antonio, TX.

Pavlos Michaels is Assistant Professor of Marketing at North Carolina A & T State University, Greensboro, NC.

Linda J. Morris is Associate Professor of Marketing in the College of Business and Economics at the University of Idaho, Moscow, ID.

C. P. Rao is University Professor of Marketing and Wal-Mart Lecturer in Strategic Marketing at the University of Arkansas, Fayetteville, AR.

Nina M. Ray is Assistant Professor of Marketing in the Department of Marketing and Finance at Boise State University, Boise, ID.

Ilkka A. Ronkainen is on the faculty of Marketing and International Business in the School of Business Administration at Georgetown University, Washington, DC.

Mary Ellen Ryder is Assistant Professor of Linguistics in the Department of English at Boise State University, Boise, ID.

Paul L. Sauer is Assistant Professor at the State University of New York at Buffalo, Amherst, NY.

Stanley V. Scott is Associate Professor of Marketing at The University of Alaska, Anchorage, AK.

Alan T. Shao is affiliated with the Department of Marketing in the College of Business Administration at the University of North Carolina at Charlotte, Charlotte, NC.

Dale H. Shao is affiliated with the Department of Management Information Systems in the College of Business Administration at East Carolina University, Greenville, NC.

Lawrence P. Shao is affiliated with the Department of Finance in the Graduate School of Business Administration at Fordham University, New York, NY.

Kristina Stephan is affiliated with The Ohio State University, Columbus, OH.

H. Rao Unnava is Assistant Professor at The Ohio State University, Columbus, OH.

Oliver Yau is Senior Lecturer in the Graduate School of Management at the University of Queensland, St. Lucia, Australia.

Murray A. Young is Assistant Professor at the University of Denver, Denver, CO.

CONTENTS

Foreword

Globalization of virtually all business sectors is having a dramatic impact on the flow of goods and services which, in turn, is speeding up the internationalization process of the world economy. From capital markets to production and resource sourcing, corporate executives have expanded their horizons to scan the world for optimum markets in which to operate. In response, national boundaries have been opened to service the needs of today's ever diverse markets. Enhanced global competition, the emergence of new industrialized economies, rising standards of living, and an increased awareness on the part of global consumers are major forces that underlie where and in what form goods are produced and where and in what form they are marketed.

The standardization of component parts, which could be used in the assembly/production of similar products on a world-wide scale, led to the interchangeability of parts in competing products. This paved the way for a wide range of industries to compete on a global basis utilizing identical components and making available less expensive replacement parts. It is logical, therefore, with identical or at least similar products competing effectively in markets throughout the world, that attention should shift from a primary focus on the globalization of industrial products and industrial markets to globalization of consumer products and, hence, to consumer markets. In fact, technology transfers by multinational firms, combined with the desires and expectations of well-informed consumers throughout the world, will speed the pace of globalization forward at a rapid pace throughout this decade and into the twenty-first century.

Responding to this change, in *Globalization of Consumer Markets: Structures and Strategies*, 33 authors, many of whom are world renowned scholars, provide major new insights into an array of decision areas confronting international marketing managers on an almost daily basis. Questions addressed are: whether or not a product can be extended across several markets or whether there is need for adaption; how a product should be priced in the various consumer markets; what the appropriate type of promotion is; what the existing channels are and how new channels can be developed; how strategies used in domestic markets are the same as those used in foreign markets–or how they must be adapted; what the best method of sourcing is; and, to what extent culture impacts on marketing decisions. Finally, issues such as just who the consumers are and what their preferences are–are they the same for Koreans as for Germans–are analyzed. In addressing these and other issues, several empirical studies, as well as case examples with marketing management implications, are included that will assist executives in managing more effectively in a rapidly changing global consumer marketplace and adjusting to structural changes taking place within individual markets.

The editors of *Globalization of Consumer Markets: Structures and Strategies* are well-recognized scholars and authorities in both academia and the private sector. Professors Salah S. Hassan and Erdener Kaynak have been strong contributors to marketing literature for more than a decade. Their combined travels have taken them to over 50 countries in all regions of the world, including many of the newly emerging nations of Eastern Europe, Latin America, Africa, and Asia. Their knowledge and insights provide an exciting blend of talents that are reflected in this most practical and useful text of readings.

Even the most casual observer cannot help but recognize how the global market place has changed in an era of a new consumer revolution. McDonald's has gone global and flourishes from Moscow to Jakarta. Kentucky Fried Chicken serves millions of Chinese customers each week as an alternative to their staple diet. Levi Jeans are a status symbol in Eastern Europe as are T-shirts with the logos and faces of the newest rock bands. There are more Rolls Royce and Mercedes automobiles in Guangzhou than there are in Hong Kong, and European designer watches (real, not fake) grace the wrist of many government officials and businessmen in the developing countries of Africa, the Near East, and Southeast Asia.

Take one country as an example: Vietnam. In January of 1990, few consumer products from abroad were evident in the marketplace. Noticeably evident, however, were a variety of Japanese, Korean, and Taiwanese made television sets, radios, record players, and video cassettes that joined with the most popular brands of American, European, and Japanese cigarettes and hard liquors. Bicycles were a status symbol, good restaurants were few in number, and, with the exception of the Floating Hotel, accommodations were at best fourth rate. Now in mid 1993, almost anything that is sold anywhere in the world can be purchased in key cities of Ho Chi Minh and Hanoi. New European, Japanese, and South Korean automobiles ply the streets fighting to get through the traffic jams of motor bikes and motorcycles (even including a few Super Harley Davidson varieties). It is not uncommon to see a well-dressed young woman wearing Revlon lipstick and having a Chanel or other designer scarf to accent her prim hat, western style dress, and high heels as she rides by on a shiny new motorcycle with a Gucci bag flapping in the breeze.

In spite of the U.S. embargo, if you need an IBM PC, a Hewlett Packard Laser Jet III Printer, or a replacement part for your 1950 Ford truck, Caterpillar tractor, or Carrier Air Conditioner, it can be obtained without much hassle. A pizza washed down with Singapore's "Tiger" or the Philippines' "San Miguel" beer has replaced rice and vegetables at lunch time for many. What is being experienced here is what one may observe elsewhere in the world: If it sells in New York, Paris, or Hong Kong, it can sell almost anywhere. Who would have believed ten years ago that specialty shops in Beijing would have difficulty keeping brand named goods such as Dior, Lanvin, Chanel, Gucci, and Louis Vitton on the shelves to meet the demands of the new cash rich society that has emerged.

Market structures will be altered considerably during the remainder of this decade and changes will be phenomenal. Consequently, marketers must not only continue to revise previous strategies for new product development, advertising, and channels for placing goods in the global marketplace, but also develop new strategies that will enhance their firm's competitiveness in both old and new markets.

Globalization of Consumer Markets: Structures and Strategies is both timely and a significant contribution to the field of international marketing management. As such, it is a must read for practitioners, academics, students, and researchers who wish to have a good grasp of what is happening in the global market place and, particularly, emerging markets that transcend both cultural and national boundaries.

Faculty will find it ideal as a text in upper level MBA marketing classes, as well as for executive programs and in-house corporate training activities. In addition, it also provides essential elements that can be utilized by governmental trade and commercial officers in assisting companies in their international expansion efforts in as much as the authors provide an understanding of trends and dynamics in an ever-evolving and increasingly competitive global economy.

Phillip D. Grub, D.B.A.
Aryamehr Professor of Multinational Management
The George Washington University;
Former President, Academy of International Business

Preface

In an increasingly growing global trade, consumer markets represent a major share. As world economies grow and prosper, consumers become more sophisticated and demanding in their request for products and services. In the future, successful international firms will be the ones that respond effectively to changes and developments taking place in the global market environment.

We developed this anthology on *Globalization of Consumer Markets* to address the issues related to various aspects of world consumer markets. The book treats the subject area within 15 chapters divided into five sections. In the introductory section, we set the tone for the book by examining critically issues and concepts that are related to globalizing consumer markets. In the second section, there are three chapters that look at degrees of globalization. The third section is devoted to market behavior and development. Section four is aimed at the study of marketing programs and processes in global consumer markets. The final section draws on managerial implications of globalizing consumer markets.

We extend our sincere thanks and appreciation to the contributors of this volume for providing such outstanding chapters. Thanks are due to The Haworth Press, Inc. of New York, London, and Norwood (Australia) for commissioning and publishing pioneering works in the frontiers of knowledge. In particular, we gratefully acknowledge the assistance, cooperation, and expert guidance of Bill Cohen, Publisher, and Bill Palmer, Managing Book Editor. We also appreciated the professional assistance of the editorial staff at The Haworth Press, Inc. Any errors or omissions found in this volume are our responsibility.

Salah S. Hassan,
Washington, DC

Erdener Kaynak,
Hummelstown, PA

Credits

This book's theme is based on two Special Issues of the *Journal of International Consumer Marketing* (Vol. 3, No. 2 and Vol. 3, No. 4, 1991). These two issues on "The Globalization of Consumer Markets" were guest edited by Salah S. Hassan. Related articles that fit the globalization theme were selected from other issues of *JICM*.

The chapters presented here were first published in the following issues of *JICM* and copyrighted by The Haworth Press, Inc.; all rights reserved: "The Globalizing Consumer Markets," Vol. 3(4), © 1991; "The Globalization of the U.S. Economy: Consumer Market Implications," Vol. 3(4), © 1991; "Identification of Global Consumer Segments." Vol. 3(2), © 1991; "International Product Rollout; A Country Cluster Approach," Vol. 4(1/2), © 1991; "The Processes Behind the Country of Origin Effect, Vol. 3(2), © 1991; "The Impact of Modernization on Consumer Innovativeness in a Developing Market," Vol. 3(4), © 1991; "Consumer Involvement in Services: An International Evaluation," Vol. 3(2), © 1991; "Conceptualization of India's Emerging Rural Consuming Systems," Vol. 3(4), © 1991; "Consumer Nondurable Products: Prospects for Global Advertising," Vol. 3(2), © 1991; "Are Global Markets with Standardized Advertising Campaigns Feasible?," Vol. 4(3), ©1992; "Winning the Global Advertising Race: Planning Globally, Acting Locally," Vol. 3(2), © 1991; "Toward an Understanding of the Use of Foreign Words in Print Advertising," Vol. 3(4), © 1991; "The Changing South Korean Marketplace: Product Perceptions of Consumer Goods," Vol. 2(3), © 1990; "Implications of Standardization in Global Markets," Vol. 3(4), © 1991; "A Values Comparison of Future Managers from West Germany and the United States," Vol. 4 (1/2), © 1991.

SECTION I.

INTRODUCTION

Market Globalization: An Introduction

Salah S. Hassan
Erdener Kaynak

Globalization is a watchword to be reckoned with throughout the 1990s and beyond. In view of the emergence of trading blocs in Europe, North America, East Asia, and elsewhere, we are also witnessing globalization of consumer markets. In particular, the so-called triad countries (Europe, North America, and Japan) account for approximately 14% of the world's population but they represent over 70% of the gross national product. As such, these countries absorb the major consumption of consumer products, as they are the most advanced consuming societies in the world. Not only do most of the product innovations take place in these countries, but they also serve as opinion leaders and mold the purchasing and consumption behavior of the remaining 86% of the world's population.

On a global scale, consumption patterns are being influenced by key trends such as: adoption of open access policies for foreign investments by many governments, increases in share of manufactured exports by newly industrialized countries, advances in telecommunications technologies, and expansion in world travel. These trends are influencing consumption behavior in a variety of ways; for example, many consumer products are becoming global in nature, such as consumer electronics, automobiles, fashion, home appliances, and beverages. Many of these products cut across national and cultural boundaries.

The challenge facing today's managers of consumer markets is to design global marketing programs that are based on meeting consumers' universal needs for products and services. Understanding of the cultural aspects of consumption, however, can be essential where unique market needs require some degree of adaptation in order to respond to certain local conditions.

Another key trend in the global marketing environment is the globalization of competition (Sheth, 1986). In today's global business environment, rivals end up buying firms instead of competing with them. Recently, Japan's Bridgestone Corporation bought most of the tire business of Firestone. Trade experts recognize that a larger share of production and export of consumer products in the U.S., for example, will occur by non-U.S. firms of U.S. affiliates abroad. This case is a reflection of a worldwide trend where sales between subsidiaries of the same firm represent a staggering 25% of global trade (Czinkota, 1989). Consequently, the global marketing environment is becoming increasingly competitive to an extent that requires firms to target their products and services at markets regardless of national boundaries.

Today, there are sizeable global markets where similar consumer segments are emerging across national boundaries. The challenge is to identify these segments on a global scale and find ways to reach them via global marketing programs. Therefore, understanding global consumer behavior is essential to the globalization of marketing.

With the standardization of manufacturing technology, spread of urbanization, advancement of telecommunications technology, interdependence in the world economy, and increased consumer sophistication and purchasing power, there is a growing belief in the "globalization" of consumer markets. Additionally, the emergence of this phenomenon is impacted by the changing political, socioeconomic, and demographic environment on a worldwide basis.

DEGREE OF GLOBALIZATION

Significant shifts have occurred in the structure and direction of world trade and financial flows in the last decade. The result has been that both policy makers and marketing managers are faced with many more dimensions in their decision horizon, yet have fewer tools to influence the new environment effectively. Czinkota and Ronkainen examine consumer market implications of the globalization of the U.S. economy.

Trade imbalance has become an increasingly important component of the U.S. economy. The growth of merchandise imports outdistanced export growth for most of the 1980s, which was especially significant in some of the consumer goods sectors such as automobiles and home electronics. The role of service industries and their increasing share in international trade flows has taken on greater importance. International competition has broadened the export base of U.S. industry to include more small- and medium-sized companies, while foreign direct investment has created a new category of U.S. exporters: foreign-held companies.

A significant shift has also occurred with respect to U.S. trading partners. Europe has decreased in its importance, while Asia has taken the lead in terms of the total U.S. merchandise flow. This has called for international marketers to change their orientations when seeking and dealing with new markets. But trade shifts are not the only indicators of dramatic change. Freedom in the international exchange of all production factors allows marketers to conduct and coordinate business functions globally.

An analysis of trends may allow the international marketer to better plan and respond to new challenges. With many more new attractive markets, products will have to be developed and their marketing programs coordinated for multiple markets simultaneously. Competitive moves are more rapid and may come from unexpected sources. The growing interdependence of economies and markets will call for a global perspective in response to change.

The chapter by Hassan and Katsanis provides an alternative approach that is based on identifying and reaching multiple market segments simultaneously. This alternative approach is in response to the globalization versus localization debate. It takes a historical perspective in analyzing developments in the body of knowledge since Levitt's thought-provoking article on the globalization of markets. There appear to be distinct trends in the global marketing literature when examined on a "historical" basis, versus a "school of thought" basis. Two consistent patterns have been found: the identification of specific global segments and the usefulness of segmentation in global marketing.

Based on this historical analysis, global segmentation variables were identified and presented in a behavioral framework for global consumer marketing. The existence of global consumer segments that are measurable and reachable must be considered as a prerequisite for the successful execution of any global marketing strategy.

Major consumption trends are examined and their effect on global markets are also identified. Two key consumer groups that may be particularly amendable to global segmentation are isolated, and their key behavioral aspects are discussed. The similarities and differences that may influence these segments are also presented. Specific corporate examples of successful efforts to reach these two segments on a worldwide basis are discussed. Implications for both researchers and managers conclude this chapter.

Herbig and Kramer examine the International Product Launch Sequence from a cultural country cluster perspective, providing arguments on why it should proceed in a certain manner. The authors also provide a step-by-step procedure on how to do so with several examples. Culturally, Juarez is years apart from Lubbock but very similar to Santiago de Chile even though Lubbock is ten times closer than Santiago. Likewise, Albany and Montreal find themselves worlds apart, although closer to each other than say Albany and Edinburgh, Scotland, or Montreal and Paris, France–yet it is the latter pair of cities that are very similar, not the former. Many marketers, though, believe geographical proximity is still the best approach to determining product launch priorities. If not geography, the determining variables in the order in which products are rolled out are usually factors such as where the company already has manufacturing facilities, distribution sites, or sales and service offices. Those companies that have graduated past geographic and logistic considerations usually emphasize financial models such as market growth rates or product portfolio models based on the GE or McKinsey Product Portfolio models. This is not to say that logistics, market share, and cash flow are not important to the health of a company and the success of a product; but in marketing a product in today's competitive environment, they are secondary to the needs and wants of a company's customers.

These culturally bound needs and wants vary from one nation or state to another. Culture is not a geographic phenomenon. France and Germany may be geographically adjacent to one another but certainly not even close culturally. A marketer rarely would be able to market a product the same way in both countries. Their cultures, like the American and Mexican (or Latino) examples above, though only separated by a scant few kilometers, are worlds apart and must therefore be treated considerably differently in the marketing of a product.

Ignoring culture, especially problems with language translations, has led to major fiascoes. Who can forget the Nova (Spanish for "no go") episode, the Pepsi campaign in China ("Pepsi brings your ancestors back from the grave"), or other equally embarrassing anecdotes. Simple oversights such as these can drastically ruin marketing efforts or jeopardize years of product development. Culture is the major dimension in international marketing; ignoring it or giving it low consideration is a sure path to failure.

MARKET BEHAVIOR AND DEVELOPMENT

In an era of globalizing markets, it is becoming more important than ever before to determine consumer behavior toward foreign products and services. The chapter by Sauer, Young, and Unnava presents three alternative processes underlying the country of origin bias effects. The first process, called the affect transfer process, assumes that the feelings people have about a country will be transferred to the products that originate from that country. Second, according to the cognitive mediation process, the cognitive processes of people are affected by country of origin information. That is, people's product attribute beliefs are first affected; these affected beliefs then cause attitude and behavioral intention differences. The third process predicts that the country of origin information affects a person's behavior directly, without affecting either beliefs or attitudes toward the product.

The research findings reported in this chapter support the cognitive mediation process. This is of particular significance to marketing practitioners because it indicates that care must be taken in choosing place of assembly. The temptation of U.S. manufacturers to move into third world countries to reduce labor and other costs associated with component manufacture and assembly must be tempered by consideration of the potential negative implications of such movement. One such negative implication is that perceived quality may decline among members of the target market if the country of assembly is generally considered to lack quality output. This study shows that this is more likely to occur when a large difference exists between countries (Japan vs. Philippines) than when a small difference exists (China vs. Philippines).

Innovativeness has been studied widely in the marketing literature. Most of the studies, however, draw conclusions only for developed nations. The empirical study by Medina and Michaels intends to shed some light with regard to the analysis of innovativeness in a developing market environment. Therefore, the objective of the study is to determine the impact of social class, individual modernism, and consumer modernism on innovativeness within the context of a developing society, Monterrey, Mexico.

A cross-sectional sample of household residents from metropolitan Monterrey, Mexico were selected for the purpose of this study. The information was collected with a structured, self-administered questionnaire. The data obtained included a measure of individual modernism, a measure of consumer modernism, a measure of social class, and a measure of innovativeness using consumer durables ownership.

A goodness-of-fit test showed that the sample was representative of Monterrey's metropolitan population along the social class hierarchy. Reliability coefficients for the study measures were "adequate" for the analysis. A path analytical model used to test the research hypotheses supported previous findings suggesting that social class is a very important influence on consumer behavior within developing market environments. Also the results suggested that values and consumption habits are not important influences on innovativeness.

The marketing of services is an increasingly global activity. A central issue of concern in this field is whether or not any standardization of marketing campaigns is feasible given the characteristics of services as products. For example, services are often described as inseparable–that is they are not fully separate from the individual who provides (performs) the service. Thus international marketers are likely to face a situation where the inseparability dimension varies from country to country in terms of customer expectations and acceptance.

In fact, most international marketing thought has been confined to physical products. This is especially ironic if one considers the economically developed nations, some 24 countries that control over two-thirds of the world's trade. In each of these countries, some 60 to 70% of the national economy is contributed by service industries. And while international trade in services is roughly at the 30% level, all signals are that it will continue to grow faster than physical goods trading.

Consumer behavior research has been focusing on service marketing for some time. Recently, scholars have started to extend the construct of involvement to services from product marketing research. However, to date there has not been any empirical evidence that demonstrates that involvement is a suitable construct to add to the arsenal of service marketing management techniques. Nor has involvement been empirically validated as a suitable measurement construct cross-culturally.

Relying on research conducted in Australia and the U.S., the chapter by Dahringer, Frame, Yau, and McColl-Kennedy analyzes whether involvement is suitable to apply to services. It also examines whether it is appropriate to use a measure of involvement across cultures. Finally, it discusses the international marketing implications of consistent consumer involvement in services in different nations.

The interrelationship between marketing and socio-economic development of developing countries has been of great interest to both marketing scholars and developmental economists in the post-second world war years. Research in this topic area is very extensive and growing. However, there is a paucity of research dealing with the marketing and consumption processes in the rural sectors of the developing countries. As the rural sectors constitute the largest segment of the population in many of the developing countries, a thorough understanding of the consumption patterns, the emerging changes in such patterns, and the factors that are shaping such changes will be of interest to marketers in these countries. From these perspectives, the chapter by Das and Rao attempts to identify the forces that are shaping the emerging rural consumption systems in India and to explore the marketing implications of such emerging systems. For conceptualizing the emerging rural consumptions systems in India, a series of field studies investigating the changing rural consumer behavior patterns in the various parts of the country were utilized. These field studies consisted of both quantitative economic surveys into the income and expenditure patterns and to a limited degree the qualitative consumer behavior patterns in rural India. Several consumption changes were identified. Two dominant changes or shifts were discerned in the rural consuming system in India. First, a distinct trend of increased buying of consumer durables as opposed to traditional behavior of spending incremental incomes to acquire more land and/or gold was noted. The second major trend was that the Indian rural consumers are more prone to buying more urban made consumer goods instead of the traditional approach of buying locally made consumer goods.

These rural consumption system changes do not seem to be brought about by any systematic and creative marketing efforts by marketers in the country. This conclusion is based on the fact that there is no evidence to indicate that marketers in India are making any special efforts to cultivate the rural markets systematically. Instead, some inherent socio-economic changes in the Indian rural life seem to provide the impetus for the observed consumption changes. These significant socio-economic changes in rural areas of India in recent years are: (a) a spurt in agrarian prosperity, (b) the perception of risk in agriculture, and (c) changes in the conception of ideal consumption basket. The emerging rural consumption system seems to have significant implications for marketers. The emerging rural consumption system in India seems to offer tremendous market opportunities and also marketing challenges in the form of adapting and adjusting their mostly urban marketing management practices to unique problems of rural marketing in India.

STANDARDIZATION OF MARKETING PROGRAMS AND PROCESS

The international advertising area has been controversial since the 1960s. Most debates have centered around the standardization-adaptation of international messages and there have been few empirical studies to resolve those issues. The chapter by Hill and James contains results of a 15 multinational corporation-120 subsidiary survey of consumer nondurable companies' advertising practices. Research findings show overall that there are few differences in standardization-adaptation strategies among the four industry groups comprising the nondurable sector (food-drink, pharmaceutical, cosmetic, and general consumer goods). Food-drink and pharmaceutical messages had their sales platforms adapted about two-thirds of the time against 40% for cosmetics and general consumer products. Creatives were changed more frequently and averaged over 60% adaptation, except for cosmetics.

Reasons to adapt and to standardize sales platforms and creative contexts were also investigated. Despite differences in sample sizes for the major types of nondurables, there was some consistency over the frequency with which factors were cited for each of the four products. Pharmaceutical product firms maintain more uniform brand images worldwide than manufacturers of other types of nondurables, but overall external (marketplace) factors dominated internal (corporate) factors in determining whether companies standardized promotional messages.

The chapter by Shao, Shao, and Shao examines the feasibility of standardized advertising campaigns in global markets. All multinational advertising agencies are looking for ways to reduce their costs while increasing their profit margins. One way to accomplish this is to use the same ad campaigns in each market served. This strategy may be pulled off if marketing environments are not significantly different. But to pretend that the world can be viewed as one large market asks practitioners to ignore regional and national differences, an encouragement posed by Levitt in his popular article on "The Globalization of Markets" (1983). But are these differences "superficial?" Based on this study of responses from 344 U.S. advertising agencies operating in six world regions, the answer is NO! Using chi-square tests, it was found that in most of the environmental factors examined by region, significant differences existed. Practitioners also indicated that they almost always had to adapt their sales platforms and creative contexts in their multinational campaigns. Therefore, ad agencies operating abroad are discouraged from treating the world as if it were one large market; the differences are too big to ignore.

The purpose of the chapter by Blackwell, Ajami, and Stephan is to provide managers with a guide to the major conceptual contributions in the marketing literature toward understanding global consumer behavior. The focus is upon the application of these concepts to the development of global advertising strategies and the effective implementation of global advertising programs. Examples of this focus are drawn from companies currently involved in this process, especially on the issue of how advertising agencies are changing and how agencies may be effectively organized to provide a competitive edge to firms involved in global marketing.

Thinking globally involves the ability to understand markets beyond one's own country of origin, with respect to sources of demand, sources of supply, and methods of effective management and marketing. In their chapter, the authors' focus of global consumer analysis is on structural variables associated with market attractiveness and cross-cultural analysis of lifestyles that permit advertising strategies to be planned globally but implemented locally.

In recent years, mega agencies have emerged such as Saatchi and Saatchi. Mega agencies are not always a good match for multinational enterprise because of conflicts of interest and high overhead expenses. A more efficient approach may be a network of domestic agencies linked with informal structures for sharing market information, creative ideas, and production costs.

The chapter by Ray, Ryder, and Scott discusses the use of words in a foreign language in advertising, focusing primarily on printed advertisements. Examples are presented from a number of countries, including Spain, Italy, and the United States. Several possible explanations of the function of foreign words are proposed, based on advertising and linguistic theories. The theory of script interruption suggests that when scenarios are interrupted by an unrelated set of events, the interruptions are remembered better than the main scenario itself. It is possible that the foreign words serve the same purpose. However, since past research has shown that the misunderstanding of monolingual print ads is widespread, it seems likely that advertisements containing more than one language would be open to even greater misinterpretation.

Linguistic theory provides two possible explanations for the function of foreign words in advertising. The first is that the ads are intended to be interpreted as *code-switching* texts by the readers. Code-switching is the use by fluent bilinguals of two languages within the same discourse, or even the same sentence or phrase. It seems to have several functions, including the creation of intimacy and solidarity between the speaker and the listener, and the exploitation of the emotional qualities of certain phrases in one of the two languages being used. Either of these effects could prove useful in an advertisement. However, since the majority of the consumers in many countries, especially in Italy, Spain, and the United States, are probably *not* fluent in both their native language and the foreign one used in the ads, the use of these foreign words and phrases must have other benefits.

The second possible explanation is that these foreign elements are servicing the same purpose as *borrowed words*, words permanently adopted from a foreign language into a primarily monolingual speech community. One of the major purposes of adopting such words is prestige; the user of such words is perceived as educated, elite, cosmopolitan. In addition, the perceived achievements of a culture or people strongly affect the values that culture's language suggests. For example, the present reputation of Japan and Germany for fine engineering causes Japanese and German phrases to have an "engineering" flavor. Since France has long been a center of fashion and culture, French words create impressions of elegance or beauty. While advertisers may not intend the foreign phrases they use to become permanent parts of the native language, the phrases may serve the same purpose as the borrowed ones, of creating feelings of cosmopolitanism and, depending on the language used, more specific implications about a product's technological or aesthetic qualities.

Linda Morris and John Hallaq critically look at the changing South Korean marketplace. As South Korea begins to open its trade doors, it becomes strategically important for U.S. marketers to gain an understanding of its marketplace. This country image study compares South Koreans' perceptions of consumer products manufactured in Taiwan, Japan, the United States, and South Korea from a macro and micro perspective.

From a macro perspective, i.e., a general products view, South Koreans perceive Japanese- and U.S.-manufactured products similar on 10 of the 13 dimensions taken from Nagishima's (1977) semantic differential scale. Three dimensions that Koreans view U.S. and Japanese products as significantly different were inventiveness, performance, and design. The U.S. is viewed more inventive and more concerned with functional product performance than with stylistic appearance of the product, while Japanese products have more contemporary designs. South Korean respondents perceive their products as inferior to Japanese and U.S. products, but very similar to Taiwanese products except for production and inventiveness. South Koreans consider their products as being mass-produced and more imitative of Western world products compared to Taiwan's handmade items designed for their cultural preferences.

Six familiar product categories and nine product attributes were examined to determine the importance of the country of origin factor on product selection. County of origin, classified as an extrinsic cue, was the least important factor when price, quality, styling, value, prestige, warranty, and product availability were considered for products in the low-risk and high-risk categories. Quality, an intrinsic cue that is rather difficult to define, was the primary dimension considered in product selection. However, when country of origin was used as a single cue in product selection, a home country bias was evident. This finding is quite interesting given that South Koreans perceive their products as being inferior in quality compared to Japanese and U.S. consumer goods. However, when South Korea is removed from the list, it was found that U.S. products were preferred in all categories except electronics, where a preference for Japanese products existed.

The positive image of U.S.-made products and the existing preference for U.S. products are advantages that should not be overlooked in designing entry-level marketing strategies. As U.S.-South Korea trade expands in the next decade, the most lucrative target market appears to be the educated South Korean youth segment. Although marketing-related activities are not well-established in this developing nation, it is important to note that promotional strategies should emphasize intrinsic cues, such as quality, styling, prestige, and value in consumer products. Price, an extrinsic cue, does not outweigh the importance of quality and styling in product selection. This price-quality relationship may become more important in the next decade as the per capita income levels of South Korean consumers increase.

MANAGERIAL IMPLICATIONS

Globalization has been portrayed as the necessary orientation to succeed both at home and internationally in the next decade. A review of the literature suggests that the term globalization is used in at least three different contexts. The holistic approach requires an integrated consideration of worldwide factors rather than a "multi-domestic" orientation. The second meaning is the standardization of the marketing mix rather than adaptation. The third meaning refers to the macro environment of the firm.

After a discussion of the meaning of globalization, the chapter by Barker and Aydin discusses the problems of implementation associated with standardization. The assertion that markets are becoming more homogeneous (convergent) in terms of consumers' tastes is a rather exaggerated view.

Instead of helping to compete better, standardization of the marketing mix may even mislead firms. Standardization (1) ignores niche marketing, (2) gives a false sense of security against competitors, and (3) may result in missed opportunities in penetrating new markets. It is very dangerous to attempt to generalize the standardization argument across different markets without verification of the environmental specifics such as product-industry characteristics, the infrastructure, and differences in the patterns of usage and purchase.

Firms that tailor their programs specifically to their markets are likely to achieve a competitive advantage. The actual strategies need not be identical but must be based on the same global perspective. The elements of the marketing mix should be grounded in the needs and the environment of the customer in order to ensure long-term success. The implementation of the strategy and the program require paying careful attention to the organization (both the people and the structure) at the headquarters and the subsidiaries.

Past and present research in the academic and professional literature shows a change in values within West Germany and the United States. This has been exacerbated by the recent German unification;

however, empirical research shows no future trends. A sample of 614 business students from both countries were tested on four value profile scales (i.e., Acceptance of Authority, Need-Determined Expression versus Value-Determined Restraint, Equalitarianism, and Individualism) and compared to historical and recent anecdotal evidence to determine future trends.

The research by Fraedrich, Herndon, and Ferrell showed that business students becoming future West German managers are less accepting of authority, more individualistic, and more independent of authoritative power sources than their U.S. counterparts. This suggests a West German competitor who is likely to approach the business world in an egoistic, rather than nationalistic, manner. It also suggests a new freedom to compete in innovative ways on the world stage, at a time when an economic merger of East and West Germany will probably leave future West German managers in charge of many East German (i.e., German Democratic Republic) corporate activities and perhaps as much as 22% of Western Europe's economy. The increase in independence may also imply that West German managers may do what is best for their firm or their country regardless of potential harm to the larger world or European Community; the potential coalignment of both personal egoistic and national interests suggests a formidable business competitor.

Because of historical evidence and our findings, we expect future West German managers to be very protective of market share and similar gains for their businesses, but to do so in innovative ways, less respectful of traditional business practices and less respectful of business superiors. This suggests a more open decision-making style characterized by freer discussions with senior managers and less regimented thinking. Because the growth of executive recruitment in West Germany for cross-border managers is increasing (executive recruitment was illegal in West Germany until the late 1970s), the increase in equalitarianism could make future West German managers more attractive to international businesses. To the degree that cross-border experience is a prerequisite to future personal business success, this trait may increase opportunities for future West German managers.

According to Herbig and Miller, relevant cultural differences that appear to influence the different adoption behaviors of the United

States and Japan appear to include: collectivist (Japan) versus individualistic (United States); status consciousness (Japan) versus egalitarianism (United States); risk avoidance (Japan) versus risk acceptance (United States); heavily aggressive/competitive (Japan) versus mildly aggressive-competitive (United States); extremely homogeneous society (Japan) versus heterogeneous population (United States); and a long-term perspective (Japan) versus short-term views (United States).

Unknown (new) goods/ideas are risky in Japan. But at the same time, once acceptability has been shown (by seniors, bosses, or production internally), then adoption should be fairly quick, otherwise one will lose face and appear different; this one cannot have if one is to be Japanese. Americans, being more individualistic, with a risk-prone mentality, are more adept to experimenting, trying things out earlier. However, adoption is an uneven and a longer term process in America than Japan due to the heterogeneity not present in Japan. The typical hesitancy rate is longer for the Japanese than for the American, while the internal adoption rate is quicker. These findings can easily be explained via differences between the two cultures. These cultural attributes appear to occur in a cluster; all or none are usually present within a society. As a generalization, by including cultural attributes into the country entry decision, the marketing manager gains additional information to assist him in determination of hesitation rate, internal adoption rate, and maximum diffusion rate for countries he is considering, as well as insight regarding what marketing mix would be most successful for that particular country and individual product.

REFERENCES

Czinkota, M. R. (1989). "Trade Trends from U.S. and Global Perspectives." Presentation in a Special Session on Global Consumer Marketing at the Academy of Marketing Science Annual Conference held in Orlando, FL.

Levitt, T. (1983). The Globalization of Markets, *Harvard Business Review*, (May/June), pp. 92-102.

Nagashima, A. (1977). A Comparative "Made in" Product Image Survey Among Japanese Businessmen, *Journal of Marketing*, 41, (July), pp. 95-100.

Sheth, J. (1986). Global Markets or Global Competition? *Journal of Consumer Marketing*, (Spring), 3(2), pp. 9-11.

Chapter 1

The Globalizing Consumer Markets: Issues and Concepts

Salah S. Hassan
Erdener Kaynak

INTRODUCTION

The "globalization" phenomenon is being impacted by the changing political, socio-economic, and demographic environment on a worldwide basis. On a global scale, trends influencing consumption behavior can be cited as follows: increases in GNP per capita, steady rises in life expectancy, rapid increase of literacy and education levels, increases in share of manufactured exports by newly industrialized countries, advances in transportation, and expansion in world travel. These macro-forces and mega-trends are influencing consumption behavior in a variety of ways; for example, many consumer products are becoming global in nature, such as consumer electronics, home appliances, fashion, and automobiles. Many of these products cut across national boundaries.

For today's consumer marketing managers, it is necessary to understand the dynamics of what is happening on a global scale in terms of consumption patterns and trends in order for their firms to remain competitive. For example, retailers are globalizing what used to be a true domestic industry. Fashion retailers like The Limited and Benetton were able to build their own global image. Benetton, as Europe's leading producer of knits, was able to operate in many key markets as a local store with a global vision and scale of operations. Benetton's competitiveness is based on understanding of worldwide consumption trends such as the globalization of the teenage market and its emergence as the first true global segment. Globalization of the teenage market was the base for competitively launching the "United Colors of Benetton" advertising campaign.

These enhanced levels of globalization of markets and competition have prompted a willingness to market consumer products through aggressive global strategies. In an increasingly globalized environment, most managers of consumer markets have to think globally, otherwise competition is going to hit them where they are, in their own domestic markets. Therefore, this chapter provides a framework for understanding key issues and concepts related to the development of competitive strategies in the globalizing consumer markets.

FRAMEWORK OF COMPETITIVENESS IN THE GLOBALIZING CONSUMER MARKETS

Globalization is becoming a reality for many industries competing in the world consumer marketplace. Consumer electronics, automobiles, and watches are a few examples of global industries. The globalization of these industries is attributed in part to technological advancement, buyer needs, and the advantages gained from creating a competitive position in different markets that cut across national boundaries. In these *global industries,* "a firm's competitive position in one nation significantly affects (and is affected by) its position in other nations" (Porter 1990, p. 53). The competitive advantage of these firms is a function of four major factors: (1) supply side conditions, (2) demand side factors, (3) scope of segmentation, and (4) degree of globalization (see Figure 1.1).

From the *supply side,* firms may employ globalized strategies in order to achieve high levels of economies of scale and market penetration. Certain global firms are assumed to have achieved high levels of market penetration and fixed cost control. To these firms, global competitiveness is demonstrated via the ability to standardize research and development, product design, manufacturing, assembly, and packaging procedures. Global sourcing for labor also can serve as an example of how companies cut down on

FIGURE 1.1. Framework of Competitiveness in the Globalizing Consumer Markets

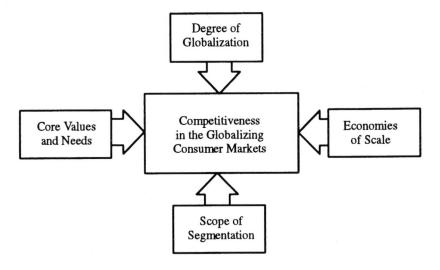

manufacturing costs as a result of shifting production from U.S. and Europe to low-wage Asian and Latin American countries. Enormous economies of scale have been achieved by companies due to their ability to think globally when it comes to sourcing decisions.

In such global industries, firms are compelled to think globally in order to maximize competitive advantage in a given industry segment. Porter (1990) identifies a global approach to strategy that is based on gaining competitive advantage via: (1) configuration of the firm's activities in many nations in order to serve markets on a global scale, and (2) coordination among the dispersed activities. Further, he points out that choosing a global strategy will depend on the extent of globalization in any given segment of the industry.

From a *demand side*, competitiveness in the globalizing consumer markets will not be achieved without carefully understanding and responding to the core values and needs of the consumer. Global firms win competitive battles only when they are armed with consumer-oriented strategies. Managers of global consumer markets will win many of these battles if they are able to "think of global similarities and adapt to local differences" (Hassan, 1991).

Today, companies operating in key consumer markets on a global scale must get close to the consumer and build competitive strategies based on commonalities and differences. A global firm like Coca-Cola was able to become global in vision and in scale of operations and to stay close to local markets. For example, with business operations in 160 countries and commanding a 47% share of the soda pop consumed on a worldwide basis, the Coca-Cola Company still manages to treat the Indonesian and Filipino teenagers with local flavors of soda pop *(The Wall Street Journal,* 1989). This "global customization" approach is based on serving the needs of the local consumer segments on a global scale.

A new market reality points to the direction of globalization of key segments in many consumer industries. *Scope of segmentation* is a key determinant of strategic competitiveness. The importance of segmentation to the global strategy is consistent with two key trends: the emergence of specific global segments, and the usefulness of segmentation to global strategy (Porter, 1986; Douglas and Wind, 1987; and Jain, 1989). The identification of target segments within countries (country groups and buyers within countries) and physical product configurations would both assist in the determination of global marketing strategy (Porter, 1986).

Global marketing strategy needs to be an integral part of the overall global strategic focus of the firm. For Porter, the role of marketing in the overall strategy of the firm is three-dimensional: it involves the geographic concentration or dispersion (in one country or a lot of different countries) of certain marketing activities; the coordination of dispersed marketing activities; and the use of global marketing strategy to gain competitive advantage.

The existence of global segments is a key condition for the success of any global marketing strategy (Douglas and Wind, 1987; Hassan and Katsanis, 1991). Several global segments that transcend country boundaries were identified and profiled, such as: the consumer segment that seeks premium and luxury products on a global scale (Quelch, 1987; Martensen, 1987; Hassan and Katsanis, 1991); the global teenagers (Feinberg, 1989; Hassan and Katsanis, 1991); and on a regional scale, environmentally conscious "green" consumers *(The Economist,* 1989; Rolfes, 1990) and the six clusters of the new "Euro-consumer" (Vandermerwe and L'Huillier, 1989). Clearly, determining the strategic attractiveness of any global segment is a prerequisite for the successful deployment of marketing programs. Determination of global segment attractiveness can be based on criteria factors such as: measurability, reachability, profitability, and receptivity to the standardized marketing.

The issue of focusing on strategically attractive global market segments, in the context of competitive strategy of the firm, is linked to developing and managing standardized marketing "program" and "process." Development and assessment of the most competitive standardized marketing programs and processes available to target global segments is a major challenge facing today's global firms.

Degree of globalization is the final factor to be considered in gaining a competitive advantage in the increasingly globalizing consumer marketplace. The globalization scope achieved in the particular industry in which the firm is trying to gain global competitive advantage dictates the degree of standardization of the marketing program and process.

The standardized marketing program is defined in terms of the various aspects of the marketing mix: product, promotion, price, and place. On the other hand, Jain (1989) introduced the concept of standardized "process," which implied the use of tools that assist in the development and implementation of global programs.

The degree of standardization of the marketing program incorporates other factors in addition to the marketing mix, such as: target market, market position, and environmental and organizational elements. For many global firms, some aspects of the marketing program (i.e., the core product) may have greater standardization potential than others. Standardization of the marketing process involves the overall planning process, including the firm's basic marketing philosophy. It incorporates a systematic analysis of the firm's marketing, knowledge, capability, and objectives. Standardization of marketing process implies consistency in applying the firm's capabilities and strategies to achieve common objectives at acceptable levels of pre-established procedures on a worldwide basis.

SUMMARY OF ISSUES AND CONCEPTS

The globalizing consumer market reality presents a number of issues for marketing managers to consider in creating, maintaining, and/or improving on their firm's international competitive position. The vast number of issues associated with global consumer markets are consolidated in this conceptual framework (see Figure 1.2).

Some of these issues include the ability to objectively develop sound and action-oriented standardized marketing programs. Other important issues are: determination of key consumer and industry trends that influence the degree of globalization; identification of demand structures at different markets on a worldwide basis; and characterization of levels of technological change, socio-economic change, and market/segment development.

It is essential for today's managers of consumer markets to be on the "cutting edge" of knowledge about how the structure of global markets is changing. It is equally important for top managers to get involved in understanding and monitoring how the global marketing concept is being moved from corporate offices to the actual marketplace.

FIGURE 1.2. Summary of Issues and Concepts

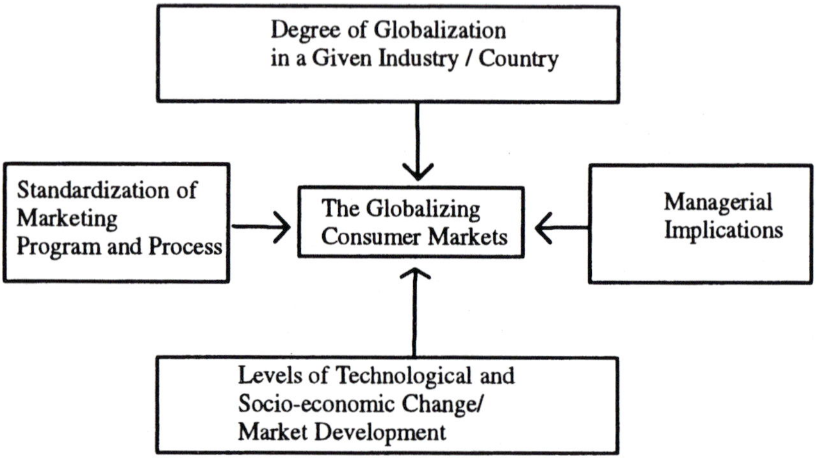

REFERENCES

Douglas, S. P. and Wind, Y. (1987). "The Myth of Globalization," *Columbia Journal of World Business,* (Winter), pp. 19-30.

The Economist, (1989). "Greening Europe," (October 14), pp. 21-24.

Feinberg, A. (1989). "The First Global Generation," *Adweek,* (February), pp. 18-27.

Hassan, S. (1991). "A Strategic Framework for Identifying and Reaching Intermarket Segments." In *World Marketing Congress,* Vol. V, edited by K. D. Frankenberger et al. Copenhagen, Denmark: Academy of Marketing Science, pp. 34–37.

Hassan, S. and Katsanis, L. (1991). "Identification of Global Consumer Segments: A Behavioral Framework," *Journal of International Consumer Marketing,* (Spring), 3(2), pp. 11-28.

Jain, S. C. (1989). "Standardization of International Marketing Strategy: Some Research Hypotheses," *Journal of Marketing,* (January), 53, pp. 70-79.

Martensen, R. (1987). "Is Standardization of Marketing Feasible in Culture Bound Industries? A European Case Study," *International Marketing Review,* (Autumn), pp. 18-28.

Porter, M. E. (1990). *The Competitive Advantage of Nations,* New York: Free Press.

Porter, M. E. (1986). "The Strategic Role of International Marketing," *Journal of Consumer Marketing,* (Spring), 3(2), pp. 17-21.

Quelch, J. (1987). "Marketing the Premium Product," *Business Horizons,* (May/ June), pp. 38-45.

Rolfes, R. (1990). "How Green Is Your Market Basket?"*Across the Board,* (January/February), pp. 49-51.

Vandermerwe, S. and L'Huillier, M. (1989). "Euro-Consumer in 1992," *Business Horizons,* (January/February), pp. 34-40.

The Wall Street Journal, (1989). "The Real Thing: Tough and Consistent, Coke Excels at Global Marketing and Keeps an Eye on Youth," (December 19), pp. A1 & A6.

SECTION II.

DEGREE OF GLOBALIZATION

Chapter 2

The Globalization
of the U.S. Economy:
Consumer Market Implications

Michael R. Czinkota
Ilkka A. Ronkainen

SUMMARY. This chapter presents an overview of the sweeping changes that have taken place in the global economy. Subsequently, the effects of these changes on U.S. consumer goods marketers are discussed. By linking together the implications of growing competitiveness, larger financial flows, and increasing foreign direct investment, the authors then suggest possible scenarios for future developments in consumer goods trade.

Significant changes have occurred in the global marketplace and the resultant newly defined macro framework in which consumer goods markets and marketers have to operate has to be assessed. The objective of this chapter is to provide sufficient background information so that consumer goods marketers may be better able to anticipate and adjust to the new realities of the global marketplace.

International business has forged a network of global linkages around the world which have an effect on multiple levels–country, organizational, as well as individual. Global trade volumes have reached unprecedented heights. Financial linkages have altered the

The authors greatly appreciate the analytical support of David Barton of the United States Department of Commerce.

directional flow and value of international funds and reduced the domesticity of stock markets and interest rates. The execution of global investment and production strategies has dramatically increased manufacturing interdependence. Countries which until recently had never been thought of as major participants in international business, such as the newly industrializing countries in Asia, have emerged as major economic powers (Czinkota and Ronkainen, 1990).

Both the willing and the unwilling are becoming participants in global business affairs. Due to the interdependence between economic conditions and activities between nations, most facets of an economy are affected directly or indirectly by the economic and political developments that occur in the international marketplace. More is to be expected: in the last five years, international trade has led economic growth, increasing at a rate of 6.4%, compared with increases of 3.1% in world production and consumption. The beginning integration of Eastern Europe into the world trade community is likely to trigger another spurt in international trade.

As a result of this globalization, the U.S. economy faces an international business imperative. In order to survive in this world of abrupt changes and discontinuities, of newly-emerging forces and challenges, of unforeseen influences and opportunities from abroad, active responses need to be developed both at macro and micro levels. New strategies need to be envisioned, new plans need to be made, and the way of doing business needs to change. At the very basis of this adjustment must be an attitude change to accommodate the growing importance of foreign markets and the growing influence of foreign organizations and individuals. Table 2.1 summarizes the factors driving the globalization of the U.S. economy and extrapolates possible implications for both the structure and focus of consumer markets. The body of this chapter will explicate in detail the significant trends and directions in the offing for consumer marketers.

GROWING TRADE VOLUMES

During the last fifteen years, total U.S. merchandise trade growth has vastly outdistanced domestic U.S. nominal gross national prod-

TABLE 2.1. Globalization Drivers and Implications

Factor driving globali-zation of U.S. economy	Implications	
	Market structure	Market focus
Growing trade volume	Expanding participation in int'l business Foreign investors as exporters Increased import competition U.S. as a world manufacturing base	Export opportunity
New competitive players	Opportunity for strategic alliances New negotiation environments	New export markets New sources for imported products
Changed composition of trade	Client-driven partnerships	Increasing dominance of mfg goods imports Service exports
Broader int'l business scope	Increased coordination of research, design, production, and marketing functions	Foreign investment supplanting trade in finished products Increasing intra-firm trade in components/semi-finished goods Rapid diffusion of new products Decreasing sensitivity to country of origin
New impact of financial markets		Currency impact Liquidity problems

uct increases. As a result, international trade comprises a gradually increasing proportion of U.S. GNP. Furthermore, from 1981 to 1988, the growth of U.S. participation in world trade has greatly outpaced the growth of overall world trade. During this period, the value of world trade in goods measured in constant dollars increased by 8%, yet for the U.S., the increase was 24%.

The increase in U.S. trade participation, however, has not been uniform. As shown in Figure 2.1, over the past decades, the U.S. share of world exports has been declining. At the same time, major increases have occurred in the U.S. share of world imports. Therefore, the U.S. role as a supplier to the world has diminished, while at the same time, the U.S. role as a marketplace for the world has increased.

The vast majority of U.S. industries has been affected by these developments. Over the period 1972 to 1985, percentages of goods and services exported increased for 88% of all U.S. manufacturing-sector industries. At the same time, import percentages increased for 75% of all manufacturing industries. Typically, capital goods industries boast the largest export ratios, while consumer goods industries report the highest import ratios (Moore, 1989). However, increases in imports have been larger, resulting in major and persis-

FIGURE 2.1. U.S. Share of World Exports and Imports (in percent)

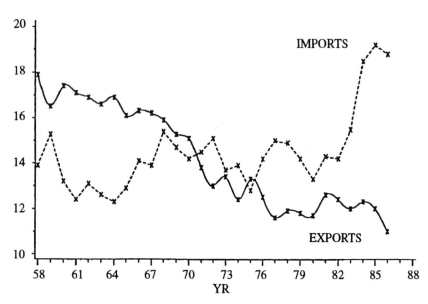

Source: International Statistics (1988), International Monetary Fund, Washington, DC

FIGURE 2.2. U.S. Merchandise Trade ($ billions)

Top 10 Product Surpluses & Deficits, 1988

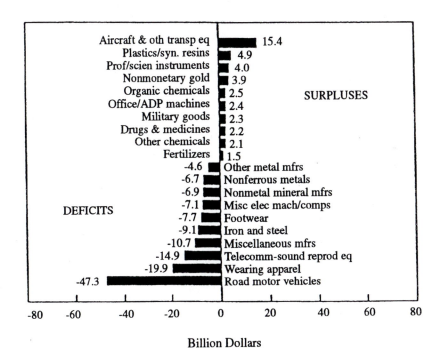

Billion Dollars

Source: United States Trade Performance in 1988, U.S. Department of Commerce, International Trade Administration, 1989, Washington, DC: 25

tent U.S. trade deficits. As can be seen in Figure 2.2, the major losers have been mainly in the consumer sector; cars, textiles, and apparel, as well as electronics.

Increasingly U.S. companies are getting involved in international trade. Although the conventional wisdom that the 250 largest multinationals dominate U.S. exports is still true, small and medium-sized companies are getting involved as well. A total of 100,000 exporters exist in the U.S., with some 10,000 whose exports are growing rapidly (U.S. House, 1988). Since the growth in foreign competition no longer assures U.S. companies domination of their own markets, they are forced to diversify their marketing efforts internationally.

Foreign direct investment in turn assists in transforming the U.S. into a world manufacturing base. Many U.S. companies have been acquired and turned into strong international competitors. While some exports by these foreign-held companies may be image-building gestures–such as SONY's, Toshiba's, and Honda's exports of U.S.-made picture tubes, televisions, and cars–some companies such as Electrolux, are major exporters. The share of U.S. manufactured exports generated by foreign-owned companies increased steadily in the 1980s, and accounts now for a fifth of U.S. exports (U.S. Department of Commerce, 1988, p. 46). The global market expertise of many foreign direct investors, together with the fact that many of these investments are occurring in consumer goods industries, may portend a phoenix-like rise of U.S. consumer goods exports–conducted by foreign-owned firms from their U.S. base.

NEW COMPETITIVE PLAYERS

The past decade has also witnessed major economic growth rate changes around the world. Gross domestic product growth rates among the traditional trading partners of the U.S. have been outpaced by the growth rates of Asian countries. For example, during the period of 1975 to 1985, France, West Germany, and the United Kingdom had ten-year gross domestic product changes of 24%, 26%, and 18%, respectively. At the same time, South Korea reported growth rates of 107%, Pakistan 89%, and Thailand 84%. Overall, the gross domestic product of the world grew by 34% during this period, while Asian developing countries registered 71%.

The substantial growth rates of Asian countries resulted in a significant shift in their international trade interaction with the United States, drastically altering the importance of the European trading partners. In 1962, for example, out of 118 trading partners, China's rank as importer to the United States was 111, Singapore's 72, South Korea's 78, and Taiwan's 40. By 1987, Singapore had taken position 13, China position 12, South Korea position 6, and Taiwan ranked as the 4th largest importer into the United States. The changes in rankings have mainly been brought about by increases in U.S. imports of consumer goods, often stimulated by U.S. firms. For example, GM imported $910 million worth of autos from Japan in 1987, while Ford doubled its imports of Korean-made cars to $225 million, and Chrysler was a net importer to the tune of $750 million, mainly from Japan (Hampton and Schiller, 1988).

This shift in position has also signified the opening of new markets for U.S. firms. For example, during the same time period, China's rank as a market for U.S. exports rose from 116 to 17, while Singapore rose in rank from 55 to 14 (see Table 2.2). Similar changes may be seen in the U.S. trade relations with the newly emerging democracies (NEDs). With the NEDs conversion to hard currency-

TABLE 2.2. U.S. Largest Trading Partners, 1987 ($ billions)

Imports		Exports	
World	420.07	World	243.86
Japan	87.44	Canada	57.00
Canada	71.27	Japan	26.90
Germany, West	28.01	Mexico	14.05
Taiwan	26.36	United Kingdom	13.14
Mexico	20.01	Germany, West	10.92
Korea, South	17.89	Netherlands	7.87
United Kingdom	17.58	France	7.50
Italy	11.47	Korea, South	7.49
France	10.94	Taiwan	7.02
Hong Kong	10.47	Belgium and Lux	5.94
Brazil	8.17	Australia	5.33
China	6.85	Italy	5.31
Singapore	6.37	Brazil	3.89
Venezuela	5.67	Singapore	3.87
Sweden	4.96	Hong Kong	3.75
Saudi Arabia	4.86	Venezuela	3.48
Belgium and Lux	4.32	China	3.46
Switzerland	4.30	Spain	3.05
Netherlands	4.21	Saudi Arabia	3.01
Nigeria	3.77	Switzerland	2.48
Indonesia	3.65	Israel	2.07
Australia	3.24	Malaysia	1.87
Spain	3.05	Sweden	1.77
Malaysia	3.02		

Source: Survey of Current Business, March 1988, U.S. Department of Commerce, Bureau of Economic Affairs, Washington, DC

based trading and their pent-up need for consumer products, virgin market territories are emerging, and opportunities exist for both exporters and marketers interested in forming strategic alliances (Czinkota, 1991).

Overall, rapid economic growth in Asian countries, combined with significant lower growth elsewhere, has resulted in a major shift of U.S. international trade flows. As Figures 2.3 and 2.4 show, Europe has decreased in its importance in the total U.S. merchandise trade flow, while Asia has taken the lead. Therefore, in the long run, adjustment is needed both by the U.S. government and U.S. firms. At the governmental level, an adjustment must be made to accommodate different negotiation environments, given that many of the emerging countries in the Pacific Rim are plan-driven rather than free-trade driven in their international trade stances (Choate and Linger, 1988). Firms similarly need to change their orientations when seeking new markets and new customers. Some companies

FIGURE 2.3. Percentage of U.S. Exports to Asia and Europe

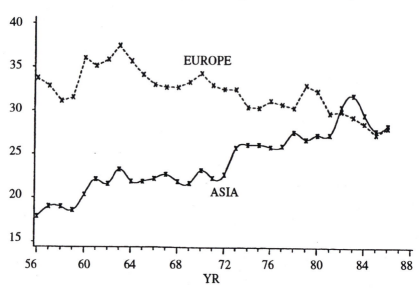

Source: International Statistics (1988), International Monetary Fund, Washington, DC

FIGURE 2.4. Percentage of U.S. Imports from Asia and Europe

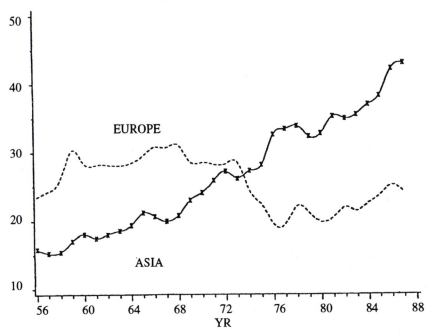

Source: International Statistics (1988), International Monetary Fund, Washington, DC

that at one time only imported from the Far East are now using their accumulated market experience to export from the U.S. to those markets boosted by the declining value of the dollar.

CHANGED COMPOSITION OF TRADE

The past two decades have also produced a substantial shift in the composition of international trade flows. In the 1960s and early 1970s, the U.S. dominated world agricultural exports due to the high volume and efficiency of production. Concurrently, U.S. manufactured products were also a highly competitive mainstay of U.S. exports, due to U.S. technology and mass-production capability.

As Table 2.3 shows, however, in the past two decades, the domestic importance of agriculture, industry, and services has

TABLE 2.3. Composition of GDP by Income and Year (percent of total)

	Agriculture		Industry		Services	
	1965	1986	1965	1986	1965	1986
Low-income economies	42	32	28	35	30	32
China and India	42	31	31	39	27	30
Other	43	38	18	20	41	41
Developing economies	29	19	31	36	38	46
Lower middle-income	30	22	25	30	43	46
Turkey	34	18	25	36	41	46
Thailand	35	17	23	30	42	53
Upper middle-income	18	10	37	40	46	50
Korea	38	12	25	42	37	45
Brazil	19	11	33	39	48	50
Industrial market economies	5	3	40	35	54	61
U.S.	3	2	38	31	59	67
Japan	9	3	43	41	48	56
Federal Republic of Germany	4	2	53	40	43	58

Source: World Development Report 1988. World Bank, Washington, DC

changed. Globally, the proportion of gross domestic product resulting from agriculture has declined, with the U.S. boasting the lowest percentage of agricultural employment. Since this decline has taken place in an era of large population and therefore consumption increases, it indicates that global agricultural production has become more efficient. During the same time, low-income, developing countries have derived an increasing proportion of the gross domestic product from industrial production. Concurrently, this proportion has declined in the industrial market economies, with the U.S. again taking the lead. The resulting slack has been taken up by the service economy.

By necessity, these developments have been reflected in international trade flows. U.S. agricultural exports have declined significantly. Manufactured exports by other economies have increased precipitously. For the U.S., the role of service industries, and their increased participation in international trade flows has taken on greater importance. As a result, the success of multilateral negotiations on liberalizing services trade is especially important for the U.S. as more U.S. service companies are internationalizing their efforts.

The growth of international business travel, for example, is changing the travel-agency sector in the United States from single-unit agencies to global ones. Major U.S. agencies have acquired or opened offices or formed partnerships with other agencies around the world. The moves have largely been client-driven as the U.S. companies selling their products abroad want the same type of travel service abroad that they get at home (*The Washington Post,* 1989).

BROADER INTERNATIONAL BUSINESS SCOPE

Trade flows, however, reveal only a part of the global economic shifts that have taken place. More freedom in the international exchange of the production factors of capital, technology, and labor, coupled with modern, low-cost communication capabilities, have permitted the global separation of ownership, management, and production. Never before has it been so easy for firms to conduct and coordinate worldwide the research, design, production, marketing, and distribution functions.

In 1986, 98 of the 100 largest U.S.-based firms each had more than $1 billion of foreign revenues. The 25 largest U.S. multinational firms obtained 1986 foreign revenues of $252 billion, an amount that exceeded the total value of U.S. exports that year. Most of these revenues resulted from foreign direct investment. Such investment has both supplanted traditional trade of finished products by resulting in more production abroad and stimulated intra-firm trade in components and supplies as inputs in the foreign production process. For example, during the 1982-85 overall decline in U.S. exports, U.S. exports to affiliated firms abroad grew by 25% (U.S. Department of Commerce, 1988, p. 46).

Over time, foreign investments carried out by U.S. firms have shifted dramatically in terms of their focus. As Table 2.4 shows, during the last 30 years, U.S. foreign direct investments have gradually moved from the Western Hemisphere to Europe. During this period, U.S. foreign direct investment in the Americas has declined by 36.7 share points. At the same time, Europe's position increased by 32.3 share points.

Yet, this shift has only occurred with a significant time lag following the shift in trade flows. These lags are still in existence today and have resulted in a major mismatch between trade and foreign direct investment. Data in Table 2.5 show that only in the case of Canada are trade and U.S. foreign direct investment equally balanced. In the case of Europe, U.S. investment significantly exceeds trade flows, while in the case of Japan and the newly industrialized countries of the Pacific, investment flows are substantially underrepresented.

TABLE 2.4. U.S. Foreign Direct Investment by Region and Year (in percent)

Region	1956	1976	1987
Canada	33.8	24.7	18.4
Other Western Hemisphere	35.0	17.1	13.7
Europe	15.9	40.7	48.2
Japan	0.6	2.8	4.6
Other	14.7	14.6	15.1

Source: Survey of Current Business, March 1988, U.S. Department of Commerce, Bureau of Economic Affairs, Washington, DC

TABLE 2.5. U.S. Total Trade and Foreign Direct Investment Shares by Region, 1987 (in percent)

Region	Merchandise Trade	Foreign Direct Investment
Canada	19.3	18.4
Japan	17.2	4.6
Pacific-NIC	16.0	5.4
Europe	25.6	48.2
Other	21.9	23.4

Source: Survey of Current Business, March 1988, U.S. Department of Commerce, Bureau of Economic Affairs, Washington, DC

Strong investments by the British, Dutch, and Japanese, especially in the late 1980s, have pushed foreign ownership of assets in the United States to $304.2 billion–almost as much as the $329.9 billion U.S. companies have invested overseas (U.S. Department of Commerce, 1988, pp. 17-50). some of the largest acquisitions have been in the consumer sector; e.g., SONY's purchase of Columbia Pictures and CBS, Grand Metropolitan's acquisition of Pillsbury, and Unilever's purchase of Chesebrough Pond's.

In terms of trade statistics, the effects and benefits of foreign investment activities are reflected only to a limited extent. For example, the benefits accruing to the U.S. from the writing of large insurance contracts abroad are reflected in the international accounts only to the extent to which actual funds are transferred back to the U.S. Similarly, only the repatriated profits of a foreign production subsidiary will show up in the international accounting system. Therefore, the true impact of the extent of U.S. international activities is only partially reflected in trade statistics. Looking at past patterns however, it is reasonable to expect that over the next decade, more U.S. firms will be investing in Asia rather than in Europe, while Asian firms are more likely to invest in the U.S. Such investment can, in turn, be expected to lead to a reduction in the rate of growth in bi-regional trade flows.

A NEW IMPACT OF FINANCIAL MARKETS

Historically, currencies have served as financial intermediaries to facilitate trade. Exchange rates, in turn, have reflected the volume and balances of trade flows since trade flows were the pacing mechanism for the resulting subsequent financial flows. Major changes have taken place to alter this relationship. The international shift from fixed to floating exchange rates in the 1970s, combined with an increased liberalization of financial markets (which started in the U.S. and continued through the 1986 Big Bang in London), and the relaxation of overseas investment restrictions in Asia have resulted in a rapid increase in the volume of international financial flows. Today, the size of the international financial markets dwarf the value of international goods markets. For example, 1.4 days of foreign exchange trading in New York, London, and Tokyo equaled all of U.S. exports in 1988. The global integration of world financial markets and the rapid movement of funds between financial centers around the globe have resulted in an environment in which financial flows determine exchange rates. As a result, trade has increasingly become subject to the influence of financial markets, and firms, both in their long-term planning and their day-to-day operations, are affected by major exogenous and volatile shifts in currency values. These shifts in turn affect both the costs and price structure as well as the profitability of the international marketer.

In addition, the direction of world financial flows has had a major impact on some markets. Due to the liquidity problems in less-developed countries, imports into countries experiencing problems in servicing their debt decreased by 32% from 1979 to 1985, while their exports scored rapid increases. As a result, Latin America's role in U.S. trade has changed dramatically. In 1980, the U.S. had a $6 billion surplus in goods and services, which, by 1987, had turned into a deficit of $15 billion, largely due to debt crisis' impact on the region's purchasing power. This swing alone accounted for 10% of the total U.S. trade gap in 1987. Furthermore, the lack of liquidity has led to a new rise in the ancient form of countertrade, obviating, at least to some extent, the need for money but precipitating and encouraging economic inefficiencies.

IMPLICATIONS FOR CONSUMER
GOODS MARKETERS

World trade has become more important to the U.S. as a nation and to its firms and citizens. Growing linkages in the planning, production, and distribution of products increasingly blur the borders between domestic and international business activities, and have raised a host of new questions for policy makers and business executives. The highlighting of some of the new issues posed may enable consumer goods marketers to better conduct the planning and responsiveness of their marketing activities.

Historically, many firms have entered the international market in a gradual fashion, introducing new products first in highly industrialized nations, and subsequently expanding sales to other countries. For consumer goods, the argument in favor of such strategy was that other countries needed to catch up in their demand situation to the more industrialized nations. International markets were therefore used mainly as a strategic tool to delay market saturation by lengthening the life span of products. Today, however, it appears that such strategy is obsolete. Products and innovations are disseminated much more quickly, often leading to an almost simultaneous introduction in global markets. This development is a function of improved information flows due to tight international communication linkages. Furthermore, the increased level of wealth in emerging nations around the globe makes it easier and more likely for consumers to adopt new products. However, at the level of the firm, such a strategy also introduces greater risk factors, since failure may now occur at the global rather than the local level, with carryover to existing brands and business relationships. Holding back, however, may mean losing out to competitors who have acted more quickly.

At the same time, global products and strategies require greater coordination across markets. If, for example, harmonization of product and service standards is not accompanied by equalization of prices, phenomena such as gray marketing will remain as problems to international marketers. Gray markets in the United States alone constitute $10 billion of all retail sales and are typically in consumer product categories such as photographic equipment, cosmetics, and watches (Cespedes, Corey, and Rangan, 1988). Similarly, gray markets in Japan affect mainly consumer products such as cameras, film, and watches (Weigand, 1989).

The mobility of production factors introduces further new dimensions for the consumer goods marketer and policy maker. Policies and activities that once were inflexible now can become variable. For example, plant locations can be shifted and sourcing policies can be altered much more quickly than in the past. It seems reasonable to expect that consumers will grow less sensitive to the issue to country of origin since the traditional demarcations of "origin" are becoming blurred or even unrecognizable. For example, is a car produced by foreign owners in a U.S. plant with 70% domestic content more or less American than a car produced by U.S. owners in a U.S. plant with only 50% domestic content? Are joint ventures more domestic if the partners are all from the U.S. but producing abroad, versus foreign partners producing in the U.S.?

As a result, constant monitoring of the changing environment and the actions of competitors is required together with rapid responsiveness to change. Governments in turn are increasingly faced with the new notion of a "competitive platform" which, if inhospitable, will precipitate major shifts in economic activity.

Of great relevance will also be the role of the consumer and consumer costs. In "capitalist" countries, consumer sovereignty has traditionally played a major role. To provide a greater variety of products to consumers at a lower price was seen as a paramount step to improving the quality of life. "Socialist" economies paid much less attention to the individual consumer and rather stressed the importance of society and the group Now, as the iron curtain has been removed, a whole new era of concern is ushered in. The newly emerging democracies are displaying more concern about the individual consumer at the same time that the traditional industrialized nations are discovering the importance of societal issues such as global warming or pollution, and are beginning to differentiate between standard of living and quality of life.

This chapter does not aim to predict the detailed consumer market environment of the future. However, given the fundamental shifts that are occurring in the world today, it seems clear that traditional approaches to marketing may be dangerous to take. Global interdependence means less insularity and the need for a greater international awareness and responsiveness. Consumer goods marketers must incorporate the global perspective into their plans and action in order to have the benefits of this interdependence outweigh its drawbacks.

REFERENCES

Cespedes, F. V., Corey, E. R., and Rangan, V. K. (1988). Gray Markets: Causes and Cures. *Harvard Business Review*, 66(4), 75-82.

Choate, P. and Linger, J. (1988). Tailored Trade: Dealing with the World as It Is. *Harvard Business Review*, 66(1), 86-93.

Czinkota, M. and Ronkainen, I. (1990). *International Marketing,* 2nd Ed., Hinsdale, IL: The Dryden Press, 5.

Czinkota, M. R. (1991). The Impact of European Integration on Outsiders: The

Case of Eastern Europe. In *Corporate Strategy After the Free Trade Agreement in Europe 1992*, edited by A. Rugman and A. Verbeke. Greenwich, CT: JAI Press.

Hampton, W. and Schiller, Z. (1988, February 29). The Long Arm of Small Business. *Business Week*, 63-66.

Moore, J. (1989). Highlights of the 1989 Industrial Outlook. *U.S. Industrial Outlook*, Washington, DC: U.S. Government Printing Office, 21.

U.S. Department of Commerce. (1988). *International Direct Investment: Global Trends and the U.S. Role*. Washington, DC: U.S. Government Printing Office.

U.S. House of Representatives, 1988 Hearings on Small Business Obstacles to Exporting, Committee on Small Business, One Hundredth Congress, Second Session, October 4.

U.S. Travel Agencies Going Global. (1989, December 29). *The Washington Post*, p. F3.

Weigand, R. E. (1989). The Gray Market Comes to Japan. *Columbia Journal of World Business*, 24(3), 18-24.

Chapter 3

Global Market Segmentation Strategies and Trends

Salah S. Hassan
Lea Prevel Katsanis

SUMMARY. This chapter underscores the importance of segmentation as a global consumer marketing strategy. It outlines a historical perspective of global market segmentation that shows the current developments of this concept. Major consumption trends and their effect on global markets are also identified. Two key consumer groups that may be particularly amenable to global segmentation are isolated, and their key behavioral aspects are discussed. The similarities and differences that may influence these segments are also presented. Specific corporate examples of successful efforts to reach these two segments on a worldwide basis are discussed. Implications for both researchers and managers conclude the chapter.

INTRODUCTION

This chapter provides an alternative to the globalization versus localization framework. Current marketing literature indicates that this dichotomy is not a true reflection of real-life situations (Jain, 1989). It is essential to look from an eclectic perspective at both similarities and differences in evaluating consumer markets on a global scale. Today, consumer marketers are expected to think of global similarities and adapt to local differences as they develop

47

and implement targeted marketing programs. This perspective helps in determining similarities across national boundaries while assessing domestic (within-country) differences.

The challenge facing today's marketing academics and practitioners alike is to identify and respond to consumers' universal needs, wants, and expectations for products and services. Equally challenging is addressing cultural differences and other unique market conditions that require certain adaptations in any marketing program. Therefore, the perspective of this chapter is based on the analysis of similarities and differences in international consumer markets as the basis for identification of global segments that cut across national boundaries.

Within this general framework, the objectives of this chapter are: to evaluate recent developments in the global marketing literature; to introduce and define segmentation of global consumer markets; to present examples of emerging global consumer segments; and to illustrate with corporate cases how these profiles are being targeted. Finally, the chapter draws conclusions for consumer marketing academics and practitioners.

GLOBAL SEGMENTATION: A HISTORICAL REVIEW

This review of the literature will not revisit the debate between the two schools of thought on international marketing strategy: standardization versus adaptation. Others in the field have done an excellent job in analyzing the positions of these two groups. This discussion, rather, will take a historical perspective in analyzing developments in the body of knowledge since Levitt's (1983) thought-provoking article on the globalization of markets. There appears to be a distinct trend in the academic literature when examined on a "historical" basis, versus a "school of thought" basis. The pattern is that of segmentation, and it will have significant implications for the development of global marketing.

The "World Segment" Strategy

As the chief proponent of globalization, Levitt (1983) claimed that advancement in technology had affected communications, transportation, and travel; this, in turn, led to the convergence of consumer markets worldwide. He described this phenomenon as the "proletarianization" of world consumer markets. What he described, in fact, was the existence of a "world" segment; one for whom low-price and high quality would be common buying elements. This increase in market homogeneity on a global scale was caused by what Levitt (1983) referred to as "segment simultaneity," or the appearance of similar market segments in different countries at the same time. This appears to be the beginning of the concept of global segmentation, on a limited basis.

Several of Levitt's key sentiments are echoed by Porter (1986) in his work on global marketing strategy. He added, however, the consideration of integrating marketing strategy into the overall strategy of the firm. For Porter, the role of marketing is three dimensional: it involves the geographic concentration of certain marketing activities; and the use of marketing strategy to gain competitive advantage. The importance of segmentation, however, is where his work is of greatest importance. He pointed out that both identification of target segments within countries (country groups and buyers within countries) and physical product configuration, would assist in the determination of global marketing strategies. He does not, however, define specific segments.

Some researchers have acknowledged the effect of overall firm strategy, e.g., merger and acquisition activity, on global segmentation strategy. Also considered important are aspects such as product safety and quality standards. Sheth (1986) built a segmentation model based on both the similarities and differences of market needs and market resources. Included in his model are specialty segmentation, product segmentation, and market segmentation.

The "Country Cluster" Segmentation Strategy

Other authors (Kotler, 1986; Wind, 1986) have taken the approach of "country segments" i.e., countries as a specific market segment on their own. For example, Kotler challenged the concept of a "world segment," and developed a "customization index." He based this on the identification of countries and their dissimilarities on the following factors: products, buyers, and environmental factors. He argued that each element of the marketing mix must be matched against a specific target country. This ensures that specific differences would be identified in advance, and thus, built into new product design. Wind (1986) also discussed the "cluster of countries" concept in his research. Specific groups of countries may or may not possess similarities that are reachable through a single strategy. He viewed this clustering approach as an interim point between pure standardization and pure adaptation. This form of segmentation may have merits of its own, outside the considerations of the standardization/adaptation debate.

One "country segment" study of particular interest involved examination of 21 industrial nations to test for products with "universal," (i.e., global) appeal. Huszagh, Fox, and Day (1986) clustered countries into five groups on the basis of economic and demographic data. A product rating scale was developed for 27 different consumer product categories; and the results examined for cluster differences. Their findings suggested the existence of segments across countries, or country clusters. They found that the more "high touch" the products, the more consistent the acceptance rates were within a cluster. Additionally, products with no close substitutes, or necessities, also tend to have universal appeal.

An area related to country clusters is that of regional markets (e.g., the EC). Daniels (1987) proposed the use of cross-national strategies as a way of identifying market regions. This suggestion is similar to that of country clusters discussed in other research. He viewed this grouping as a means of pooling company resources and taking advantage of synergies in regions for improved competitiveness.

Additional research on this type of segmentation includes a "two-stage" segmentation approach recommended by Kreutzer (1988). This method included first grouping countries based on environmental indicators, such as technology, culture, ecology, and law. Second, within-country segmentation based on behavioral attributes such as consumption patterns, information processing, and brand name loyalty, was suggested.

Psychographic Segmentation Strategies

Arguments have been made for the use of psychographic variables in global segmentation strategies, rather than economic/demographic data. Domzal and Unger (1987) argued for four themes that appear universal throughout the world: materialism, heroism, play, and pro-creation, through the use of a "high-touch"/"high tech" continuum. However, this study was not based on empirical data.

A variety of industry organizations and individuals have produced empirical studies that focus on specific global segments across country boundaries, such as Rena Bartos' study on female consumers worldwide (1989). Among the most popular type of study conducted by major corporations and advertising firms is that of the psychographic segment profile. Two recent studies in this vein are by Goodyear Tire and Rubber (*Marketing News*, 1988) and by Ogilvy and Mather (*Marketing News*, 1989).

Goodyear Tire developed six different consumer profiles: the Prestige Buyer, the Comfortable Conservative, the Value Shopper, the Pretender, the Trusting Patron, and the Bargain Hunter. Different marketing mixes and promotional programs are utilized for these groups, which overlap country boundaries.

Ten segments based on lifestyle characteristics were developed by Ogilvy and Mather's Futures Division: Basic Needs, Fairer Deal, Traditional Family Life, Conventional Family Life, Look At Me, Somebody Better, Real Conservatism, Young Optimist, Visible Achiever, and the Socially Aware. As in the Goodyear study, these segments can be found across countries.

Cross-National Segmentation Strategies

Several researchers have examined the possibility of cross-national segmentation strategies, such as "strategically equivalent segments," cultural segmentation, and pro-trade segments. The concept of "strategically equivalent segments," or SES, was introduced by Kale and Sudharshan (1987). An SES represents a group of consumers who may cross national boundaries, but respond in the same fashion to a firm's marketing mix.

Cultural segmentation is viewed as a potentially sound segmentation strategy. Whitelock (1987) found a positive relationship between product adaptation and success in export markets based on cultural factors. The more developed the market in terms on consumption patterns, the stronger the pattern.

Pro-trade consumer segments are another way of defining global segments. This group has been empirically identified by Crawford,

Garland, and Ganesh (1988). They defined pro-trade consumers as those who show a preference for imported goods. Demographics, personal characteristics, and experience with imported products were the variables used to predict pro-trade tendencies.

Verhage, Dahringer, and Cundiff (1989) presented the strongest evidence to date for segmentation strategies across countries/markets. Their empirical study examined the energy conservation behavior of four countries, using cluster analysis to identify specific categories of behavior. The results suggested that neither a single global strategy nor a strategy across clusters would be justified. However, they determined that segmentation across countries within a cluster might be possible.

Synthesized Views of Segmentation

Several researchers in the field have attempted to bring together the various perspectives on global segmentation. Jain (1989) has posited that globalization is the way of the future, and suggests a framework for determining marketing programs in the global context. His conceptual framework emphasized the importance of segmentation in determining target markets, market positions, nature of products, and environmental and organizational factors. Other aspects, such as the consideration of culture, economy, and customer perceptions of specific markets were considered in his framework.

More recently, Wills, Samli, and Jacobs (1991) have recommended a global strategy decision model, which they define as the "be global, act local" model. They incorporate the theories of learning, involvement, diffusion/adoption, and culture context as the dimensions of a global product and subsequent strategy development.

These synthesized views of segmentation are adding to the sophistication of segmentation tools, and to a better understanding of how a firm can utilize segmentation strategies to better reach global markets.

OVERALL PATTERNS OF GLOBAL SEGMENTATION

This review of the literature reveals two consistent patterns: the identification of specific global segments, and the usefulness of segmentation in global marketing. The global segmentation strategies presented in Table 3.1 show how these patterns have developed since 1983: the move from one world segment to cross-national segments. This examination of the research, in fact, shows that there is more commonality within the literature than might be apparent from examining dichotomous viewpoints (e.g., standardization versus adaptation).

There has been an increase in the number of empirical studies to support the existence of global segments. For example, statistical analyses such as cluster analysis, perceptual mapping, and correspondence analysis are proving to be useful tools for segment identification. The emerging issue in the global marketing area at this time is as follows: global marketers need to identify measurable and reachable segments that transcend national boundaries. In order to attain this objective, a definition of global market segmentation is necessary.

GLOBAL MARKET SEGMENTATION DEFINED

Based on the past literature, it appears that a restatement of global market segmentation is in order. The authors propose that global market segmentation be defined as *the process of identifying specific segments, whether they be country groups or individual consumer groups, of potential consumers with homogeneous attributes who are likely to exhibit similar buying behavior.* The existence of global consumer segments that are measurable and reachable must be considered as a prerequisite for the successful execution of any global marketing strategy.

Traditionally, international marketers segmented world markets based on geopolitical variables (i.e., country segments). This approach presents three potential limitations: (1) it is based on country variables and not consumer behavioral patterns, (2) it assumes total homogeneity of the country segment, and (3) it overlooks the existence of homogeneous consumer segments that exist across national boundaries.

As discussed in the literature review, several studies (Kale and Sudharshan, 1987; Kreutzer, 1988) have presented managerial models for segmentation of global markets. Although it is not with-

TABLE 3.1. Global Segmentation Strategies

Segment Name	Author/ Date	Segment Description
World Segment	Levitt 1983	Low price + high quality part of a world homogenous market
Specialty, Product, and Market Segments	Sheth 1986	Products adapted to local market; different segments across different markets; product modified from country to country
Country Segments	Kotler 1986	Individual countries represent separate segments
Country Groupings or Clusters	Porter, 1986 Wind, 1986 Huszagh, Fox, & Day, 1986	Identification of country groupings with similar demographic, cultural, and buyer behavior similarities
Regional Segments	Daniels 1987	Identification of regions (country groupings) with similar characteristics for economics of scale (similar to clustering)
Psychographic Segments	Domzal & Unger, 1987	Segmentation across countries based on lifestyle factors and product benefits
Cultural Segments	Whitelock 1987	Identification of similar cultural values and attributes across country boundaries
"Strategically Equivalent" Segments	Kale & Sudharshan 1987	Segmentation to respond to a specific marketing mix
Pro-trade Segments	Crawford, Garland, & Ganesh, 1988	Segmentation on the basis of attitudes toward imports in developed and developing countries
Two-stage Segments	Kreutzer 1988	Stage 1: segment by environmental indicators Stage 2: further segment by buyer behavior indicators
Attitude Clusters	Verhage, Dahringer, & Cundiff, 1989	Similar consumer attitudes for specific products across countries

in the scope of this chapter to model the process of segmenting global markets, it is our intention to present profiles of two emerging global consumer segments. These two profiles will be presented with examples of how global firms are responding to current trends in consumption patterns. Additionally, there will be a discussion of criteria used in the identification of these segments across cultures and/or countries.

CONSUMPTION TRENDS IN GLOBAL MARKETS

It is essential to analyze all elements of commonalities and differences that may exist in today's global consumer markets. On a global scale, trends influencing consumption behavior can be cited as follows: increases in GNP per capita; steady rises in life expectancy; rapid increase of literacy and education levels; growth in industrialization and urbanization among developing countries; increases in share of manufactured exports by newly industrialized countries; advances in transportation; and expansion in world travel. These trends are influencing consumption behavior in a variety of ways. For example, some consumer products are becoming more widely accepted globally, such as consumer electronics, automobiles, fashion, home appliances, food products, and beverages.

Many of these products respond to needs and wants of consumer segments that cut across national boundaries. The challenge facing international marketers is to identify these segments and reach them with marketing programs that meet the common needs and wants of these consumers. However, uniqueness of certain market characteristics will also require understanding of cultural differences. It may be necessary to introduce certain modifications (e.g., language) to accommodate these differences. Consequently, success in global market segmentation efforts will be based on an eclectic perspective of both similarities and differences in evaluating global markets. Consumer marketers, in particular, should "think of global similarities and adapt to local differences" (Hassan, 1990). This is, in fact, the essence of global segmentation. This perspective helps any manager of consumer markets to determine similarities across national boundaries while assessing domestic (within-country) differences. Several case examples are presented here in order to illustrate how global firms identify and meet the needs of the globally segmented consumer markets.

THE "GLOBAL ELITE" SEGMENT

A growing market segment on a global scale is composed of consumers aspiring to an "elite lifestyle." The emergence of this global consumer segment has been attributed to increased wealth and widespread travel; this, along with other influencing factors, has stimulated the desire to own universally recognizable products. Products with prestige images that fit the expectation of being recognizable will be considered as universal in nature. Global marketers may identify commonality in prestige segments and target them accordingly. For example, European retailers such as Harrods, Ferragamo, and Galleries Lafayette reach U.S. consumers with upscale and unique leading-edge style fashions. These retailers target consumers directly through telemarketing/catalogue retailing without having physical presence, and with relative ease.

Today, global telemarketing is dramatically changing; for example, AT&T International 800 services are now available from 41 countries (Butkus, 1989). Toll-free calls are now available and being accepted from international consumers. In developing such global telemarketing programs, some adjustments may have to be introduced to the marketing strategy in response to differences such as language and calling-time zones.

Other global marketers targeted the elite consumers with product offerings that fit the image of exclusivity such as:

1. global durable goods such as Mercedes Benz, an automobile with perceived status;
2. global nondurable goods such as Perrier, a natural soft drink with a prestige image;
3. global services such as an American Express Gold Card, which offers financial services with the privileges of status and membership; and,

4. global retailers that carry products by Ralph Lauren's Polo franchises.

Such premium products can be targeted internationally to consumer segments that aspire to the images of leadership, exclusivity, high quality, and status in the same way that they are currently targeted in their home market (Quelch, 1987). Elite consumers often differentiate themselves through buying and using products that are distinguishable from those bought and used by mainstream consumers (Hassan, 1990). Identification of behavioral factors related to media, selection, information, acquisition, and purchasing decisions can be essential to successful global marketing efforts. For example, the marketing mix should be managed in a way that will target this segment with high quality and high-priced products that are promoted and distributed through selective channels, in order to build and maintain the image of exclusivity. Douglas and Wind (1987) argued for the emergence of this consumer segment that seeks premium or luxury products on a global scale. The existence of global segments is key condition for the success of global marketing programs and strategies.

Table 3.2 presents these criteria, as well as other variables that are being used in profiling this global segment. It is, however, important to recognize that this profile is rather broad for such a mega-segment on a global scale. Other variables such as sex, age, region, and product benefits sought must still be examined to identify elite consumers who are part of certain micro-segments in order to reach them by niche strategies. Further segmentation typically means that consumer needs are being addressed more closely and that brings higher profit margins for the firm (Quelch, 1987).

THE "GLOBAL TEENAGER" SEGMENT

Teenagers on a global scale, particularly in western and newly industrialized societies, are experiencing intense exposure to television media, international education, and frequent travel. Global

TABLE 3.2. Behavioral Aspects Related to the Identification of Global Consumer Segments

Name of Global Segment:	Global Elites	Global Teenagers
Shared Values:	wealth, success, status	growth, change, future, learning, play
Key Product Benefits Sought:	universally recognizable products with prestige image, high quality products	novelty, trendy image, fashion statement, name brands/novelty
Demographics:	very high income, social status and class/well-travelled/well-educated	age: 12-19, well-travelled, high media exposure
Media/Communication:	up-scale magazines, social selective channels (i.e., cliques), direct marketing, global telemarketing	teen magazines, MTV, radio, video, peers, role models
Distribution Channels:	selective (i.e., up-scale retailers)	general retailers with name brands
Price Range:	premium	affordable
Targeted by Global Firms such as:	Mercedes Benz Perrier American Express Ralph Lauren's Polo	Coca-Cola Co. Benetton Swatch International Sony PepsiCo, Inc.
Related Micro-Segments/ Clusters:	affluent women, top executives, highly educated professionals, professional athletes	pre-adolescents female teens male teens adolescents
Factors Influencing the emergence of the segment:	increased wealth, widespread travel, advancement of communication, technology	television media international education travel music

teens from New York, Tokyo, and Hong Kong to those from Paris, London, and Seoul are sharing memorable experiences that are reflected in their consumption behavior. Young consumers, whose cultural norms have not become ingrained, and who can share universal needs, wants, and fantasies, may be easily influenced by similar marketing programs (Hassan, 1990).

The "teenage culture" on a global scale shares a youthful lifestyle that values growth and learning with appreciation for future trends, fashion, and music. Teenagers are very self-conscious about the way they look, and role models act as an important influence on their choices (Guber, 1987). For example, MTV Network, the cable company for youth, broadcasts its English-language programming in 25 countries. Music is becoming an effective tool in communicating globally with teenagers, and the Coca-Cola Company responded to this fact by introducing its first global advertising campaign, "You Can't Beat the Feeling" (Feinberg, 1989). Also, in recognition of the growing similarities among teenagers, regardless of nationality, Benetton introduced colorful Italian knitwear based on its global advertising campaign, "The United Colors of Benetton." Other examples of global firms that meet the universal needs and wants of the teenage segment include Swatch International, Sony, Pepsico, and Gillette.

It is projected that in the 1990s, the size of the global teenage market will reach 1.37 billion. According to recent estimates, the purchasing power of the young consumers in the U.S. alone increased from $30 to $55 billion in recent years (Hall, 1987; Sellers 1989). Sony has responded to this booming market segment by introducing "My First Sony" line of audio products for children. (Such teenage products are being targeted globally in response to homogeneous teenage consumer desire for novelty, trendier designs, and image.) Often with aloof attitudes, teenage consumers tend to respond to peer pressure and resist parental control in accepting fads and name brands. Swatch International responded to these behavioral patterns by marketing watches that are trendier in design and that make a fashion statement.

The global teenager segment for blue jeans is the fastest growing demographic segment in the apparel industry. In fact, it is somewhat of a truism to discuss jeans, in that they are a basic teen clothing staple around the world. In 1991, jeans sales worldwide grew 25.2% to young men, and 9.9% to young women. The message to teens worldwide is that jeans are down-to-earth apparel that can be worn anywhere. The most popular jeans around the world are the most basic styles: an overwhelming 45% of teen males select Levi's, while the highly fragmented teen female market chooses Lee's at 9.5% (Underwood, 1992).

Table 3.2 illustrates the major product benefits sought by this global segment and shows other behavioral variables related to information acquisition, media exposure, and purchasing decisions. Unlike the elite consumers segment, global teenagers are confined by their age range of 12-19. However, further segmentation into clusters by age (e.g., pre-adolescents and adolescents) or by sex can be accomplished. In this context, it is important to recognize that today's teenagers may become tomorrow's global-brand loyal consumers.

IMPLICATIONS

There are several fertile areas for research that his study has uncovered on the subject of global consumer segmentation. They are: (1) identification of other potential global segments; (2) quantitative research of the elite and teen segments to determine their size, composition, and location; (3) profiling the teen and elite segments, as well as other identified segments on variables such as psychographics; (4) development of products needed by these segments; (5) in-depth qualitative research on the buying behavior of these segments and the identification of commonalities and characteristics of their purchase habits.

Additionally, managers need to consider the ramifications of global consumer segmentation, such as: (1) the "reach" factor: how marketers actually communicate with regular frequency to these audiences; (2) key tactical decisions: the media and promotional tools that will most effectively influence these segments (catalogs, radio, video productions, global magazines); (3) the organizational considerations: multinationals in particular will need to harness their subsidiaries for the most efficient use of resources; (4) new product development issues: the type of products and brands that will meet the needs of these global segments; and, (5) the potential economies of scale and profit implications that may result from this type of global segmentation.

CONCLUSIONS

It is essential for academics and practitioners of consumer marketing to be on the "cutting edge" regarding how the structure of global markets is changing. It is a major challenge for marketers to identify segments that transcend national and cultural boundaries on a global scale. However, this challenge is even greater when it necessitates dealing with the actual implementation of global marketing strategies. This chapter is only a start toward the understanding of how the global marketing concept can be moved from corporate offices to the actual marketplace.

REFERENCES

Bartos, R. (1989). *Marketing to Women Around the World*, Cambridge: The Harvard Business School Press.
Butkus, R. (1989). Global Telemarketing, *Export Today*, (December), pp. 5-7.
Crawford, J. C., Garland, B., and Ganesh, G. (1988). Identifying the Global Pro-Trade Consumer, *International Marketing Review*, (Winter), 3(4), pp. 25-33.
Daniels, J. D. (1987). Bridging National and Global Marketing Strategies Through Regional Operations, *International Marketing Review*, (Autumn), 2(3), pp. 29-44.
Domzal, T. and Unger, L. (1987). Emerging Positioning Strategies in Global Marketing, *Journal of Consumer Marketing*, (Fall), 4(4), pp. 23-40.
Douglas, S. P. and Wind, Y. (1987). The Myth of Globalization, *Columbia Journal of World Business*, (Winter), pp. 19-30.
Feinberg, A. (1989). The First Global Generation, *Adweek*, (February), pp. 18-27.
Guber, S. (1987). The Teenage Mind, *American Demographics*, (August), pp. 42-44.
Hall, C. (1987). Tween Power: Youth's Middle Tier Comes of Age, *Marketing & Media Decisions*, (October), pp. 56-62.
Hassan, S. (1990). Dynamics of Global Consumer Marketing in *Global Business Management in the 1990's*, edited by R. Moran et al., pp. 199-203. Beacham Publishing Inc.
Huszagh, S. M., Fox, R. J., and Day, E. (1986). Global Marketing: An Empirical Investigation, *Columbia Journal of World Business*, (Winter–Twentieth Anniversary Issue), 20(4), pp. 31-43.

Jain, S. C. (1989). Standardization of International Marketing Strategy: Some Research Hypotheses, *Journal of Marketing*, (January), 53, pp. 70-79.

Kale, Sudhir H. and Sudharshan, D. (1987). A Strategic Approach to International Segmentation, *International Marketing Review*, (Summer), pp. 60-70.

Kotler, P. (1986). Global Standardization–Courting Danger, *Journal of Consumer Marketing*, (Spring), 3(2), pp. 13-15.

Kreutzer, R. T. (1988). Marketing Mix Standardization: An Integrated Approach in Global Marketing, *European Journal of Marketing*, 22(10), pp. 19-30.

Levitt, T. (1983). The Globalization of Markets, *Harvard Business Review*, (May/June), pp. 92-102.

Marketing News (1988). Attitude Research Assesses Global Market Potential, (August), pp. 10,11.

Marketing News (1989). Value Segments Help Define International Market, (Fall), 17.

Porter, M. E. (1986). The Strategic Role of International Marketing, *Journal of Consumer Marketing*, (Spring), 3(2), pp. 17-21.

Quelch, J. (1987). Marketing the Premium Product, *Business Horizons*, (May/June), pp. 38-45.

Sellers, P. (1989). The ABC's of Marketing to Kids, *Fortune*, (May), pp. 114-120.

Sheth, J. (1986). Global Markets or Global Competition? *Journal of Consumer Marketing*, (Spring), 3(2), pp. 9-11.

Underwood, E. (1992). Jean-etics 101, *Brandweek*, (August 17), 33(31), pp. 14-15.

Verhage, B. J., Dahringer, L. D., and Cundiff, E. W. (1989). Will a Global Marketing Strategy Work? An Energy Conservation Perspective, *Journal of the Academy of Marketing Science*, (Spring), 17(2), pp. 129-136.

Whitelock, J. M. (1987). Global Marketing and the Case for International Product Standardization, *European Journal of Marketing* (U.K.), 21(9), pp. 32-44.

Wills, J., Samli, A. C., and Jacobs, L. (1991). Developing Global Products and Marketing Strategies: A Construct and Research Agenda, *Journal of the Academy of Marketing Sciences*, (Winter), 19(1), pp. 1-10.

Wind, Y. (1986). The Myth of Globalization, *The Journal of Consumer Marketing*, (Spring), 3(2), pp. 3-26.

Chapter 4

International Product Rollout:
A Country Cluster Approach

Paul A. Herbig
Hugh E. Kramer

SUMMARY. In this, the global age of marketing, no astute business executive can avoid international competition. If a company is to survive it must be global in scope, actively marketing its products to the entire world. Launching a product internationally is a rather complex task, requiring different considerations than doing so domestically. Most marketers prefer to roll out products either geographically, by considering national growth rates, or by using elaborate matrices such as McKinsey product portfolios. Cultural reasons are usually given little or no attention.

In this chapter, we offer a modified approach to international product launch activities: a country cluster approach that utilizes cultural similarities as the basis for prioritizing timing decisions in the introduction of new products in world markets.

NATIONAL CHARACTERISTICS

Culture gives the people of any society a sense of common identity and a means of relating to one another, a common sharing within the same group but distinct from that of another culture. Patterns of personality do exist for groups that share a common

---

Paul A. Herbig is indebted to the East-West Center of Honolulu, Hawaii for their support of this paper while he was an intern there in Spring 1990.

culture. In the process of being socialized, the individual picks up the knowledge, the ideas, the beliefs and values, and the phobias and anxieties of the society. Some of this is taught explicitly; most of it is absorbed subconsciously. Americans value time and efficiency, and place emphasis on individual achievement. The Japanese place emphasis on the group, and value and honor complex sets of obligations with regard to status, age, and place in society. Mexicans learn to treat time less frenetically, and to value human response and feelings and close personal relationships. A culture preconditions its members to perceive and value social relationships and, in fact, all aspects of daily life and interactions in terms of the norms of their cultures. We tend to project our own motives to the behaviors prevailing in other cultures and naively assume our way of thinking about our society is universal.

Stereotyping occurs when assumptions about collective properties of a group are applied to a particular individual. Mr. X is Japanese; Mr. Y is American. Mr. Y assumes that Mr. X adheres to collectivist values. Mr. X likewise is convinced Mr. Y as an American is a rugged individualist. These are stereotypes and they may be unwarranted. Stereotyping is not useful for describing individuals but can be useful when outlining the social system the individuals live in. Social systems do not refer to the exceptional individual, but to the dominant values and behavioral characteristics of the majority of its people (Hofstede, 1990). Cultural stereotypes do provide clues on what to expect generally with members of that culture. For example, when a businessman wishes to enter the Italian market, it helps if he assumes that the Italian people are culturally relatively homogeneous and builds his marketing strategy around a basic set of stereotypes about the Italian people's motivations and behavior. This would, indeed, be far more successful and economical than to start with no cultural concept at all. Nonetheless, although accurate in the aggregate, like a bell-shaped curve, the Italian market is comprised of millions of different individuals. In reality, no two humans belonging to the same culture respond in the same way.

In international marketing, we likewise enter the French or Italian market as if they were similar in all aspects. We know it isn't totally true and that many deviations may occur, but our assumption is in a general sense accurate and makes more economic sense than to try to custom market every product. Marketers frequently have used segmentation strategies to divide mass markets based on common geographic, demographic, psychographic or behavioral, and lifestyle characteristics in order to gain a greater competitive advantage and market share. Marketers, therefore, tend to understand the usefulness and limitations of stereotyping better than managers from other functional areas.

We often associate cultural stereotypes with national characteristics. We say the French are egotistical, the Italians late, the Germans punctual and efficient, the English refined and cool, the Americans brashly independent and individualistic, and the Japanese so collectivist that they travel only in groups all wearing the same uniforms. Can we really do so? Each of us can probably cite instances of Japanese who are fiercely individualistic and risk-taking, as well as of Americans who are risk avoiders and think in collectivist concepts. Can one abstract meaningful cultural characterization in the aggregate for a society?

Numerous cross-cultural studies have been conducted to resolve this question. Haire, Ghiselli, and Porter (1966) evaluated 3,641 managers from 14 countries. They determined that two-thirds of the variance can be explained by national differences. The responses in their study consistently and significantly differed from country to country. England, Negandhi, and Wilpert (1974), in their study, found that culture or nationality explained one-third of the variance by national differences. Bass and Burger (1979) surveyed managers in twelve countries on eleven attributes and found the mean scores between nationalities were significantly different, also confirming Haire's results. Sirota and Greenwood (1971) administered a questionnaire to 13,000 employees working in 46 countries of a multinational manufacturer of electrical equipment. Significant differences between countries and clusters were reported. The Anglo cluster scores highest on goals pertaining to individual achievement and low on the desire for security. The French give greater importance to security and less importance to challenging work. Managers in Nordic countries are less oriented towards achievement or recognition and more towards tangible forms of accomplishment.

Ronen and Kraut (1977) studied 4,000 technicians in 15 countries of a multinational electronic organization (with a United States headquarters) concerning 22 work goals and also analyzed Haire's and Sirota and Greenwood's data. Three factor analyses were made of their own data and compared with Haire's and Sirota and Greenwood's data. Clusters found in all three cases included an Anglo cluster (in one of the three instances including Ireland and Israel), a Germanic cluster, a Nordic cluster, a Latin European cluster, a Latin American cluster and several independent segments (Brazil, Israel, Japan, and Sweden). Griffeth et al. (1980) studied 1,768 managers in 15 Western countries of an international manufacturing company (USA headquarters). Only three superclusters appeared in their data: an Anglo cluster consisting of UK and British-speaking Canada; a Germanic-Nordic cluster; and a Latin European cluster (which strangely enough included the Netherlands). The Germanic-Nordic cluster was primarily Protestant, while the Latin European cluster was dominated by Catholic nations.

In by far the most comprehensive survey ever attempted, Hofstede (1984) analyzed the data from questionnaires given in 20 different languages to 116,000 IBM employees from 72 countries at two different time frames (1968, 1972). He found significant differences between countries and the existence of similar country clusters that appear to confirm the earlier studies. Hofstede defined four basic dimensions that accounted for over 50% of the variance. They were: (1) Individualism versus Collectivism–the extent to which the individual prefers personal freedom versus the acceptance of responsibility to family, tribal, or national groups; (2) Power Distance–the degree of tolerance to, and inequality in, wealth and power indicated by the extent to which centralization and autocratic power are accepted and executed; (3) Risk (also called Uncertainty Avoidance)–the extent to which the society avoids risk and creates security by emphasizing technology and buildings, laws and rules, and religion; and (4) Masculinity versus Femininity–the extent to which the society differentiates roles between the sexes and places emphasis on so-called masculine values of performance, aggression, and visible achievement. These dimensions have been confirmed by many other subsequent studies. Their wide acceptance is indicative of their validity and usefulness as a manageable number of dimensions.

Ronen and Shenkar (1985) examined eight empirical studies that used value surveys or attitudinal data to cluster countries. The common base of the Anglo nations, the Germanic-Nordic tie can be explained by language and religion similarities as can the Roman Empire's influence in Latin Europe. Geography, however, cannot be the dominative factor. (See also Ohmae's [1990] concept of the "equidistant manager," who no longer distinguishes between home and overseas markets and views all key customers as equally important and "equidistant" from the corporate center.) The wide geographic flow found in the Anglo cluster can only mean that the spread of English colonialism and the resulting influence of language and religion played an important part. Their analysis seems to confirm the existence of cultural clustering by countries, even though geographic divergence does exist.

All the surveys cited previously do not only support the existence of common cultural attributes, but also indicate an amazing predominance of clusters by countries and common dimensionality of attributes. All countries within a cluster are similar to one another and dissimilar to those outside the cluster. Ronen and Shenkar (1985) made the case for a synthesis of clusters by countries. This, then, brings together all the clustering results as transpired in their survey. Their clusters are depicted as a "Motivational World Map" in Figure 4.1 and described below:

Anglo-American: This cluster is composed of the United States, Great Britain, Australia, Canada, New Zealand, Ireland, South Africa, and other former British colonies. It is characterized by a cultural focus on motivation through personal, individual success in the form of wealth, public recognition, and self-actualization. It is very high on individual achievement, but relatively low on the desire for security. These countries score high on Individualism, low on Power Index, moderate to high on Masculinity, and low on Uncertainty Avoidance.

Nordic: This cluster is composed of the Scandinavian countries of Denmark, Norway, Sweden, and Finland. It is characterized by a cultural focus on motivation being achieved through success and belonging. Success is measured partly as collective success and in the quality of human relationships and the living environment. It is less oriented than other clusters toward personal advancement and

FIGURE 4.1. A Synthesis of Country Clusters

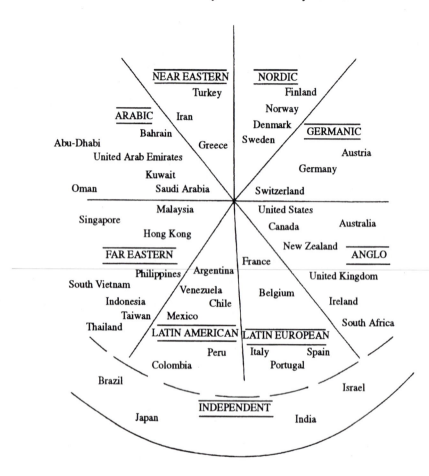

recognition and more oriented toward job accomplishments. Here people exhibit more concern with the immediate environment (friendly and efficient) and less with the organization as a whole (working for a successful company and contributing to the company). People in the Nordic culture place emphasis on the condition that jobs should not interfere with their personal lives. Scandinavia is above average in risk tolerance; emphasis here is on maturity and steadiness, with a premium placed on tolerance and sociability.

Femininity is combined with weak Uncertainty Avoidance and a low Power Distance.

Germanic: This cluster is composed of Germany, Austria, and Switzerland. It is characterized by a cultural focus on motivation through personal success and individual security as measured by wealth, hard work, and public esteem. These countries are low in tolerance for risk, with an emphasis on self-realization, leadership, and independence as life goals. They are highly competitive with little regard being placed on patience and reliability. They score relatively high on the Masculinity index but low on Power Distance.

Latin-European: This cluster is composed of France, Spain, Italy, Portugal, and Belgium, as well as the Latin American countries. It is characterized by a cultural focus on motivation through security and belonging. Individual wealth and achievement is less important than group solidarity. The Latin European cluster follows the old Roman empire boundaries and tends to be highly correlated with the Catholic religion. These countries scored high on Uncertainty Avoidance, moderate to high on Power Distance, low to medium on the Masculinity index, and relatively high on Individualism.

Japan: The Japan cluster follows a rather unique pattern in that many of the goals that ordinarily are related to one another do not appear to be so here. Japanese are more motivated than others by their desire for earnings opportunities. On the other hand, their desire for advancement is less developed. They know their position in society and in their company. The Japanese appear to score very high on challenge but low on autonomy. They place a low value on conflict and open expression of feelings. Japanese place strong emphasis on working in a friendly and efficient department and on having good physical working conditions. These apparent contradictions are in line with the teachings of Oriental philosophy. Japan is high on both Masculinity and Uncertainty Avoidance and relatively high on Power Distance but extremely low on Individualism.

Far Eastern: This cluster includes Malaysia, Hong Kong, Singapore, Philippines, Indonesia, Taiwan, and Thailand. The PRC–mainland China–would fall in here but was not surveyed at the time. This cluster has high Power, low to medium Uncertainty Avoidance, low Individualism, and a medium level on the Masculinity-Femininity index. Pakistan and India in many studies join this cluster. Nations in this cluster tend to be autocratic and paternalistic, with a centralized decision-making style and a strong task orientation. The people are concerned with rules, emphasize patience and modesty, are low in risk tolerance, and deemphasize pleasure. No doubt, Korea would also fall into this cluster.

Arabic: This cluster includes Bahrain, Abu-Dhabi, Oman, Kuwait, Saudi Arabia, and the United Arab Emirates. This cluster is geographically concentrated, Moslem in religion, and has numerous historical and traditional similarities. Although not included due to lack of survey results, Egypt, Morocco, Libya, Tunisia, and Algeria would also probably fall into this cluster.

Near Eastern: This cluster includes Greece, Turkey, Yugoslavia, and Iran. This cluster has high Power, high Uncertainty Avoidance, low Individualism, and low to medium Masculinity-Femininity. It is diverse in all aspects except geography. This cluster tends toward centralized decision making, and highly personalized, strong leaders. Little delegation or task orientation exists. Emphasis is on family and status.

Independents: This cluster includes India, Brazil, Israel, and Pakistan. Throughout the surveys, the responses from Belgium sometimes mixed with the Latin cluster, once with the Germanic one, and oftentimes showed independence. Since southern Belgium was once part of France, still speaks French, and has a Catholic heritage, this could account for its clustering with Latin-European countries. Northern Belgium, being Flemish with its Protestant history and more closely affiliated with the Netherlands than France, is more likely to be associated with Germanic/Nordic countries than Latin countries. Switzerland with its multicultural heritage also showed no general pattern. This confirms the image that cultural heritage rather than nationally was being defined in the studies.

An analysis of the Anglo-American cluster by particular cultural attributes indicates almost uniform similarity. A comparison of the countries within Hofstede's four dimensions (see Figure 4.2) shows that they all have medium Power indices (35 to 40), low Uncertainty Avoidance (Risk) indices (35-51), and high Achievement Scores. The highest score is related to Individualism (80 to 91), the highest of any countries in the world. In all three matrices (a matrix being

FIGURE 4.2. Index Values and Rank of Fifty Countries and Three Regions on Four Cultural Dimensions

Country	Abbre- viation	Power Distance Index (PDI)	Rank	Uncertainty Avoidance Index (UAI)	Rank	Individualism Index (IDV)	Rank	Masculinity Index (MAS)	Rank
Argentina	ARG	49	18-19	86	36-41	46	28-29	56	30-31
Australia	AUL	36	13	51	17	90	49	61	35
Austria	AUT	11	1	70	26-27	55	33	79	49
Belgium	BEL	65	33	94	45-46	75	43	54	29
Brazil	BRA	69	39	76	29-30	38	25	49	25
Canada	CAN	39	15	48	12-13	80	46-47	52	28
Chile	CHL	63	29-30	86	36-41	23	15	28	8
Colombia	COL	67	36	80	31	13	5	64	39-40
Costa Rica*	COS	35	10-12	86	36-41	15	8	21	5-6
Denmark	DEN	18	3	23	3	74	42	16	4
Equador*	EQA	78	43-44	67	24	8	2	63	37-38
Finland	FIN	33	8	59	20-21	63	34	26	7
France	FRA	68	37-38	86	36-41	71	40-41	43	17-18
Germany (F.R.)	GER	35	10-12	65	23	67	36	66	41-42
Great Britain	GBR	35	10-12	35	6-7	89	48	66	41-42
Greece	GRE	60	26-27	112	50	35	22	57	32-33
Guatemala*	GUA	95	48-49	101	48	6	1	37	11
Hong Kong	HOK	68	37-38	29	4-5	25	16	57	32-33
Indonesia*	IDO	78	43-44	48	12-13	14	6-7	46	22
India	IND	77	42	40	9	48	30	56	30-31
Iran	IRA	58	24-25	59	20-21	41	27	43	17-18
Ireland	IRE	28	5	35	6-7	70	39	68	43-44
Israel	ISR	13	2	81	32	54	32	47	23
Italy	ITA	50	20	75	28	76	44	70	46-47
Jamaica*	JAM	45	17	13	2	39	26	68	43-44
Japan	JAP	54	21	92	44	46	28-29	95	50
Korea (S.)*	KOR	60	26-27	85	34-35	18	11	39	13
Malaysia*	MAL	104	50	36	8	26	17	50	26-27
Mexico	MEX	81	45-46	82	33	30	20	69	45
Netherlands	NET	38	14	53	18	80	46-47	14	3
Norway	NOR	31	6-7	50	16	69	38	8	2
New Zealand	NZL	22	4	49	14-15	79	45	58	34
Pakistan	PAK	55	22	70	26-27	14	6-7	50	26-27
Panama*	PAN	95	48-49	86	36-41	11	3	44	19
Peru	PER	64	31-32	87	42	16	9	42	15-16

FIGURE 4.2 (continued)

Country	Abbre-viation	Power Distance		Uncertainty Avoidance		Individualism		Masculinity	
		Index (PDI)	Rank	Index (UAI)	Rank	Index (IDV)	Rank	Index (MAS)	Rank
Philippines	PHI	94	47	44	10	32	21	64	39-40
Portugal	POR	63	29-30	104	49	27	18-19	31	9
South Africa	SAF	49	18-19	49	14-15	65	35	63	37-38
Salvador*	SAL	66	34-35	94	45-46	19	12	40	14
Singapore	SIN	74	40	8	1	20	13-14	48	24
Spain	SPA	57	23	86	36-41	51	31	42	15-16
Sweden	SWE	31	6-7	29	4-5	71	40-41	5	1
Switzerland	SWI	34	9	58	19	68	37	70	46-47
Taiwan	TAI	58	24-25	69	25	17	10	45	20-21
Thailand	THA	64	31-32	64	22	20	13-14	34	10
Turkey	TUR	66	34-35	85	34-35	37	24	45	20-21
Uruguay*	URU	61	28	100	47	36	23	38	12
U.S.A.	USA	40	16	46	11	91	50	62	36
Venezuela	VEN	81	45-46	76	29-30	12	4	73	48
Yugoslavia	YUG	76	41	88	43	27	18-19	21	5-6
Regions:									
East Africa*	EAF	64	(31-32)	52	(17-18)	27	(18-19)	41	(14-15)
West Africa*	WAF	77	(42)	54	(18-19)	20	(13-14)	46	(22)
Arab Ctrs.*	ARA	80	(44-45)	68	(24-25)	38	(25)	53	(28-29)

*Based on data added later.

Source: G. Hofstede, "National Cultures in Four Dimensions," International Studies of Management and Organization, 13(2):52 (1983).

the comparison of countries using two of the four Hofstede dimensions), the Power-Individualism matrix (Figure 4.3), the Power Distance-Uncertainty Avoidance (Figure 4.4), and the Masculinity-Femininity Uncertainty Avoidance (Figure 4.5), the Anglo-American countries provide concise and consistent cultural clusters.

The findings clearly suggest that culturally, the United States, Canada, Australia, and the United Kingdom are similar. This is understandable since all are derived from a common land with

FIGURE 4.3. The Position of the 50 Countries on the Power Distance and Individualism Scales

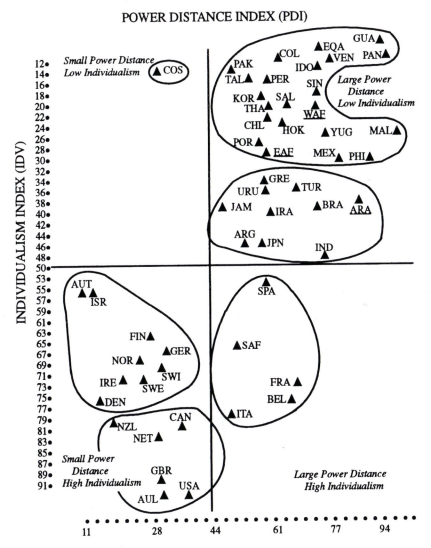

A POWER DISTANCE ×
INDIVIDUALISM–COLLECTIVISM PLOT
for 50 countries & 3 regions

FIGURE 4.4. The Position of the 50 Countries on the Power Distance and Uncertainty Avoidance Scales

A POWER DISTANCE ×
UNCERTAINTY AVOIDANCE PLOT
for 50 countries & 3 regions

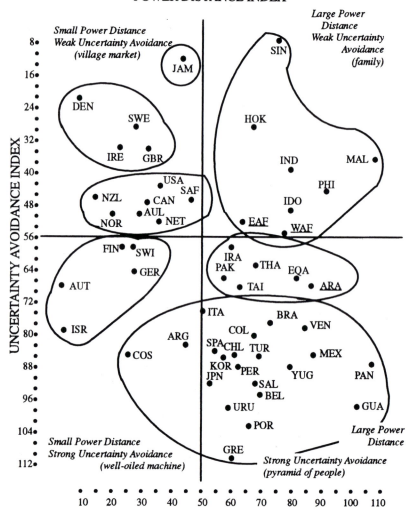

POWER DISTANCE INDEX

FIGURE 4.5. The Position of the 50 Countries on the Uncertainty Avoidance and Masculinity Scales

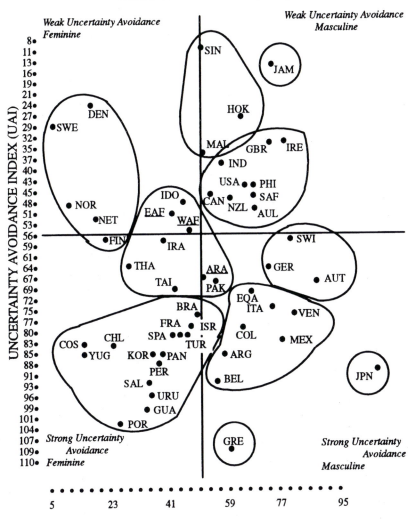

A MASCULINITY-FEMININITY ×
UNCERTAINTY AVOIDANCE PLOT
for 50 countries & 3 regions

MASCULINITY INDEX (MAS)

common heritage, language, and laws with the point of departure being only a few hundred years ago.

Usage of this country cluster as well as the others defined above appears to be reasonable and justified for international marketing planning. This includes market clustering based on cultural similarities and differences.

DESIGNING A GLOBAL MARKETING STRATEGY BY COUNTRY CLUSTERS

How can managers put this concept of cultural clusters to work in their strategic planning and day-to-day operations? The following procedure suggests a step-by-step method of using the country-cluster approach. It is summarized in Figure 4.6 of the exhibits.

1. *The effective manager when applying the Cultural Cluster Strategy. . . . Assesses the cultural identification,* i.e., the cultural cluster to which his company belongs. Even so-called Multinationals tend to have a predominant cultural leaning. Where is the corporate headquarters located? Where is the majority of business done? What is the nationality of the majority of the executives? Is there a principal language spoken? From which lab or manufacturing facility are the major products coming? He identifies his home country and primary cluster. If he is with a German firm, then his cultural cluster is Germanic; if he is with a predominantly Swedish firm, his cluster is Nordic; if he is with an Australian multinational firm, his primary cluster would be Anglo.

2. *. . . Will start* expanding his marketing effort first in his home country or in the cultural home cluster of his company. This can be done regardless of geographical boundaries or limitations. The effective manager proceeds from cultural, not geographic, reference points. For example, if his home country is France, he should market to the French cultural community, which includes not only France but the French-speaking parts of Belgium, Switzerland, Italy, and eventually even the French satellites of New Caledonia, Tahiti, and Quebec. He will subsequently expand his marketing activities to the *entire* French cultural community. The effective manager for other cultural entities such as German, Italian, or Span-

FIGURE 4.6. Designing a Global Marketing Strategy by Country Clusters

Steps	Issues	Procedures
		The effective Manager
Step 1:	Cultural Cluster Identification	... **Assesses Cultural Affiliation** of the company and key managers based on country clusters in Figure 4.1.
Step 2:	Cultural Cluster Selection	... **Selects** cultural target cluster in line with company's or top managers' cultural heritage.
Step 3:	Country Evaluation within Cluster	... **Proceeds** to examine marketing the product in countries of his own cultural cluster.
Step 4:	NonCultural Environmental Analysis	... **Analyzes** non-cultural opportunities and constraints for company business in each country of the target cluster in terms of a. geographic opportunities and constraints, e.g., location, transportation, climate b. political-legal opportunities and constraints c. demographic opportunities and contraints, e.g., number of people, potential customers, by target gender, age group, race, household size and income d. economic . . . e.g., purchasing power, discretionary income, balance of payments, stage of business cycle, distribution channels, communications media, currency exchange, restrictions, infrastructure, availability of local capital for financing, technology, utilities.
Step 5:	Cultural Match	... **Establishes** the new product's and total company product portfolio's cultural match. a. Currently discernible and latent (potential) market demand for product and other lines. b. Present product lines (strengths and weaknesses) of other companies, which compete directly with the new product and other company products, also nature and likelihood of competitors' counter strategies. c. Present product lines (strengths and weaknesses) of other companies, which compete indirectly; also nature and likelihood of competitors' counter strategies. d. Accessibility of distribution channels to handle the new product, expected mark-ups and promotion and financial support. e. Availability and Cost of communication media and their expected effectiveness and efficiency to inform and persuade the target markets. f. Estimate of the present and future market potential and why consumers would prefer the new product over competitors' offerings.

FIGURE 4.6. (continued)

Steps	Issues	Procedures
		The effective Manager
Step 6:	Corporate Goals And Marketing Objectives	... **Sets** <u>corporate goals and realistic Marketing objectives</u>, which can be measured and supported by resources.
Step 7:	Prioritizing National Markets	... **Prioritizes** each country of the relevant target cluster for a phased roll-out strategy with approximate dates of entry, entry budgets to allocate, etc.
Step 8:	Global Marketing Plan	... **Designs** the <u>global</u> strategic marketing plan in terms of a. Product Strategy b. Promotion Strategy c. Price Strategy d. Place Strategy (preferred distribution channels and physical distribution)
Step 9:	Differentiated National Marketing Plans	... **Designs** <u>Differentiated National Marketing Plans</u> (if needed) to comply with the national and/or regional peculiarities.
Step 10:	Contingency Plans	... **Prepares** <u>Contingency Plans</u> in case unexpected constraints or environmental changes require a revision of the plan.
Step 11:	Go/No Go Decisions, Timing & Execution	... **Decides** on a <u>go or no-go</u> and the <u>timing</u> of the implementation of the roll-out strategy. In case of a go decision, he carefully yet forcefully, <u>executes</u> the marketing plan.
Step 12:	Feedback & Control	... **Monitors** the results and <u>takes corrective actions</u> whenever needed; also <u>revises</u> the global and differentiated national plans and makes sure that unbiased realistic feedback is continuously provided.
Step 13:	Secondary & Tertiary Country Clusters	... **Evaluates** the potential of other (secondary and tertiary) <u>country clusters</u> & prioritizes them for future expansion via steps 14 through 17. Repeats steps 4 through 12 for each country within target clusters.
Step 14:	Product Characteristics	... **Determines** the salient characteristics of the product.
Step 15:	Chooses Next Cluster	... **Targets** the Product Launch and Introduction activities to the closest cluster from his primary cluster.

Steps	Issues	Procedures
		The effective Manager
Step 16:	Repeats Prioritization Procedure for each country and cluster	. . . **Repeats** Steps 4 through 12 for each cluster and each country in the cluster, prioritizing and creating individual marketing plans for each one as necessary.
Step 17:	Continues	. . . **Continues** the procedure (and repeating Cluster Process [the reprioritizing steps]) choosing those clusters nearest his home cluster on the appropriate dimensional matrix.
Step 18:	Locating	. . . **Locates** his multinational competitors and Competitors and evaluates them on the same cultural dimensions.
Step 19:	Competes With Major Competitors	. . . **Competes** head on with multinational competitor in the competitor's home cluster or country only after all other nearby clusters have been attacked and penetrated.

ish will likewise expand his marketing operation to the German, Italian, or Spanish cultural community.

3. . . . *Proceeds* to examine the potential of marketing the product in rest of the countries in his cultural cluster. For the French or Spanish or Italian manager, this means focusing on the Latin European and Latin American markets. The evidence is overwhelming that those within a country cluster are similar in cultural traits and this similarity extends into all dimensions of business. This should not be interpreted as if the marketing programs and advertising campaigns can be transferred directly from one country to another without changes. The cultural similarities provided by a cluster merely mean that the differences are smaller than going to outside clusters that are much further away from your primary cluster.

For example, the Latin European cluster includes Spain, Portugal, Italy, and France. If the effective manager is based in France, the initial marketing programs will be in French. Languages are different and the advertising and promotional materials must be translated into Spanish, Portuguese, or Italian. Perhaps even some minor nuances must be changed. The underlying differences in people's perceptions and motivations, however, will still be minor. Less marketing effort and changes from the marketing plan created in the home country are needed than if one were to go to another cluster. The different languages may require a translation, but the culturally conditioned, persuasive core of the message will probably be kept relatively intact. This is what belonging to the same primary cultural cluster really means: minimal changes in the marketing promotional and advertising campaign of the product.

The effective manager analyzes the countries within a cluster by following Steps 4 through 12.

4. . . . *Analyzes non-cultural opportunities and constraints* for company business in each country of the target cluster in terms of:

  a. geographic opportunities and constraints, e.g., location, transportation, climate, and topography;
  b. political-legal opportunities and constraints;
  c. demographic opportunities and constraints, e.g., number of people, potential customers, by target gender, age group, race, household size, and income;
  d. economic, e.g., purchasing power, discretionary income, balance of payments, stage of business cycle, distribution channels, communications media, currency exchange, restrictions, infrastructure, availability of local capital for financing, technology, utilities

5. . . . *Establishes* the new product's and total company product portfolio's *cultural match.*

  a. currently discernible and latent (potential) market demand for product and other lines;
  b. present product lines (strengths and weaknesses) of other companies that compete directly with the new product and other company products; also nature and likelihood of competitors' counter strategies;
  c. present product lines (strengths and weaknesses) of other companies that compete indirectly; also nature and likelihood of competitors' counter strategies;
  d. accessibility of distribution channels to handle the new product; expected mark-ups and promotion and financial support;
  e. availability and cost of communication media and their expected effectiveness and efficiency to inform and persuade the target markets;

f. estimate of the present and future market potential and why consumers would prefer the new product over competitors' offerings

6. . . . . *Compares corporate goals and sets realistic marketing objectives* for the chosen country that can be measured and supported by resources.

7. . . . *Prioritizes* each country of the relevant target cluster for a phased roll-out strategy with approximate dates of entry, entry budgets to allocate, etc.

8. . . . *Designs* the individual country strategic marketing plan in terms of:

a. product strategy
b. promotion strategy
c. price strategy
d. place strategy (preferred distribution channels and physical distribution)

9. . . . *Designs Differentiated National Marketing Plans* for each country in the cluster (if needed) to comply with the national and/or regional peculiarities.

10. . . . *Prepares Contingency Plans* in case unexpected constraints or environmental changes require a revision of the plan.

11. . . . *Decides on a go or no-go* and the *timing* of the implementation of the roll-out strategy. In case of a go decision, he carefully yet forcefully *executes* the marketing plan.

12. . . . *Monitors* the results and *takes corrective actions* whenever needed; also *revises* the global and differentiated national plans and makes sure that unbiased realistic feedback is continuously provided.

13. . . . *Evaluates* the potential of other (secondary and tertiary) *country clusters and* prioritizes them for future expansion. He does this by following steps 14 through 17.

14. . . . *Determines* the salient characteristics of the product. The best way to do so is in terms of the Hofstede dimensions described earlier. They have been shown to be well-correlated and manageable in business practice. Indices have been established for over seventy countries (see Figure 4.2). So the data is accessible and proven to be quite accurate and usable.

Questions the effective manager may wish to ask regarding the product and its usage may include: Is there risk involved in its use? Is it a status-oriented product? Is it used more by one of the two genders or by both? Is it a faddish product that is subject to peer or group pressure? The effective manager then selects the two primary characteristics that distinguish his product from those of competitors and that are relatively easy to communicate to his target market. For example, Hofstede's first dimension deals with the cultural issue of how much people are guided in their behavior by individualistic or collectivist values. The other dimensions as previously described are related to power distance, the willingness to accept risk, and the gender role in consumption patterns. For practical purposes, the selection of two, instead of four, major dimensions usually suffices to provide guidance in strategic planning. This is in line with Hofstede's own recommendations. These two dimensions serve as the axis of a market matrix on which the cluster indices can be plotted and compared to each other. Figure 4.2 provides indices for fifty countries and three regions for the four Hofstede dimensions. Figures 4.3, 4.4, and 4.5 illustrate matrices for selected pairings of Hofstede dimensions to indicate clusters and distances from other clusters.

15. . . . *Targets* the product launch and introduction activities to the closest cluster from his primary cluster. If there are several country clusters in the proximity to choose from, the effective manager selects the cluster that displays the most similar key dimension. In Figure 4.3, Japan and Latin America display a similar Power Distance but a great difference in Individualism compared to the primary cluster. The Nordic and Germanic clusters were likewise similar in the Individualism index but dissimilar in Power Distance. The critical question the effective manager raises is what is the key dimension for marketing his product? If it is a status-oriented product, he would tend to proceed in the direction of common Power; in this case, market to Japan and Latin America before proceeding to Nordic and Germanic countries. If it is a faddish product, he would tend to proceed first to market and penetrate the Nordic and Germanic countries before expanding to the Japanese and Latin American markets, since the Individualism indices are more closely related. Note that although the Anglo countries appear to be similar to

the others in distance from the Latin Europeans, they differ considerably in both Individualism and Power and should be approached only after the other 4 cultural clusters have been sufficiently penetrated.

Once again observe that in moving to the next cluster, the successful international marketer does not merely translate his advertising and marketing documents into different languages. The key to understanding a cultural cluster approach is not that the same marketing campaign can be used from cluster to cluster, but that the cultural changes that must be made in a marketing program will be smaller when moving from one cluster to another culturally close cluster than if one were to proceed geographically. Cultural differences are more subtle and harder to detect than geographic, demographic, commercial, and economic dissimilarities. Yet, since they involve behavioral, perceptual, and motivational differences, they are frequently crucial to the successful launch of a new product in a foreign market.

16. . . . *Repeats* Steps 4 through 12 for each cluster and each country in the cluster, prioritizing and creating individual marketing plans for each one as necessary.

17. . . . *Continues* the procedure (and repeats the reprioritizing steps), choosing those clusters nearest his home cluster on the appropriate dimensional matrix. He markets to and penetrates those countries within that cluster before proceeding to the next distant cluster. He remembers cultural changes must be implemented for each country and that the same marketing strategy, campaign, and advertising materials will not be usable from one country to another. However, he also knows that the changes will be smaller and more manageable if one moves to culturally similar clusters.

18. . . . *Locates* his multinational competitors and evaluates them on the same cultural dimensions. What is their home country, their primary cluster? This is probably where they are the strongest. He examines the cluster spacing. He may decide not to compete initially in their cluster and to postpone head-on competition there until he has marketed and penetrated other more similar and convenient cluster markets. He concentrates in the clusters nearest his home cluster but furthest from his major competitors. He takes the easy ones first. He builds strength, market share, volume, and expertise

from those clusters nearest his home cluster but far from the major competition before tackling the war zone of the home cluster or home country of any of his multinational competitors. He makes his mistakes where it won't hurt him.

For example, in Figure 4.5, if he is a manager in a French firm with major German, Japanese, and American competitors, he has an advantage with the Latin American cluster in that they are culturally much closer to him than to his competition. Therefore, marketing his products in these markets would be easier to accomplish for him than for his major competitors. He could also use these markets as test sites, to test the marketing or functionality of the product, or he could proceed to compete on more culturally distant fronts and leave the Latin American country cluster to pick up at a more appropriate time when resources and time are available.

19. . . . *Competes* head on with multinational competitor in the competitor's home cluster or country only after all other nearby clusters have been attacked and penetrated. If a choice exists between the home cluster of a competitor and a neutral cluster, he chooses the neutral cluster. As a general rule, his competitor will have the advantage and expertise within the competitor's own cluster and he will only be throwing money and resources into a protracted battle with limited results. Instead, he proceeds to other clusters first.

TWO CASES IN POINT

Example 1

You are an executive with a British firm who has created an innovative status-oriented consumer good. It is somewhat unique and stylish and could well start a fad. Its two key dimensions appear to be Power and Individualism. The primary dimension, in your opinion, is Power. You are, therefore, aiming your marketing towards status-conscious consumers. The applicable matrix is depicted in Figure 4.3, measured by the Power Distance axis versus the Individualism-Collectivism axis. Since this is a new product, there are presently no direct competitors. However, you feel the

Japanese would copy this product in short order, if it is a success, and mass-produce it.

Following the Product Launch Guidelines described earlier, the international product launch sequence should be:

1. Britain, as the home country to the multinational;
2. the countries in the Anglo-American cluster;
3. the Germanic cluster, since power distance is most similar;
4. the Nordic cluster, since power distance is quite close;
5. the Latin-European cultural cluster;
6. Japan would be the next logical country based upon its cluster position. However, if strong competition has shown up there by the time the Japanese market would be next on the product launch list, a wiser alternative would be to pass Japan by and come back when the other markets have been penetrated. In addition, most authorities on doing business in Japan recommend to always find a strong local partner for a joint venture in Japan (McCall and Warrington, 1989). The stronger you are in your worldwide franchise of your product, the better your negotiating position and the chance that you will eventually end up with a stronger local partner;
7. the Latin American cluster as an extension of the Latin-European culture;
8. the Near Eastern cluster, which is composed of the markets in Greece, Turkey, and Iran;
9. the Far Eastern mixture of cultures. Each country–Hong Kong, Singapore, Taiwan, Thailand, the Philippines, Indonesia, and Malaysia–is in a different stage of economic development;
10. and finally Japan, if not done earlier during Step 6.

By doing so, you can build your marketing strengths from market cluster to cluster. In proceeding this way, any changes in the marketing programs can be minimized and mistakes corrected more easily.

Example 2

You are the marketing manager of a multinational computer firm based in the United States. Your company has just developed an innovative computing device for the industrial sector. Your sales pitch emphasizes that it is a new and unique product (low on the Uncertainly Avoidance scale). It is also powerful, authoritative, and provides the user a sense of control over his actions he has never seen before (highly Masculine on the Masculinity-Femininity scale). Thus, the two relevant dimensions are Uncertainty Avoidance and Masculine-Feminine, with the key dimension being the former. In Figure 4.5 the applicable matrix is depicted. Your major multinational competition is derived from Japan, who you know will pick up on your successful efforts and begin marketing their own version of the device.

In what order should the product be introduced? Apart from other imponderabilia such as competitive structure, a country's economic infrastructure, currency convertibility, political stability, and patent and trademark laws, the marketing roll-out strategy would most effectively be based on the cultural cluster concept, beginning with the culturally more similar and ending with the most dissimilar markets. These are, in terms of the method described earlier:

1. The United States
2. the rest of the Anglo countries
3. Germanic
4. Far East Asian countries
5. Latin American
6. Nordic
7. Latin European
8. Middle Eastern
9. Japan

In this case, the Japan cluster is culturally the widest distance away from the United States or Anglo cluster and thus would be the cluster reserved for the last phase in an international roll-out strategy. If the competition from Japan does develop and the Japanese would also use a similar approach, one would expect that their roll-out strategy would subsequently target first the Latin American countries followed by the Germanic clusters. Therefore, these clusters should get a higher priority. If competition does start to develop, special efforts can then swiftly be focused on the markets in these countries. Note that the Nordic cluster is culturally rather distant from Japan. It can therefore be marketed relatively at will from the United States according to the premises described earlier.

SUMMARY AND CONCLUSIONS

This chapter dealt with the arguments in favor of using cultural clusters across political borders in determining and prioritizing market potentials in the launch of a new product on a worldwide scale. To keep costs under control, it is critical to identify those markets that offer least resistance to the introduction of a new product. Selecting countries by cultural similarities helps management avoid marketing mistakes based on cultural differences. Not only the size of a market but correctly perceiving underlying reasons for a latent or manifest market demand gives a company its competitive edge in world markets. Using a roll-out strategy based on cultural clusters by countries is both a more effective and more efficient approach to introducing new products in world markets.

REFERENCES AND RECOMMENDED READINGS

Bass, B. M., and P. C. Burger (1979), *Assessment of Managers: An International Comparison*, New York: The Free Press.

Brown, I. C. (1982), *Understanding Other Cultures*, Englewood Cliffs, New Jersey: Prentice Hall.

England, G. W., A. R. Negandhi, and B. Wilpert (1974), *Organizational Functioning in a Cross Cultural Perspective*, Kent, Ohio: Kent State University Press.

———— (1978), "Managers and Their Value Systems; A Five Country Comparative Study," *Columbia Journal of World Business*, 13(2), 35-44.

Gatignon, H., and T. Robertson (1985), "A Propositional Inventory for New Diffusion Research," *Journal of Consumer Research*, vol. 11 (March), 849-867.

Griffeth, R. W., P. W. Hom, A. Denisis, and W. Kirchner, (1980), "A Multivariate Multinational Comparison of Managerial Attitudes," paper presented at the annual meeting of the Academy of Management, Detroit (August).

Haire, M., E. Ghiselli, and W. Porter (1966), *Managerial Thinking: An International Study*, London: John Wiley & Sons.

Hofstede, G. (1983a), "National Cultures in Four Dimensions: A Research Theory of Cultural Differences Among Nations," *International Studies of Management and Organization*, 13 (Spring-Summer), 52.

———— (1983b), "Dimensions of National Cultures in Fifty Countries and Three

Regions," in *Expiscations in Cross Cultural Psychology*, Lisse, Netherlands: Swets and Zeiltinger.

_____ (1984), *Culture's Consequences*, London: Sage.

_____ (1990), *Software of the Mind*, (unpublished).

McCall, J. B., and M. B. Warrington (1989), *Marketing by Agreement: A Cross Cultural Approach to Business Negotiations*, 2nd ed., New York: John Wiley & Sons.

Ohmae, K. (1990), *The Borderless World: Power and Strategy in the Interlinked Economy*, New York: Harper Business.

Redding, S. G. (1982), "Cultural Effects on the Marketing Process in Southeast Asia," *Journal of the Market Research Society*, 24(2), 98-114.

Rogers, E. M., and F. F. Shoemaker (1971), *Communication of Innovations*, New York: Free Press, 135-157.

Ronen, S., and A. I. Kraut (1977), "Similarities Among Countries Based on Employee Work Values and Attitudes," *Columbia Journal of World Business*, 12(2), 89-96.

Ronen, S., and O. Shenakar (1985), "Clustering Countries on Attitudinal Dimensions: A Review and Synthesis," *Academy of Management Review*, 3, (July 10), 435-454.

Sirota, D., and J. M. Greenwood (1971), "Understand Your Overseas Workforce," *Harvard Business Review*, January-February, 53-63.

SECTION III.

MARKET BEHAVIOR
AND DEVELOPMENT

Chapter 5

The Processes Behind
the Country of Origin Effect

Paul L. Sauer
Murray A. Young
H. Rao Unnava

SUMMARY. This chapter presents and tests three alternative processes through which country of origin information affects attitudes toward and intentions to purchase a product. Results support a cognitive process in which beliefs about ad-derived attributes are affected by country of origin cues. Belief effects mediate the effect on attitudes. Halo effects on inferential beliefs are not observed. Though an interaction between countries in the binational test is not significant, a simple main effect is observed that supports separate country of design and country of assembly effects.

In an era when businesses are expanding into international operations, one of the important challenges they face is the acceptance of foreign products by consumers. A substantial body of literature has accumulated showing that consumers adjust their attitudes toward a product according to its country of origin. This bias may be categorized as either "home country bias" or "foreign country bias." With "home country bias," consumers prefer products made in their own country to identical products made in foreign countries (Schleifer and Dunn, 1968; Schooler, 1965; Schooler and Wildt, 1968). "Foreign country bias" exists when differential preferences are expressed for products made in different foreign countries (Kaynak and Cavusgil, 1983; Schooler, 1965; Wang and Lamb, 1980, 1983).

Although country of origin effects have been investigated over the past several years, methodological and conceptual problems, discussed in the next section, render the findings of this research of limited value to both academicians and practitioners, because of their atheoretical nature (Obermiller and Spangenberg, 1988). The main objective of the research reported here is to examine the cognitive/affective processes by which country of origin information influences an individual's evaluation of a product in a theoretical structure. At a more pragmatic level, another problem that is only recently beginning to impinge on country of origin studies is multi-country input to the manufacturing and marketing of a single product (Han and Terpstra, 1988; Obermiller and Spangenberg, 1988).

Therefore, a second objective of this research is to develop a better understanding of the country of origin effect by separately examining the effects of the country of design of a product and the country of assembly of a product. The issue of country of design vs. country of assembly is important given the movement of the production facilities of several brand name manufacturers into third world countries where labor is cheaper. Despite an increasing trend in such movement, there is little research to date that has sought to separately examine the effects of country of design and country of assembly of a product (Han and Terpstra, 1988).

A CRITIQUE OF PRIOR RESEARCH

In their review of country of origin research, Bilkey and Nes (1982) raise several concerns that question the validity of the findings in this area. We echo their concern and add several more concerns regarding research on the country of origin bias.

First, several of the studies used a single cue paradigm where the respondents were given only information concerning the country of origin (e.g., Nagashima, 1970; Schooler, 1965; Wang and Lamb, 1980). In such an informationally impoverished environment, presenting only the country of origin cue may lead subjects to establish a stronger connection between country of origin and the dependent measure, such as attitude, than would occur in a more realistic purchase setting. Any results obtained might bias results compared with those observed in more realistic and informationally enriched multiple cue environments. Asking subjects to respond to a single cue has the potential of generating results caused more by demand artifacts than by the treatment itself. Most studies do not report debriefing procedures that could have revealed the existence of such a connection in the minds of subjects.

A second concern involves measurement issues. Most studies have not used validated scales to measure the dependent variable. Furthermore, for the most part, the dependent variables used in various studies have ranged from beliefs to choice, in part because little attention has been paid to theoretical structure. This diversity renders generalization across studies difficult. Exceptions include Erickson, Johansson, and Chao (1984) and Johansson, Douglas, and Nonaka (1985), where cognitive structure theory (Fishbein and Ajzen, 1975) was used to develop both the process and measurement properties.

Third, only recently have efforts begun to be made in the literature to clarify what the term "country of origin" actually means to a consumer (Han and Terpstra, 1988). Specifically, does country of origin imply the country where the product was designed or the country where the product was assembled? In this research, country of design shall be used to mean the country in which the corporate headquarters are based, product design usually takes place, some manufacture of one or several key components may occur, marketing efforts are initiated, and hence brand name associations are highest. Country of assembly is used to mean the country where some or all component manufacture and all final assembly occurs. Country of assembly is usually not associated with the brand name and is only identified on most products with a small label in an unobtrusive area of the product where the serial number and date of manufacture may sometimes be found. Due to increasing emphasis on this type of distinction, the uni-national "country of origin" label is not applicable to all products. Complex products are more likely to be bi- or multinational in origin, where "origin" refers to all countries that contribute to the design, manufacture, and sale of a product. Multinational origin raises concerns in a consumer's mind about the quality and value of product design- and assembly-related factors.

Finally, only one attempt has been made to develop a theoretical understanding of the processes by which country of origin information affects people's evaluations of products (Han, 1989). Some researchers have argued that country of origin labels affect evaluations directly because of image effects resulting from stereotypes consumers have about different countries (Lillis and Narayana, 1974; Han, 1989; Nagashima, 1970; Reierson, 1967). This will be termed the affect transfer process. An alternative approach proposes that evaluations are mediated by country of origin effects on the belief structure (Erickson, Johansson, and Chao, 1984; Johansson, Douglas, and Nonaka, 1985; Han, 1989; Obermiller and Spangenberg, 1988). This will be called the cognitive mediation process. A third possibility is that country images may condition behavior directly rather than affecting evaluation of the brand/product. This will be termed the direct behavioral process. This theoretical issue is discussed in more detail in the following section.

Cognitive/Affective Structures

Affect Transfer Process

Though consumers may react positively to a product's features, they may at the same time evaluate the product negatively if it originates from a country that is negatively evaluated by them. This affective theory holds that the feelings consumers have about the country of the product's origin are transferred directly to their overall evaluation of the product. That is, consumers' beliefs about the product do not change due to the country of origin information, only their overall product evaluations are affected. Figure 5.1 depicts this type of an effect of country of origin information on consumer's evaluations of products.

This is a type of "mere effect" exposure mechanism (Obermiller, 1985; Zajonc and Markus, 1985) in which the name of the country is the cue that triggers positive or negative feelings. This differs from Han's (1989) summary construct model in that the country of origin cue is not modeled as mediating the effect of beliefs on

FIGURE 5.1. Affect Transfer Process

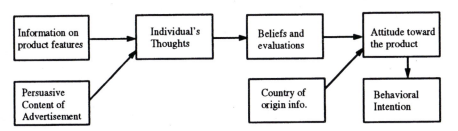

attitude, but rather as an alternative construct to attribute beliefs that effect a change in attitude toward the product. The country name acts as a triggering cue that when encountered creates positive or negative affect without the person recalling the specific cognitive beliefs that at one time created this negative or positive attitude. These latent feelings endure beyond the time when the underlying beliefs are recallable or perhaps even recognizable. These attitudes are more stable than attribute information directly impacting product beliefs, and hence override the belief effect on attitude as occurs in the cognitive mediation process. Therefore, it is hypothesized that:

H1a: A country of origin (design/assembly) cue will directly affect attitude toward the product, but not the beliefs concerning attributes of the product.

Cognitive Mediation Process

Other researchers have argued that the effect of country of origin information on attitudes is not due to "affect transfer" as described above, but is *cognitively mediated* (Erickson, Johannson, and Chao, 1984; Johansson, Douglas, and Nonaka, 1985; Han, 1989; Hong and Toner, 1988; Obermiller and Spangenberg, 1988). According to the cognitive mediation argument, beliefs about a product's features or attributes are directly affected by the product's country of origin information. These affected beliefs mediate changes in attitude toward the product. Changes in product attribute beliefs occur when consumers encode information about a product (Greenwald, 1968) in response to advertisement content concerning the product. Figure 5.2 depicts this process suggested by the cognitive mediation process.

Support for this process comes from recent studies. Erickson, Johannson, and Chao (1984), using measures of beliefs about and attitudes toward automobiles made in different countries, found that the country of origin effect on attitudes was mediated by country of origin effects on subjects' beliefs about the various brand attributes. Similarly, Han, (1989) found that the cognitive mediation process held for both automobiles and television sets, but that the effect applied to Korean and U.S. products, but not Japanese products.

A critical issue is whether this is an advertisement specific "halo" effect that applies only to attributes contained in a target advertisement for a brand, or a more global "halo" effect in which inferential beliefs about attributes not specifically addressed in the ad would be affected by the country of origin cue. Han's (1989) study does not test this "halo" effect distinction, as telephone interviews were used and no treatment advertisements employed.

Another concern with both the Han (1989) and Erickson, Johannson, and Chao (1984) studies is the use of existing brands. Specifically, when existing brands are used in research, confounds related to experience with and prior knowledge about the brands can affect the results. Han (1989) attempts to resolve this by using ownership, past and present, to assess familiarity. Similarly, Erickson et al. (1984) on the other hand incorporated two familiarity measures. However, in their regression model, Erickson et al. hypothesized an effect of familiarity (or experience) directly on attitudes, and not through beliefs (see their discussion on p. 695).

FIGURE 5.2. Cognitive Mediation Process

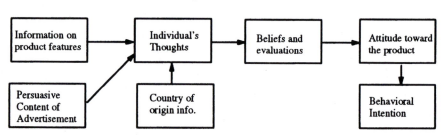

Fishbein and Ajzen (1975), in contrast, argue that experience with an attitude object results in strongly held beliefs about the object. More recent research by Fazio and his colleagues (Fazio, 1985; Fazio and Zanna, 1981) also supports the claim that information in the form of direct experience results in beliefs that are held more confidently compared to other forms of information. However, because Erickson et al. (1984) did not test for the direct effect of familiarity on beliefs and Han (1989) used it as a moderating variable that was confounded with country, it is not clear what proportion of the country of origin effects they found in their research are attributable to the past experience of subjects. Despite this limitation, both studies are of considerable value because they demonstrate that the country of origin impact on attitude was effected through beliefs about the attributes of the product. Therefore it is hypothesized that:

H1b: A country of origin (design/assembly) cue effect on attitude toward a product will be mediated by effects on beliefs about attributes of the product.

Direct Belief Process

A third possible process by which country of origin information impacts behavior is through the direct effect on behavior without mediating effects of product attributes or attitudes (Obermiller and Spangenberg, 1988). An example of such a process is where an individual holds positive *product attribute* beliefs and a subsequent positive attitude toward a Japanese car, but ends up buying an American car because of "buy-American" pressure that stems from his/her reference group. For example, peer pressure among unionized blue collar workers who may face loss of jobs from superior, competitive foreign products may override *product attribute* beliefs and attitudes that acknowledge superior Japanese quality automobiles. In this case, the effect of the country of origin on behavior is direct and is depicted in Figure 5.3. Therefore it is hypothesized that:

FIGURE 5.3. Direct Behavioral Process

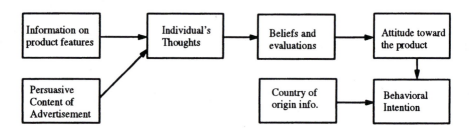

H1c: A country of origin (design/assembly) cue will directly affect intentions to buy a product, but not beliefs about or attitudes toward the product.

It is possible that country of origin labels affect consumer response through each of the three processes described above. Han (1989), for example, finds that both his "halo" model and "summary construct" model hold for the same product, but which is valid is dependent upon the country from which the product originates.

Binational Country of Origin Effects

The second important issue that is examined in this research pertains to the effects of country of design and country of assembly of a product. As mentioned earlier, past research on country of origin effects has not unambiguously defined the term "country of origin." It is possible that country of design and country of assembly affect consumers' evaluations independently. Bilkey and Nes (1982) present anecdotal evidence on a German firm that faced the problem of selling products manufactured by its Brazilian subsidiary to its industrial customers. Customers were reluctant to buy the products manufactured and assembled in Brazil even though the German firm that designed and produced them attached their name to the products. Such reluctance reflects the fears consumers may have about the quality of workmanship that goes into a product when it is assembled in a technologically inferior country.

Evidence on multiple country contribution effects on consumer choice behavior has been discussed by Khanna (1986) with regard to the sensitivity of Indian consumers to television sets whose components originated in different countries. When color television was introduced for the first time in India in 1983, the only televisions available in the market were those assembled in India from components imported from Germany or Korea. Indian consumers were so particular about not buying television sets made from Korean picture tubes that they had the retailers open the back cover of the television set they were planning to buy to confirm that the picture tube was made in Germany.

The most recent as well as most conclusive multi-country study involved a 2 × 2 design in which U.S. and foreign brands represented the country of origin and U.S. and foreign-made represented the country of manufacture and assembly. The dependent measure was perceived quality. In this study, Han and Terpstra (1988) found that country of manufacture had a more powerful effect than country of origin. They also found that country cues in general affected product attributes differentially (supporting a cognitive mediation argument), and that this affect on attributes tended to be similar across product classes. Thus, it appears that place of assembly and place of design exert separate influences on consumers' evaluations of products. The Khanna (1986) results also indicate that the country in which components to be assembled were manufactured–assuming the country is different from that of assembly–may also affect beliefs and attitudes toward a product. For purposes of the current study, only the distinction between country of assembly and country of design will be investigated. In this study, all component manufacture as well as assembly are considered to be performed in the "country of assembly" as in the Han and Terpstra (1988) study.

Place of assembly and country of design may not affect a person's evaluations additively or linearly. That is, it may not be possible to make up for the loss in "favorableness" due to design in an inferior country by assembling the product in a positively evaluated country. Also, when design and assembly are done in different countries that are viewed as equally advanced or inferior, assembly effects may be absent. For example, when Japanese-designed products are assembled in Germany, the effect of place of assembly may be absent because consumers may view both Japan and Germany as equally superior in industrialization. On the other hand, when products designed in Japan are assembled in a country that is not well-industrialized (e.g., Philippines), consumers may view the product less favorably. Thus, place of assembly effects may be found only when country of design and country of assembly are different in terms of consumers' perceptions with respect to industrial development. The above arguments lead to the following hypothesis:

H2:   The country of assembly and the country of design of a product interact to affect the attitudes toward a brand of a product.

This hypothesis is based on the logic that consumers are sensitive to both design- and assembly-related differences between countries in that perceived differences affect their evaluations of products. It should also be pointed out that hypotheses H1 (a, b, and c) propose alternative processes by which the effect summarized in H2 may occur. In other words, the effect of place of assembly and country of design on consumer evaluations and/or behavioral intentions may occur through an affective, a cognitive, or a more direct behavioral process. Such a test is beyond the scope of this study.

METHOD

Experiment

An experimental study was undertaken to test these research hypotheses. This experiment possesses several advantages over prior research. First, we provided subjects with several advertisements that they had to use in a purchase choice task. The ads were based upon ads for real products. As such they were both persuasive and informative and provided the subjects with substantial attribute information in a multiple cue environment (cf. Ettenson, Wagner, and Gaeth, 1988). Second, to remove effects of prior experience (cf. Han, 1989 and Erickson et al., 1984), we provided subjects with neutral brand identifiers (i.e., A, B, C, and D). Third, we measured subjects' product attribute beliefs to see if country of origin effects on attitudes were mediated by those beliefs. Finally, we used a between-subjects design to reduce demand effects and followed the study with a thorough debriefing procedure to ascertain the existence of demand artifacts.

Design and Subjects

The influence of place of assembly and country of design on the evaluation of a target product was tested in a 2 (country where the product was designed–China or Japan) × 2 (place of assembly–same as country of design or the Philippines) between-subjects design. Seventy-two subjects from an introductory marketing class participated in this research for extra course credit.

An alternative way to study effects of assembly and design may be a 2 × 2 factorial design where country of design and place of assembly are orthogonally manipulated. We were, however, also interested in demonstrating the lack of assembly effect when design and assembly were done in countries viewed as not very different. Past research suggested countries where the assembly effect may be absent. Wall and Heslop (1986), using Canadian consumers, found that products from China and the Philippines were ranked about equally low (p. 32, Table 4), and significantly lower than products from Japan. Informal pretesting on a sample of subjects from our student population indicated that this ranking should hold for U.S. subjects too. Thus, the use of Japan, China, and the Philippines in our design enabled us to test the interactive nature of the effects of country of design and country of assembly. If place of assembly was salient only when the country of design and country of assembly were perceived as being significantly different, our manipulation of place of assembly should affect attitudes only when the product was designed in Japan, not when it was designed in China.

Stimulus Materials

The stimulus materials consisted of four ads for four color TV brands named simply A, B, C, and D. The ads were arranged in alphabetical order with the last brand (brand D) being the target brand in this research. Because a between-subjects design was used, the order of brands remained constant across subjects with the ad for target brand D always the last of the four. All the ads were about

150 words in length and were developed based on existing magazine ads and descriptions of televisions contained in a *Consumer Reports* issue dealing with TV sets.

The country of origin information was included in the ad for the target brand as part of a sentence in the middle of the ad. To make it as unobtrusive as possible, the phrase "designed and made in Japan (China)" or "designed in Japan (China) and assembled in the Philippines" was inserted in a sentence that contained other product information for the brand. The sentence for the experimental condition, in which the TV was designed and made in Japan read as follows: "Brand D televisions, designed and made in Japan, actually enhance the broadcast signal to give you optimum sharpness, clarity, contrast, and color." The ad for brand D was identical in all treatment conditions except for changes in the country of design and place of assembly/manufacture information. All ads were typed on 8 1/2 × 11 inch paper and were devoid of illustrations.

Procedure

The study was conducted in a classroom during the first part of the lecture hour. The student subjects were told that their task was to *choose one* of four color TV sets *based on information* presented in the ads. The information on the four brands was presented as four advertisements with each ad appearing on a separate page. Based on pretest findings from the same subject population that showed no large differences in reading speed between subjects, participants were given 1.5 minutes to read each ad. Subjects were told that if they finished reading before the allotted time was over, they should wait until instructed to turn the page. This procedure gave more control in terms of equal exposure time for all subjects, which was an important concern given our interest in country of origin effects when other information was available.

After reading the four ads, subjects were asked to write the name of the brand they would choose on the back of the booklet. This made the choice task a more externally valid response to ad exposure than if choices had followed the remaining tasks, which focused the subject's attention on brand "D" and required reprocessing brand D information from memory, which likely would have biased the choice toward brand D. This choice measure also provided support for our cover story because subjects were asked to choose between brands.

Following the choice measure, subjects were asked to open the questionnaire booklet. The first question asked subjects to write down all the thoughts that went through their mind when they read the ad for brand D. The thought listing task was employed to develop a better understanding of the cognitive processes that contribute to country of origin biases. The subjects were given three minutes to list their thoughts. Following this, they were instructed to rate each thought as to whether it was a positive, negative, or neutral thought. Subjects' rating of their own thoughts has been shown to be a reliable and valid method of assessing the valence of thoughts (cf. Petty and Cacioppo, 1981).

Next, the subjects' attitude toward brand D was measured using a six-item semantic differential attitude scale (seven-point scales anchored by good-bad, nice-awful, harmful-beneficial, desirable-undesirable, inferior-superior, and pleasant-unpleasant). Following the attitude measure, subjects responded to two questions that measured their intention to buy brand D if it were available locally and if they needed a TV (two seven-point scales anchored by likely-unlikely, probable-improbable). Subjects were then asked to recall all the information that they remembered from the brand D ad. The recall measure was used to check whether the subjects remembered the information on the country of design and assembly of the target product. This measure was also used to check for differences between groups on the recall of this information. The lack of differences between groups would argue against a possible alternative explanation that subjects in different groups were differentially attentive to assembly and design information. If they were differentially attentive, then their recall data should reflect these differences in attention. If country of origin conditions evaluations of beliefs, then it is possible that if country of origin is a more salient cue, it would affect processing of information. If country of origin is very important to evaluation of a product and is perceived in either a positive or negative way, then processing (reading) of other cues may cease with choice based mainly on country of origin. If country of origin is marginal, then other cues are needed to make the evaluation.

Finally, subjects also responded to a set of Likert scales that measured beliefs about the attributes of brand D (five-point scales anchored by strongly agree and strongly disagree). Specifically, four attributes were derived from the ad for brand D:

1. Brand D actually enhances the broadcast signal.
2. Brand D gives optimum sharpness and clarity in the picture.
3. Brand D has excellent color compatibility.
4. Brand D's color TV series are technological masterpieces.

In addition to the four attributes that were discussed in the ad, belief measures on two attributes that were not discussed in the ad were also included (Brand D TV is very reliable, and, Brand D TV is very durable). The inclusion of these two attributes served a very important purpose. It enabled us to test whether the country of design and assembly information affected only the attributes that were presented in the ad, or whether the effect generalized to other attributes as well. If attributes not presented in the ad were also affected, then it would suggest that negative affect toward the country of origin (design or assembly) was being generalized in all attributes of the target product, irrespective of the content of the target ad. On the other hand, if the attributes mentioned in the ad were affected by the country of origin (design or assembly) of the product, but other attributes were not affected, then it would suggest that the subjects' responses to the belief measures were not based on a generalized negative affect toward the country of origin (design or assembly). This is because if subjects were responding to all the belief measures based on their negative feeling toward the product's country of origin (design or assembly), and not on their thought processes, then they should rate all attributes of the target product negatively, irrespective of whether they were discussed in the ad or not.

After completing the questionnaire, all subjects were asked to guess what the purpose of the experiment was. Several explanations were offered by subjects, but the issue of country of origin was not mentioned by any subject. Subjects were then debriefed and normal classroom activities were resumed.

RESULTS

Recall

The recall protocols were examined to see if the country of origin information was recalled. About 60% of the subjects recalled that the brand was designed by a Japanese (Chinese) company, and about 66% of the subjects recalled the place of assembly of the target brand. The incidence of recall was examined for differences between experimental conditions. A Chi-square test of the relationship between recall and country of origin (design/assembly) revealed no significant differences ($^2 < 1.00$ in both cases) between experimental conditions. The lack of differences between experimental conditions suggested that no one experimental group had paid more attention to the country of origin information than the other groups.

Process Models and Inferential Beliefs

To test each of the hypotheses H1a, H1b, and H1c, as well as the effect on inferential beliefs, the arithmetic mean of the four ad-derived belief measures (coefficient alpha = 0.74) was used to form an ad-derived belief index, and the two inferential belief measures (correlation = 0.85) were similarly averaged to form an inferential belief index. These two indices were used in all the analyses where tests involving beliefs were used.

The ad-derived belief index was subjected to an analysis of variance with country of assembly and country of design as independent variables. The analysis revealed a significant ($p < 0.035$) country of assembly effect. Subjects held more favorable product attribute beliefs when brand D television was assembled in Japan or China ($M = 2.9$) than when it was assembled in the Philippines ($M = 2.4$). No other effects approached significance. The finding that subjects' product attribute beliefs were affected by place of assembly manipulation argues against both affect transfer and behavior explanations of country of origin bias (H1a and H1c). The cognitive mediation argument (H1b), however, is supported.

A similar analysis performed on the inferential belief index produced different results. Neither country of design nor place of assembly had any effect on the inferential beliefs of subjects (all p-values > 0.25). Brand D was rated equally durable/reliable whether it was assembled in Japan or China (M = 3.1) or in the Philippines (M = 3.0). It appears that country of origin information results in changes only in those product attribute beliefs that are specifically discussed in the ad, and not in other beliefs about the product. This finding further argues against an affect transfer (H1a) explanation of country of origin bias, because if the underlying process were affect transfer, then all attributes of the product should be affected by country of origin manipulation.

Design-Assembly

Attitude Effects

The reliability of the six-item attitude scale was found to be high (Cronbach's alpha = 0.91). Based on this, the mean attitude score was computed for each subject by averaging the score across the six items of the scale. These scores are presented by experimental group in Table 5.1 and plotted in Figure 5.4.

According to H2, country of assembly and country of design should interactively affect subjects' attitudes toward the TV. Specifically, subjects' evaluations should be affected when country of design and place of assembly were perceived to be different in terms of the level of technological development of each country. Assuming that China and the Philippines are perceived equivalent, but that Japan is perceived superior to both, then when the TV is designed in Japan, it should be rated more positively when it is assembled in Japan than when it is assembled in the Philippines. On the other hand, when the TV is designed in China, there should be no differences in subjects' evaluations whether the country of assembly is China or the Philippines. Thus, H2 called for an interaction between place of assembly and country of design in an analysis of variance of the dependent measure. In addition to the interaction, H2 also called for a significant difference between the mean attitude scores when the TV was designed in Japan and assembled in Japan versus the Philippines, whereas no difference was expected when

TABLE 5.1. Mean Attitude, Behavioral Intention and Belief Scores by Condition

Dependent	Designed In Japan		Designed in China	
	Assembled in			
	Japan	Philippines	China	Philippines
Attitude	4.95	4.23	4.87	4.51
Behavioral Int.	4.53	3.19	3.89	3.49
N	18	18	18	18
Valence of Thought				
on origin: Positive	5	0	0	0
Negative	6	10	8	8
Neutral	2	1	1	3
No thoughts on origin				
Number of Thoughts				
Positive	1.94	0.83	1.06	0.67
Negative	1.44	1.67	1.28	2.06
Belief Index:				
Product Related	2.93	2.35	2.81	2.41
Inferential	3.16	2.98	3.03	2.94

Note: All responses were recoded so that higher values mean higher evaluations. For Attitude and Behavioral Intention, seven-point scales were used. For beliefs, five-point scales were used.

the TV was designed in China and assembled in China versus the Philippines.

A 2 × 2 analysis of variance with the mean attitude score as the dependent measure and country of design and place of assembly as the factors revealed only a main effect of place of assembly ($p < 0.05$). Subjects rated TVs assembled in the Philippines less positively ($M = 4.37$) than TVs assembled in Japan or China ($M = 4.91$). No other effects were significant.

The absence of an interaction between place of assembly and country of design did not support H2. However, the basis for H2 was the hypothesized assembly effect when the country of design

FIGURE 5.4. Relation Between Attitude and Country of Origin of the Product

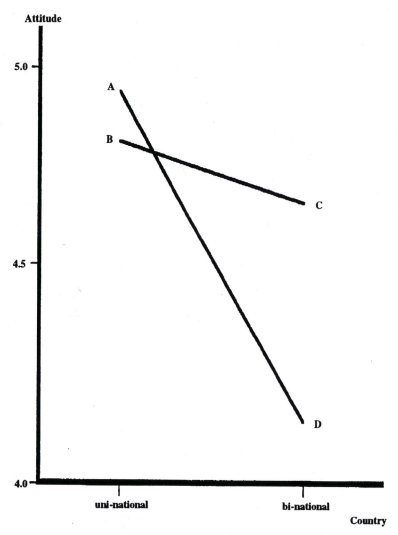

A – Designed and Made in Japan
B – Designed and Made in China
C – Designed in China / Assembled in Philippines
D – Designed in Japan / Assembled in Philippines

was Japan, and the absence of an assembly effect when the country of design was China. Therefore, simple main effects analysis was performed on the attitude scores to test for the hypothesized assembly effects for each country of design. The analysis revealed that place of assembly had no effect when the TV was designed in China ($M_{China} = 4.87$; $M_{Philippines} = 4.51$; $p > 0.25$), but a significant assembly effect emerged when the TV was designed in Japan ($M_{Japan} = 4.95$; $M_{Philippines} = 4.23$; $p < 0.05$). Thus, even though the interaction between place of assembly and country of design was not significant, the effects discussed above may be viewed as supportive of H2.

This lack of an interaction appears to result from the lack of a main effect of the country of design as expected. A TV designed in Japan ($M = 4.59$) was not rated higher than a TV designed in China ($M = 4.69$; $p > 0.25$). Subjects rated Chinese products higher than expected, which contradicted previous research studies and our own pretest results that showed Japanese products were rated significantly more positively than products made in China. To determine why Japanese products were not rated more positively than Chinese products in this study, the thoughts listed by the subjects were examined. Several subjects, in their thought listing protocols, wrote "Designed in Japan" or "Designed in China" and rated that thought with a "+" (positive) or " − " (negative). Surprisingly, more people (six) rated the thought "Designed in Japan" negatively than those who rated the thought positively (five). This net negative reaction to Japanese designed products was not expected, and might have caused the absence of a country of design effect in our experiment. However, the negative reaction to China was greater than that toward Japan in that *all* respondents who recorded the thought "Designed in China" rated it as "−." This means that the lack of a main effect for country of design was caused by the failure of "Designed in Japan" to generate a positive response among more subjects. It may be that this is a product specific effect (Etzel and Walker, 1974), and that other Japanese products such as automobiles and cameras would fare better.

Behavioral Intention Effects

The two items constituting the behavioral intention scale correlated very highly ($r = 0.92$). A mean of the score on the two items was computed to form an index of behavioral intention. The mean scores by condition are presented in Table 5.1. The behavioral intention of subjects was expected to be affected by the country of design and place of assembly manipulations in a manner similar to their effects on subjects' attitudes.

A 2×2 analysis of variance of the behavioral intention with country of design and place of assembly as the factors revealed a significant country of assembly main effect ($p < 0.02$), as occurred with attitude. Subjects indicated greater intention to buy the TV assembled in Japan or China ($M = 4.21$) than the TV assembled in the Philippines ($M = 3.31$). No other effect was significant.

A simple main effects analysis was performed again to analyze the effect of assembly for each country of design (Japan and China) separately. The effect of assembly was significant when the TV was designed in Japan ($M_{Japan} = 4.53$; $M_{Philippines} = 3.19$; $p < 0.01$), but did not even approach significance when the TV was designed in China ($M_{China} = 3.89$; $M_{Philippines} = 3.49$; $p > 0.5$). The similarity between attitude and behavioral intention effects is not surprising because of the significant intercorrelation between the index measure for each ($r = 0.55$; $p < 0.001$). It may be noted that a significant effect of place of assembly on subjects' intention to buy the target product does not support H1c, which posits a direct effect of country of assembly information on behavioral intention of subjects.

The cognitive mediation argument, as discussed before, not only predicts that subjects' beliefs would be affected, but also argues that changes in subjects' attitudes are affected by these beliefs. In other words, changes in beliefs mediate changes in subjects' attitudes. If this prediction were correct, then covarying out subjects' product attribute beliefs should eliminate place of assembly/country of design effects on subjects' attitudes. If the effect of place of assembly on subjects' attitudes does not disappear completely when beliefs are used as covariates, then this suggests that place of assembly affects attitudes both directly and by changing beliefs.

To test this prediction of the cognitive mediation argument, the analyses reported earlier for attitude and behavioral intention measures were repeated with the ad-derived belief index as a covariate. The analyses revealed that the effects of place of assembly on attitude and behavioral intention, as reported earlier, were eliminated and the belief index covariate was significant ($p < 0.05$). This finding further supports the cognitive mediation (H1b) explanation of the processes underlying country of origin bias.

DISCUSSION

The results of our experiment provide strong support for the cognitive mediation process of country of origin effects and further substantiates the findings of Erickson et al. (1984) and to the "halo model" of Han (1989). It was shown that not only were subjects' beliefs about a television set's attributes affected by country of assembly manipulation, but these beliefs were shown to mediate country of assembly effects on subjects' attitudes and behavioral intentions.

The research findings suggest that country of origin bias is not an affect transfer process. Consumers exposed to information on a product's country of origin will modify their beliefs about the product based on its country of origin. The modification of beliefs may be the result of the thoughts that people generate when they are exposed to this information. Three types of evidence provide support for this line of thinking. First, a post hoc analysis of the total positive and negative thoughts that subjects generated in our research showed that when the target brand was assembled in the Philippines, subjects generated fewer positive thoughts ($M = 0.75$) than when the target brand was not assembled in the Philippines ($M = 1.50$; $p < 0.025$). There was no significant difference, however, in the number of negative thoughts generated by the subjects whether the target brand was assembled in the Philippines or not. The result is a net increase in the proportion of negative thoughts that contributes to lower evaluations of the product. Second, the effects of country of assembly on attitude and behavioral intention were shown to occur through effects on product attribute beliefs. Finally, halo effects on inferential beliefs that were not discussed in the ad were not affected by place of assembly manipulation. Thus, in this research, the cognitive mediation explanation was supported strongly.

A second important issue examined in this research pertains to the separation of the effects of country of design and place of assembly. Even though a substantial research base has been generated in this area, previous research on country of origin bias is not clear about the meaning of the term "origin." It was argued in this research that country of design and country of assembly would interactively affect people's evaluations of products. Specifically, only when country of design and place of assembly are perceived to be different in terms of factors directly related to the product(s) considered will effects of country of assembly emerge. When assembly and design are done in countries perceived to be similar, effects of design or assembly will be absent. This argument received only weak support when it was found that a TV designed in Japan was rated less favorably when it was assembled in the Philippines than when it was assembled in Japan, while a TV designed in China was not rated differently whether it was assembled in China or the Philippines. The weakness stems from the lack of a significant interaction at the 5% level of significance, though the interaction approached significance. The relatively small sample size may account for this near but not significant interaction.

Surprisingly, country of design had no effect on subjects' evaluation of the target product. A TV designed in Japan was rated no differently than a TV designed in China. This finding, however, does not suggest that country of design has no effect on people's evaluations, because a careful examination of subjects' thought protocols showed that on average, subjects who were exposed to the ad for a TV designed and assembled in Japan were only slightly negatively predisposed toward Japan while those exposed to the ad for a TV designed and assembled in China were all negatively predisposed toward China. However, because of the average negative evaluation of Japan contrary to our expectation, our country of design manipulation was not sufficiently powerful. This weakness in manipulation resulted in the absence of a country of design effect and contributed to an absence of a significant interaction effect. While unexpected, the negative reaction to Japan is not totally surprising from hindsight, considering that the sample consisted of business majors who are likely exposed to the heavily publicized and straining trade relations between Japan and the U.S. A subsequent study of differences in evaluation of Japan and China across a variety of products indicated non-significant differences between overall product evaluation impact of these two countries of origin. One consideration, which was not explored, was the ability of subjects to distinguish between Taiwan and China. The use of other country pairs in future research should produce stronger country of design effects.

SUMMARY AND FUTURE RESEARCH

Country of origin effects are manifest even in a multicue environment where considerable information is available for people to make judgments about the product. One of the concerns expressed about past research on country of origin bias was the possibility of exaggerated effects due to the absence of information about other attributes of the experimental products used. Our research shows that even in the presence of other information, including intrinsic product attributes, country of assembly affects evaluation of a product. Thus, country is an important piece of information that people use in making judgments. The presence of country bias when other product information is available has not been demonstrated previously in the literature.

Some caveats are in order with respect to the results reported and the implications drawn here. One major limitation is the use of a sample from a student population. Use of a student sample weakens the external validity, thereby lessening the managerial usefulness of the results. This is compounded by the use of a midwestern university as a sample source, for this may bias response with respect to cultural, social, political, and racial opinions of residents of that part of the United States. Students generally represent a segment of the population affected by a different level of exposure to national issues than the more general population. On the other hand, students constitute a more homogeneous sample, which increases the internal validity of the results obtained. For example, students in this study have values conditioned by the university business school environment. They are in the same age cohort and therefore, are more likely to be similarly affected by exposure to wars, world tensions, past inferior products (e.g., Japanese products in 1950s), etc. Also, they are in more similar income and occupation cohorts and have similarly restricted exposure to news due to time constraints and peer pressures than the general population. A challenge, then, is for future research to confirm that the cognitive mediation explanation operates at a more general geographical as well as population level.

Another limitation is that only one product was used. Past research has indicated that country of origin bias is highly product specific (e.g., Etzel and Walker, 1974). It is possible that for less "technical" products, country of origin may affect people's evaluations via the affect transfer route. For example, a product like men's clothing may not be evaluated as unfavorably if it originates in a less developed country than would a complex, technical product. Furthermore, purchase conditions such as routine vs. deliberative, high involvement vs. low involvement, and high familiarity vs. low familiarity purchases and products need to be manipulated to provide a theoretically richer understanding of country of origin affects. Finally, factors specific to a country, such as economic development and political status and stability contribute to country of origin effects (Wang and Lamb, 1983). More research is needed on these issues.

The lack of a global effect on inferential as well as ad-derived beliefs may result from the proximity of ad-derived attributes to the country of origin information as well as to means-end hierarchy of attributes. The hierarchy proceeds from objectively measurable physical characteristics at the lowest level to more global, abstract characteristics such as "product quality" at the highest level (Zeithaml, 1988). Between these extremes there are varying degrees of abstractness and specificity in the product attributes. Any country effect is more likely to occur within a hierarchy of attributes than between attributes not in the same hierarchy (Gutman and Alden, 1985; Holbrook and Corfman, 1985; Reynolds and Jamieson, 1985). Future research should examine in greater detail issue of global versus attribute specific halo effects.

In addition, not only the design-assembly dichotomy needs to be investigated, but also the impact of manufacturing key components such as TV picture tubes or automobile engines in countries other than that of design or assembly (cf. Khanna, 1986). It is plausible that less complex and/or less technological products would be less susceptible to binational effects. Thus, binational effects may be more likely to occur in industrial markets than in consumer markets.

REFERENCES AND RECOMMENDED READINGS

Anderson, W. and Cunningham, W. (1972). Gauging Foreign Product Promotion. *Journal of Advertising Research*, (February), 12, 29-34.

Bilkey, W. and Nes, E. (1982). Country-of-Origin Effects on Product Evaluations. *Journal of International Business Studies*, (Spring/Summer), 89-99.

Cattin, P., Jolibert, A. and Lohnes, C. (1982). A Cross-Cultural Study of "Made In" Concepts. *Journal of International Business Studies*, (Winter), 131-141.

Casin, J. and Jaffe, E. (1979). Industrial Buyer Attitudes Toward Goods Made in Eastern Europe. *Columbia Journal of World Business*, (Summer), 74-81.

Cronin, J. and Bullard, W. (1988). Country-of-Origin Effects on Customer Service Perception: An Exploratory Investigation. In K. Bahr (Ed.), *Developments in Marketing Science*, 11 (pp. 107-111). Blacksburg VA: Academy of Marketing Science.

Erickson, G., Johansson, J. and Chao, P. (1984). Image Variables in Multi-Attribute Product Evaluations: Country-of-Origin Effects. *Journal of Consumer Research*, (September), 11, 694-699.

Ettenson, R., Wagner, J. and Gaeth, G. (1988). Evaluating the Effect of Country of Origin and the "Made in the USA" Campaign: A Conjoint Approach. *Journal of Retailing*, (Spring), 64(1), 85-100.

Etzel, M. and Walker, B. (1974). Advertising Strategy for Foreign Products. *Journal of Advertising Research*, (June) 14, 41-44.

Fazio, R. H. (1985). How do Attitudes Guide Behavior? In Sorrentino, R. M. and Higgins, E. T. (Eds.), *The Handbook of Motivation and Cognition: Foundations of Social Behavior*. NY: Guilford.

Fazio, R. H. and Zanna, M. P. (1981). Direct Experience and Attitude Behavior Consistency. In Berkowitz, L. (Ed.), *Advances in Experimental Social Psychology*, 14 (pp. 161-202). NY: Academic Press.

Fishbein, M. and Ajzen, I. (1975). *Belief, Attitude, Intention and Behavior: An Introduction to Theory and Research*. Reading, MA: Addison-Wesley.

Gaedeke, R. (1973). Consumer Attitudes Toward Products "Made In" Developing Countries. *Journal of Retailing*, (Summer), 49, 13-24.

Greenwald, A. G. (1968). Cognitive Learning, Cognitive Response to Persuasion, and Attitude Change. In Greenwald, A., Brock, T. and Ostrom, T. (Eds.), *Psychological Foundations of Attitudes*, (pp. 148-170). NY: Academic Press.

Gutman, J. and Alden, S. (1985) Adolescents' Cognitive Structures of Retail Stores and Fashion Consumption: A Means-End Chain Analysis of Quality. In Jacoby, J. and Olson, J. (Eds.), *Perceived Quality: How Consumers View Stores and Merchandise*. NY: Lexington Books.

Hampton, G. (1977). Perceived Risk in Buying Products Made Abroad by American Firms. *Baylor Business Studies*, (October), 53-64.

Han, C. M. (1989). Country Image: Halo or Summary Construct? *Journal of Marketing Research*, (May), 26, 222-229.

Han, C. M. and Terpstra, V., (1988). Country-of-Origin Effects for Uni-National and Bi-National Products. *Journal of International Business Studies*, (Summer), 19, 235-255.

Holbrook, M. and Corfman, K. (1985). Quality and Value in the Consumption Experience: Phaedrus Rides Again. In Jacoby, J. and Olson, J. (Eds.), *Perceived Quality: How Consumers View Stores and Merchandise*. NY: Lexington Books.

Hong, S. and Toner, J. (1988). Are There Gender Differences in the Use of Country-of-Origin Information in the Evaluation of Products? In Skrull, T. K. (Ed.), *Advances in Consumer Research*, XVI (pp. 468-472). Provo, UT: Association for Consumer Research.

Johansson, J., Douglas, S. and Nonaka, I. (1985). Assessing the Impact of Country of Origin on Product Evaluations: A New Methodological Perspective. *Journal of Marketing Research*, (November), 22, 388-396.

Johansson, J. and Thorelli, H. (1985). International Product Positioning. *Journal of International Business Studies*, (Fall), 16, 57-75.

Kaynak, E. and Cavusgil, T. (1983). Consumer Attitudes Towards Products of Foreign Origin: Do They Vary Across Product Classes? *International Journal of Advertising*, 2, 147-157.

Khanna, S. (1986). Asian Companies and the Country Stereotype Paradox: An Empirical Study. *Columbia Journal of World Business*, (Summer), 29-38.

Koh, A. and Brunner, J. (1988). Consumer Perceptions Towards Products Made in the People's Republic of China: Implications for Marketing Strategy. In Bahr, K. D. (Ed.), *Developments in Marketing Science*, 11 (pp. 122-126). Blacksburg, VA: Academy of Marketing Science.

Lillis, C. and Narayana, K. (1974). Analysis of "Made In" Product Images–An Exploratory Study. *Journal of International Business Studies*, (Spring), 5 119-127.

Nagashima, A. (1970). Comparison of Japanese and U.S. Attitudes Toward Foreign Products. *Journal of Marketing*, (January), 34, 68-74.

Obermiller, C. (1985). Varieties of Mere Exposure: The Effects of Processing Style and Repetition on Affective Response. *Journal of Consumer Research*, (June), 17-30.

Obermiller, C. and Spangenberg, E. (1988). Exploring the Effects of Country of Origin Labels: An Information Processing Framework. In Skrull, T. K. (Ed.), *Advances in Consumer Research*, XVI (pp. 454-459). Provo, UT: Association for Consumer Research.

Olson, J. and Jacoby, J. (1972). Cue Utilization in the Quality Perception Process. *Proceedings of the 2nd Annual Convention of the Association for Consumer Research* (pp. 167-179). Provo, UT: Association for Consumer Research.

Petty, R. and Cacioppo, J. (1981). *Attitudes and Persuasion: Classic and Contemporary Approaches*. Dubuque, IA: W. Brown.

Reierson, C. (1967). Attitude Changes Toward Foreign Products. *Journal of Marketing Research*, (November), 4, 385-387.

Reynolds, T. and Jamieson, L. (1985). Image Representations: An Analytic Framework. In Jacoby, J. & Olson, J. (Eds.), *Perceived Quality: How Consumers View Stores and Merchandise*. NY: Lexington Books.

Schleifer, S. and Dunn, S. (1968). *Journal of Marketing Research*, (August), 5, 296-299.

Schooler, R. (1965). Product Bias in the Central American Common Market. *Journal of Marketing Research*, (November), 2, 394-397.

_____ . (1971). Bias Phenomena Attendant to the Marketing of Foreign Goods in the U.S. *Journal of International Business Studies*, (Spring), 2, 71-80.

Schooler, R. and Sunoo, D. (1964). Consumer Perceptions of International Products: Regional vs. National Labeling. *Social Science Quarterly*, 886-890.

Schooler, R. and Wildt, A. (1968). Elasticity of Product Bias. *Journal of Marketing Research*, (February), 5, 78-81.

Tse, D., Belk, R. and Zhou, N. (1989). Becoming a Consumer Society: A Longitudinal and Cross-Cultural Content Analysis of Print from Hong Kong, the People's Republic of China, and Taiwan. *Journal of Consumer Research*, (March), 15(4), 457-472.

Wall, M. and Heslop, L. (1986). Consumer Attitudes Toward Canadian-Made versus Imported Products. *Journal of the Academy of Marketing Science*, (Summer), 14, 27-36.

Wang, C. and Lamb, C. (1980). Foreign Environmental Factors Influencing American Consumers' Predispositions Toward European Products. *Journal of the Academy of Marketing Science*, (Fall), 8, 345-356.

Wang, C. and Lamb, C. (1983). The Impact of Selected Environmental Forces Upon Consumers' Willingness to Buy Foreign Products. *Journal of Academy of Marketing Science*, (Winter), 11, 71-84.

White, P. (1979). Attitudes of U.S. Purchasing Managers Toward Industrial Products Manufactured in Selected Western European Nations. *Journal of International Business Studies*, 10, 81-90.

White, P. and Cundiff, E. (1978). Assessing the Quality of Industrial Products. *Journal of Marketing*, (January), 42, 80-86.

Yavas, U. (1988). Global and Attribute-Specific Attitudinal Correlates of Made-In Labels. In Bahr, K. D. (Ed.), *Developments in Marketing Science*, 11 (pp. 112-116). Blacksburg, VA: Academy of Marketing Science.

Zajonc, R. B. and Markus, H. (1985). Must All Affects Be Mediated by Cognition? *Journal of Consumer Research*, (December), 12, 363-364.

Zeithaml, V. (1988). Consumer Perceptions of Price, Quality, and Value: A Means-End Model and Synthesis of Evidence. *Journal of Marketing*, (July), 52(3), 2-22.

Chapter 6

The Impact of Modernization
on Consumer Innovativeness
in a Developing Market

Jose F. Medina
Pavlos Michaels

SUMMARY. Modernization is a macrosocial phenomenon that has been neglected in international marketing. At the same time, there is a paucity of research on the concept of innovativeness in LDCs. This empirical study uses path analysis to assess the impact of individual modernism, consumer modernism, and social class on innovativeness in Monterrey, Mexico. Innovativeness was measured by the degree of ownership of novel consumer durables. The results showed that innovativeness was overwhelmingly influenced by social class, but not by individual and consumer modernism. This suggests the greater importance of socioeconomic variables in predicting consumer behavior in developing nations.

INTRODUCTION

Adoption of innovations and the innovativeness of individual consumers have been studied widely in the marketing literature. Rogers (1983), Gatignon and Robertson (1985), and Foxall (1988) each gives a comprehensive review of the literature with respect to innovativeness. They identify 31 variables in all as possible producers of innovativeness. Of these, 9 are socioeconomic, 12 personality and attitude factors, and 10 communication behavior variables. The socioeconomic determinants of innovativeness include: social class, income, education, and age. Open-mindedness, venturesomeness, favorable attitude toward change, favorable attitude toward science, and achievement motivation are some of the personality and attitude factors that previous research has established to be associated with innovativeness (Rogers, 1983; Gatignon and Robertson, 1985; Foxall, 1988). Finally, cosmopolitanism, social participation, contact with change agents, mass media exposure, and information seeking are communication behavior variables that have been found to be associated with innovativeness (Rogers, 1983; Gatignon and Robertson, 1985; Foxall, 1988).

Adoption of innovations by members of a social system such as a market segment of a developing country requires time for behavioral and attitudinal changes to occur (Dholakia, Sharif, and Bhandari, 1988). Although consumption practices occurring in developing countries reflect the growing influence of modern consumption patterns that prevail in affluent societies, especially the United States (Freedman, 1975; James and Stewart, 1981; Hirschman, 1986), researchers have made no attempt to link this phenomenon to innovativeness.

Review of the literature reveals that the study of innovativeness in developing countries has been neglected. This chapter addresses the problem of the paucity of research of innovativeness in developing countries. It is an attempt to explore the linkages between a macrosocial phenomenon known as modernization and innovativeness. More specifically, the purpose of this chapter is to assess the interplay between social class, individual modernism, and consumer modernism with innovativeness in a developing country, Mexico.

To accomplish the purpose of this chapter, a review of the literature is pursued first. Subsequently, the chapter reports on a survey study conducted to investigate the impact of individual modernism, consumer modernism, and social class on consumer innovativeness in Monterrey, Mexico. Finally, a discussion is presented on the limitations of the study and the conclusions and implications.

LITERATURE REVIEW

Modernization and Consumption

It has long been recognized that economic growth, (i.e., the build-up and accumulation of economic resources) is but one factor in the economic development process. Other elements contributing to and symptomatic of country development are the evolution of political, economic, and social institutions on the one hand; and the development of individuals from traditional to modern outlooks and orientations on the other hand (Kahl, 1968; Inkeles and Smith, 1974).

According to Inkeles and Smith (1974), modernization in developing countries results from industrialization and technology transfer. That is, societies and individuals reorganize themselves and their institutions to sustain economic, political, and social development. More specifically, during modernization, individuals undergo psychological and behavioral adjustments to meet the requirements of the modern society. The degree to which individuals move from traditional to modern value orientations is known as individual modernism (Kahl, 1968).

In the international business literature, Korbin (1979) and Hill and Still (1980) formalized these observations and proposed a conceptual framework dealing with the impact of technology transfer in developing countries from a cultural perspective. This framework suggests that multinational corporations (MNCs), via technology transfer, foster economic development through their impact on individual and group behavior. The same scholars refer to this phenomenon as an acculturation process requiring major psychological and social changes.

One of these social changes takes place in the marketplace where modern consumer behavior appears (Freedman, 1975; James and Stewart, 1981; Hirschman, 1986). This appearance of modern consumption patterns and values has long been recognized in the international business literature as the "demonstration effect" (Nurkse, 1953). There is a "trickle-down effect" derived from the tendency of traditional groups to emulate sophisticated urban lifestyles in developing countries. Nurkse (1953, p. 59) goes on to say that, "Their knowledge is extended, their imagination stimulated;

new desires are aroused, the propensity to consume is shifted upward . . . ." This exposure to alternative products and services
causes change in consumer attitudes and purchasing behavior, especially as traditional members of the society observe how new products and services contribute to the lifestyles of the innovators (Hill
and Still, 1980; Hirschman, 1986).

The Nature of Innovativeness and Innovations

Discussing the construct of innovativeness and its significance in
marketing, Hirschman (1980) says that different consumers have
adopted innovative goods or services in their lifetime. Consequently, every consumer has some degree of innovativeness. In general,
the construct of innovativeness is defined and measured in two
ways in marketing studies (Midgley and Dowling, 1978; Assael,
1987; Engel, Blackwell, and Miniard, 1990). One of these defini-
tions is based on the time of adoption, that is, the time framework in
which persons purchase and use a product in the first x weeks,
months, and so on (Midgley and Dowling, 1978; Engel, Blackwell,
and Miniard, 1990).

Alternatively, innovativeness is measured by the number of new
products on a prespecified list, which a particular individual has
purchased by the time of the study (Summers, 1972; Midgley and
Dowling, 1978). This approach of "ownership of new products" or
"cross-sectional" method was initiated by Robertson and Myers
(1969).

The literature identifies three major categories of variables
associated with consumer innovativeness. These three categories
are: socioeconomic, personality, and communication behavior variables (Rogers, 1983; Gatignon and Robertson, 1985; Foxall, 1988).

Socioeconomic Variables. Research pertaining to socioeconomic
variables shows that people of high social status, educated, and who
are privileged relative to others in their social system tend to be
high in consumer innovativeness (Rogers, 1983; Gatignon and Robertson, 1985; Foxall, 1988). Income is almost always present in
profiles of innovators and innovativeness. People with higher income levels not only can afford to take the risk of trying new
products but they also have the financial ability to purchase more
new goods. Of course, this relationship is mainly important when

expensive products such as consumer durables are involved (Engel, Blackwell, and Miniard, 1990).

Personality and Attitude Factors. Open-mindedness or venturesomeness, higher aspirations for themselves and their children, intelligence, the ability to deal with abstractions or to be creative, and rationality are a few of the personality and attitudinal factors that have been found to be associated with innovativeness in people as consumers (Rogers, 1983; Gatignon and Robertson, 1985; Foxall, 1988). In contrast, rigidity of personality or dogmatism, and fatalism tend most likely to be related negatively with innovativeness (Rogers, 1983; Gatignon and Robertson, 1985; Foxall, 1988).

People possessing these personality-attitude attributes are more likely to seek solutions outside the context of their previous solutions to consumption problems. They are likely to seek different ways of organizing, deciding, and behaving, which in general involve some type of radical change and the incorporation of new objects, activities, and methods and techniques (Foxall and Hawkins, 1986).

Communication Behavior Variables. According to Rogers (1983), communication behavior variables that have been found to be associated with innovativeness include cosmopolitanism, social participation, contact with change agents, mass media exposure, higher amounts of interpersonal communication, active information seeking, knowledge of innovations, opinion leadership, and other variables. Communication behavior variables recognize that information contributes to an increased level of awareness, which subsequently leads to favorable attitudes and an adoption decision. For example, recent research shows that earlier adopters use both mass media and interpersonal sources of information more than later adopters (Price, Feick, and Smith, 1986).

Robertson (1969), classified product innovations according to their effects on consumer behavior. He identified three types: continuous, dynamically continuous, and discontinuous innovations. *Continuous innovations* have the least disruptive influence on established consumption patterns. They are usually alterations of established brands (e.g., fluoride in toothpaste). Although they do not involve new patterns of consumption, *dynamically continuous* innovations are more disruptive than continuous innovations. They may be totally new products or modifications of old ones. Some resistance to them occurs because traditional patterns of behavior may change. Examples include electric hairdryers and can openers. Finally, *discontinuous innovations* involve the development and introduction of previously unknown products. They produce drastic changes in behavior and consumption patterns. Examples are televisions, refrigerators, personal computers, etc.

Most innovations introduced during the industrialization of developing countries are of the dynamically continuous and discontinuous nature. Rostow (1967) predicted that as nations drive to maturity in their economic development process, they seek to extend modern technology to sustain economic progress, and consumption patterns shift toward consumer durables and services. Alternatively, Uusitalo (1979) observed that high ownership levels of consumer durables reflect individuality, personal success, and the adoption of modern economic values that occur as individuals move from traditional to modern urban surroundings. It is important to point out that many continuous innovations in developed countries can be construed as discontinuous in developing countries.

Product Adoption in Mexico

Trade and international business activities naturally affect products and services offered in developing countries. As adoption occurs, it brings increased varieties of goods and services to consumers (Kaynak, 1986). Mexico's modernization and adoption of new products has occurred mainly as a result of technologies and innovations transferred from the United States and other developed countries (Balan, Browning, and Jelin, 1973). Technologies imported from these countries through trade and direct investment have significantly affected Mexico's occupational structure, allocation of resources, and social patterns (Balan, Browning, and Jelin, 1973).

In particular, the proximity of Mexico to the United States has led to social change and the introduction of new patterns of lifestyle. For example, back in the early 1960s, the introduction of supermarkets in Mexico meant that greater varieties of consumer packaged goods were distributed to the small but growing Mexican middle and upper classes. The efficiency and convenience of supermarket shopping encouraged Mexican housewives to do the shopping themselves–

instead of having their maids do it–and pay for it by check, just like their American counterparts. This changed old habits, reducing the need for servants and leaving less leisure time for middle and upper income housewives, which leads to subsequent changes in lifestyles. As a consequence of social and lifestyle changes, consumers in Mexico have increased their ownership of durable products, selection of stores to choose from, and product information that influences their consumption behavior.

HYPOTHESES

Review of the literature shows that modernization is a socioeconomic process that affects the social, political, and economic values of a society. It helps explain changes from traditional to modern attitudes and behaviors that take place among individuals in a developing country (Kahl 1968; Inkeles and Smith, 1974). Therefore, we consider individual modernism a personality variable in our study. Also, observation of new and modern lifestyles resulting from product adoption encourages individuals to imitate modern consumption patterns (Nurkse, 1953). Modern patterns include new purchasing roles, information seeking, and packaging (Hill and Still, 1980). Therefore, we consider consumer modernism a communication behavior variable in our study. Finally, research indicates that social class is associated with innovativeness (Rogers, 1983). Social class is expected to be an important socioeconomic factor within a developing market environment (Cunningham, Moore, and Cunningham, 1974).

There is no previous documentation in the literature linking individual modernism (a personality variable) and consumer modernism (a communication variable) with innovativeness. Similarly, there is no indication that attempts have been made to determine the relationship between social class (a socioeconomic variable) and innovativeness within the context of a developing country. More importantly, there is no indication that determinants of innovativeness from the three major categories discussed have been tested simultaneously. The following hypotheses consider these relationships within the context of an industrializing country, Mexico:

H1:   Individual modernism in Mexico is positively related to innovativeness.

H2:   Consumer modernism in Mexico is positively related to innovativeness.

H3:   Social class in Mexico is positively related to innovativeness.

Figure 6.1 depicts the overall model with the major variables included in the present study, as well as their hypothesized linkages. The model indicates that social class, individual modernism, and consumer modernism have related, but independent, effects on innovativeness. Additionally, the model hypothesizes a temporal effect among these three variables, where income affects both individual and consumer modernism, and individual modernism affects consumer modernism. Since preferences underlying consumption are strongly related to consumer need-priorities, which in turn tend to be value-based (Uusitalo, 1979), consumer modernism is considered an intervening variable between individual modernism (values) and product ownership (behavior).

METHODOLOGY

Measurement Scales

A four-part structured questionnaire was developed to measure individual modernism, consumer modernism, innovativeness, and demographic and socioeconomic information on the respondents, including social class. *Individual modernism* was measured using Kahl's (1968) Individual Modernism II Scale. This measure consists of an eight-item, five-point Likert scale which has the following components: efficiency, democratic orientation, low community stratification, low integration with relatives, individualism, and preference for urban life. The measure was developed and tested originally in Mexico and Brazil. More recently, however, the scale has been used successfully in India by Dugan (1983).

Consumer modernism assesses attitudes of individuals toward modern consumption habits (Campbell, 1987). Adoption of modern

FIGURE 6.1. Overall Model Indicating Study Hypothesis and Path Coefficients

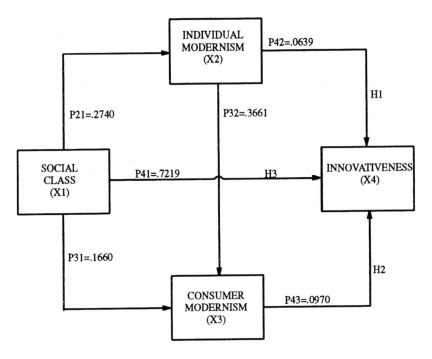

consumption attitudes and habits was measured by using a nine-item, five-point Likert scale developed by the researchers. Various sources were used to develop this scale (Hair, 1971; Green, Cunningham, and Cunningham, 1973; Cunningham, Moore, and Cunningham, 1974; Uusitalo, 1979; Green and Cunningham, 1980; Schiffman, Dillon, and Ngumah, 1981; Hill, 1984). Overall, this scale measured attitudes toward new purchasing roles, information seeking, brand evaluation and decision making, new shopping behavior, and packaging.

Innovativeness was measured on the basis of ownership of modern technological products (Robertson and Myers, 1969; Summers, 1972). This "cross-sectional" technique is one of the customary and acceptable approaches in marketing studies (Midgley and Dowling, 1978). Midgley and Dowling (1978) report that almost

40% of the investigations analyzed in their study used this technique as a measure of innovativeness.

Items used in this scale required dichotomous responses. A score of "0" indicates non-ownership and a score of "1" indicates ownership of a given product at the time of this survey study. The degree of innovativeness is judged by how many of the twenty prespecified "modern technological products" are owned by the respondents (Summers, 1972).

The twenty products used in this study are: (1) radio, (2) black and white television, (3) refrigerator, (4) range, (5) camera, (6) hair dryer, (7) toaster, (8) stereo system, (9) color television, (10) microwave oven, (11) video cassette recorder, (12) electric shaver, (13) electric mixer, (14) washing machine, (15) clothes dryer, (16) vacuum cleaner, (17) food processor, (18) electric can opener, (19) dishwasher, and (20) personal computer.

All twenty products share the following two characteristics: (1) They constitute technology transfers. The invention and development of these products can be traced to the U.S. (2) They are dynamically continuous and discontinuous innovations. They are generally disruptive when they are first introduced because they change old patterns of behavior (Cateora, 1990).

Questionnaire Translation and Validation

The method of back-translation in an English-Spanish context was used. Such a technique has been previously used with good results (Brislin, 1970; Green and Cunningham, 1980). The questionnaire was administered for validation purposes to a small group of "knowledgeable others" (all educated professionals from a major southern university), who had an in-depth understanding of both the language and the Mexican culture. Though this pretesting procedure alone is not optimal, it improves the face and content validity of the measurement instrument.

Sampling Design

The sample was drawn from Monterrey, Mexico. Monterrey was chosen because it represents a "typical" industrializing city in the developing world. It is heavily exposed to outside modern influences and technology transfer. Stratified sampling was used to ensure the data were representative of the Mexican social class structure. *Social class* was defined as a group of people with similar ranking position with respect to their socioeconomic status (Sorokin, 1962; Coleman, 1983).

The operationalization of social class had to be congruent with the process of modernization and reflective of social mobility, urbanization, and economic advancement. Therefore, the type of dwelling unit was considered to be the best indicator of social position of households in developing countries (Garza, 1985). Respondents were pre-selected into one of five social class rankings by field observations of the physical location and appearance of their dwelling units (Garza, 1985). Dwelling units are generally defined as a group of rooms or a single room occupied or intended for occupancy by a family, a group of persons living together, or a person living alone (Kish, 1965).

The sampling frame (list of all the city blocks in metropolitan Monterrey) was produced by the Instituto Nacional de Estadísticas, Geografía, e Informatica (INEGI). The primary sampling units (i.e., city blocks) were chosen through a random selection procedure. Then, within each city block all dwelling units (secondary sampling units) were surveyed.

Data Collection Procedures

Data were collected from the sample during the month of June, 1987, using a self-administered, structured questionnaire. Seven hundred and fifty questionnaires were delivered to selected dwelling units within Monterrey's metropolitan area. Each questionnaire was accompanied by a cover letter explaining the purpose of the research. In addition, basic information was given about the content of the questionnaire, including an explanation of who should qualify for filling it out. Five hundred and seven people responded with complete and usable questionnaires for a response rate of 68%.

ANALYSIS AND INTERPRETATION OF FINDINGS

Representativeness of the Sample

To test the representativeness of the sample, a goodness-of-fit test was performed. Social class population estimates from the 1980 Census were compared with sample statistics. It was assumed that social class distribution changes were not significant between 1980 and 1987 (the year this study's data was collected) because of Mexico's stagnant economy during these years. The overall results showed that the sample was representative of the social class hierarchy of metropolitan Monterrey (Chi-square = 13.15, p < .05, d.f. = 4). Table 6.1 shows the number of respondents from each social class, the corresponding percentages, and the estimated population percentages.

TABLE 6.1. Distributions of Sample Respondents and Population Estimates by Social Class

| Social Class | Sample | | Estimated[a] Population Percentages |
	Number of Respondents	Percentage	
High	100	19.7	9.9
Middle-high	119	23.5	18.0
Middle-low	115	22.7	18.4
Low	82	16.2	15.9
Marginal	91	17.9	22.1
Total	507	100.0	100.0

[a]These statistics are based on the 1980 Census of the population. Adapted from Menno Vellinga and Edgar López (1987), *Ingreso: Distribución y Redistribución, Movilidad Social y Niveles de Vida 1965-1985*, Table 13, p. 41.

Reliability of Measurement Scales

Table 6.2 shows a summary of statistics, including reliability estimates for the scales used in this study. The first scale, consumer modernism, shows a moderately low alpha coefficient (.59). Equivalent reliabilities for other studies of modernism are generally higher. For example, Inkeles and Smith (1974), using Kuder-Richardson's technique, reported reliability estimates between .55 and .91.

The consumer modernism scale was computed at .557, which is considered acceptable for a new scale. At early stages of measure development, reliability levels can range from .5 to .6 (Nunnally, 1978, p. 226).

The reliability of the social class measure was tested by estimating the strength of its association with widely used social class surrogates such as occupation, income, and education (Coleman, 1983). Because these surrogate measures are ordinally-scaled, the appropriate test statistic was Kendall's Tau-C correlation coefficient for bivariate relationships (Nunnally, 1978). This test produced values of .612, .539, and .487 for occupation, income, and education, respectively, all significant at .0001 level.

TABLE 6.2. Reliability Coefficients for the Scales Used in the Model

Scales	Number of Items	Possible Value Range	Type of Scale	Reliability
Individual Modernism	8	8-40	Interval	.590[a]
Consumer Modernism	9	9-45	Interval	.557[a]
Social Class	Preallocated	1-5	Ordinal	.612[b] .539[b] .487[b]
Innovativeness	20	0-20	Ratio	.881[a]

[a]Internal consistency reliability (Cronbach Alpha)
[b]Alternative measures reliability (Kendall Tau-C), with occupation, income, and education, respectively.

No previous reliability estimates of the innovativeness measure are reported in the literature. Thus, Cronbach alpha was computed to determine the internal consistency of this ratio-scaled measure. This turned out to attain an excellent high value of .881 (see Table 6.2).

Hypotheses Testing

Path analysis was determined as a useful tool for discerning the strength and direction of the underlying causal mechanisms (Asher, 1983). This is only possible by the computation and comparison of direct and indirect effects among the variables being evaluated. These effects are discussed in the following section.

The path analysis diagram of the total model is depicted in Figure 6.1, path analysis results are indicated in Table 6.3, and the decomposition of total associations between model variables are shown in Table 6.4. The total model has three sub-models: the innovativeness sub-model, the consumer modernism sub-model, and the individual modernism sub-model (see Table 6.3).

Innovativeness Sub-Model

The innovativeness sub-model was concerned with analyzing what factors impact varying levels of consumer durable ownership. To do this, innovativeness was regressed on individual modernism (hypothesis H1), consumer modernism (hypothesis H2), and social class (hypothesis H3). As Table 6.3 indicates, consumer modernism, individual modernism, and especially social class show definite associations with innovativeness, as derived from the obtained magnitudes of the path coefficients, $P_{43} = .097$, $P_{42} = .0639$ and $P_{41} = .7219$, respectively. Collectively, they account for 60.27% of the variance in individual innovativeness. While this looks significant, these effects are not as strong as they appear. Table 6.4 shows why.

In the description of effects, the importance of consumer modernism and individual modernism is diluted considerably because most of their attributable effects are spurious (.2185 and .2022, respectively). That is, they are due to a common cause or causes–a background variable(s) that is (are) affecting their performance on

TABLE 6.3. Path Analysis Results for the Model

Dependent Variable (X_j)	Independent Variable (X_i)	Regression Coefficient (β_{ij})	Path Coefficient (P_{ij})	R^2
X4	X3	.1002	.0970[a]	.6027[a]
	X2	.0612	.0639[b]	
	X1	2.3528	.7219[a]	
	Constant	−.9247		
X3	X2	.3404	.3661[a]	.1949[a]
	X1	.5255	.1660[a]	
	Constant	18.9130		
X2	X1	.9328	.2740[a]	.0751[a]
	Constant	26.9750		

Where: X1 = Social Class
X2 = Individual Modernism
X3 = Consumer Modernism
X4 = Innovativeness

[a]p<.01
[b]p<.05

innovativeness. These effects are significant because they account for 69% (.2185/.3155) and 67% (.2022/.3016) of their implied correlations (see Table 6.4). The temptation is to conclude that this common cause may very well be social class. That is, the correlations between innovativeness and consumer modernism, and between innovativeness and individual modernism are due to social class effects that are acting upon all of them simultaneously. The strength of the social class effect on innovativeness underscores the relatively obvious idea that as modernization occurs, incomes, educational opportunities, and occupational statuses improve. When this improvement occurs, discretionary incomes increase and consumption of durable products increases too.

TABLE 6.4. Decomposition of Total Associations Between Model Variables

					Path Analysis		
Dep. Var. (X_j)	Indep. Var. (X_i)	Zero Order Corr.	Direct Effect (1)	Indirect Effect (2)	Spurious Effect (3)	Total Effect (1+2)	Implicit Corr. (1+2+3)
X4	X3	.316[a]	.0970[a]	–	.2185	.0970	.3155
	X2	.302[a]	.0639[b]	.0355	.2022	.0994	.3016
	X1	.765[a]	.7219[a]	.0433		.7652	.7652
X3	X2	.412[a]	.3661[a]	–	.0454	.3661	.4115
	X1	.266[a]	.1660[a]	.1003	–	.2663	.2663
X2	X1	.274[a]	.2740[a]	–	–	.2740	.2740

Where: X1 = Social Class
        X2 = Individual Modernism
        X3 = Consumer Modernism
        X4 = Innovativeness

[a]p<.01
[b]p<.05

Consumer Modernism Sub-Model

The consumer modernism sub-model was set up to determine whether individual modernism (the extent of the adoption of modern values) and social class influenced the respondents' adoption of modern consumption habits. Thus, consumer modernism was regressed on individual modernism and social class. The results, shown in Table 6.3, indicate that both individual modernism and social class have significant and direct effects on consumer modernism ($P_{32} = .3661$ and $P_{31} = .1660$, respectively). However, individual modernism and social class account for only 19.49% of the variance in consumer modernism. This is low, but is explicable due to the large number of externalities acting on the consumer, including marketing stimuli (Parsons and Schultz, 1976).

Further insight is gained from Table 6.4, where a breakdown of the total association between predictor variables and consumer modernism is shown. It indicates that of the two variables, social class effects are more potent in explaining consumer modernism. Individual modernism has no indirect effects, and spurious effects account for only 11% (.0454/.3661) of the implicit correlation. On the other hand, social class has an indirect effect that accounts for 37.6% (.1003/.2663) of the total association but with no spurious effects.

These results suggest that, for example, as individuals assimilate modern economic values such as efficiency and individualism, their attitudes and consumption habits change too (e.g., favorable attitudes toward labor-saving devices, instant foods, etc.).

Individual Modernism Sub-Model

The relationship evaluated in this sub-model concerns social class association with the adoption of modern values. For this purpose, individual modernism was regressed on social class. Results shown in Table 6.3 confirm that social class has a positive direct causal effect on individual modernism (P_{21} = .2740). However, the coefficient of determination of 7.5% suggests that social class is only one of many possible variables influencing traditional or modern value orientations. It is likely that another key factor such as age, which is not specified in the model, may account for some portion of the unexplained variance.

The component breakdown for the association between social class and individual modernism is shown in Table 6.4. The absence of indirect and spurious effects confirms that this direct effect is the only one working in this relationship within the model. The direct effect of social class on individual modernism is also significant. This result suggests, not surprisingly, that individuals in the lower social classes have more traditional or conservative values and those in the upper classes tend to hold modern values.

STUDY LIMITATIONS

The following limitations apply to this study and may affect the findings and their interpretation:

1. Attempts to generalize study results for analysis of other cities in other developing countries must be made with the greatest of caution. This study was a single-city, single-country sample. This automatically reduces the generalizabilty of the findings.
2. Nonrespondent bias was not accounted for in this study. It is possible that people with less ability to understand what the study was about decided not to answer the questionnaire. This would create an "education bias" in the sample.
3. The reliability coefficients for the individual and consumer modernism scales were low. This fact can contribute to non-random measurement errors which can attenuate the results of the path coefficients (Asher, 1983).
4. While research data basically supported the hypothesized relationships in the model, it is still methodologically and philosophically difficult to infer which are the true and actual causes and which are effects.

CONCLUSIONS AND IMPLICATIONS

While hypothesis H3 (relationship between social class and innovativeness) was strongly supported by the data, there were problems in relating individual modernism to innovativeness (H1) and consumer modernism to innovativeness (H2). This supports, however, at least one previous study's contention that social class may be a primary variable in determining consumption behavior in developing countries (Cunningham, Moore, and Cunningham, 1974). It also supports another finding that economic success, as revealed by an individual's social class ranking, results in increased conspicuous consumption of consumer durables (Rostow, 1967; Uusitalo, 1979). Findings also suggest that modern values and consumption attitudes are essentially by-products of individuals' upward socioeconomic progression and not the opposite. There is indication that modern values and modern consumption habits do not play an important role in directly influencing consumer innovativeness (that is, the ownership of consumer durables) in developing countries.

Implications for Practitioners

Since in most cases successful marketing of products depends on understanding factors affecting consumer behavior, this study stands to contribute to managerial understanding of market segments in at least two ways. First, the strength of the relationship between social class and consumer innovativeness confirmed that there are, at least in urban areas of developing countries such as Mexico, important upper class segments for consumer durables. This has important implications for producers of household consumer durables such as personal computers and video cassette recorders. Marketers may need to determine the order of acquisition of consumer durables as individuals move from lower to higher social class groups. Secondly, geographical segmentation (dwelling location and appearance) in urban centers in developing countries would be a useful approach for promotional purposes. Billboards, in-transit mass advertising, and direct mail should be effective in reaching upper class neighborhoods.

Implications for Policy Makers

Although international marketing programs should be evaluated in terms of their efficiency in distributing goods and services in developing countries, they can be critically and fairly evaluated only if favorable social, economic, and political environments are produced as a result of their implementation. The study showed that ownership of consumer durables varied considerably across social class groups. This suggests that standards of living, as indicated by consumers' ability to acquire expensive products, have not improved for some population groups as a result of government industrialization programs.

Given a national strategy of economic growth through industrialization, developing nation policy makers should bear major responsibility for reducing or reversing the possible negative consequences resulting from the modernization of their markets. Consumer innovativeness (the ownership, and thus, the demand for modern consumer durables) can be seen as a socially undesirable goal for developing countries that have not reached a balanced phase of economic development. This is so because high levels of consumer innovativeness could shift domestic resources from more basic (perhaps productive) industries such as agriculture to more lucrative (perhaps inefficient) industries such as consumer electronics, with the potential detriment to the society as a whole.

Implications for Future Research

This study's point of departure was the recognition of a paucity of adequate knowledge and research in consumer innovativeness in developing nations. Hopefully, this effort will promote the generation of new knowledge on a worthwhile topic as it pertains to a particular type of market that might have a great potential and influence in the future.

Overall, the combination of variables used in this study may have significant research implications in other international consumption settings. The relevance of the employed variables may be considered in relation to other durable products and services, as well as other developing markets.

The study has a number of limitations as indicated. Therefore, we suggest that future research efforts replicate the study's methodology in other developing countries to establish its veracity. A special effort should be made to refine the measurement scales and/or develop new ones more appropriate, if so warranted.

This study is a cross-sectional one. Future research should try to capture the dynamics of changing consumer values, attitudes, and behaviors using longitudinal or intergenerational survey data. It should be recognized, however, that such a task is difficult and demands special allocation of time and resources.

REFERENCES

Asher, Herbert (1983), *Causal Modeling.* Beverly Hills: Sage Publications, Inc.
Assael, Henry (1987), *Consumer Behavior and Marketing Action*, 3rd ed. Boston: Kent Publishing Company.

Balan, Jorge, Harley L. Browning, and Elizabeth Jelin (1973), *Men in a Developing Society: Geographic and Social Mobility in Monterrey, Mexico*. Austin: University of Texas Press.

Brislin, Richard W. (1970), "Backtranslation for Cross-Cultural Research," *Journal of Cross-Cultural Psychology*, (September), 185-216.

Campbell, Colin (1987), *The Romantic Ethic and the Spirit of Modern Consumerism*. Oxford: Basil Blackwell.

Cateora, Philip R. (1990), *International Marketing*, 7th ed. Homewood, IL: Richard D. Irwin, Inc.

Coleman, Richard P. (1983), "The Continuing Significance of Social Class to Marketing," *Journal of Consumer Research*, 10 (December), 265-280.

Cunningham, William H., Russell M. Moore, and Isabella Cunningham (1974), "Urban Markets in Industrializing Countries: The Sao Paulo Experience," *Journal of Marketing*, 38 (April), 2-12.

Dholakia, R. Ror, Mohammed Sharif, and Labdhi Bhandari (1988), "Marketing and Development: Toward Broader Dimensions," in *Research in Marketing*, Vol. 4, 129-147. New York: JAI Press, Inc.

Dugan, John J., Jr. (1983), "The Relationship Between Culture and Managers' Behavioral Decisions: A Two Country Study of the Presence Formation and Choice Processes," Dissertations Abstracts International (University Microfilms).

Engel, James F., Roger D. Blackwell, and Paul W. Miniard (1990), *Consumer Behavior*, 6th ed. Chicago: The Dryden Press.

Foxall, Gordon (1988), "Consumer Innovativeness: Novelty-Seeking, Creativity and Cognitive Style," in *Research in Consumer Behavior*, Vol. 3, edited by Elizabeth Hirschman and Jagdish Sheth, 79-113. New York: JAI Press.

Foxall, Gordon and Christopher G. Hawkins (1986), "Cognitive Style and Consumer Innovativeness: An Empirical Test of Kirton's Adaptation-Innovation Theory in the Context of Food Purchasing," *European Journal of Marketing*, 20, 63-80.

Freedman, Deborah S. (1975), "Consumption of Modern Goods and Services and its Relation to Fertility: A Study in Taiwan," *Journal of Development Studies*, 12(1), 95-117.

Garza, Rosalinda (1985), "Estratificación del Area Metropolitana de Monterrey," Thesis, Universidad Autónoma de Nuevo León, Monterrey, México.

Gatignon, Hubert and Thomas S. Robertson (1985), "A Proportional Inventory for New Diffusion Research," *Journal of Consumer Research*, 11 (March), 849-867.

Green, Robert T. and Isabella Cunningham (1980), "Family Purchasing Roles in Two Countries," *Journal of International Business Studies*, 11 (Spring/Summer), 92-97.

Green, Robert T., Isabella Cunningham, and William H. Cunningham (1973), "Cross-Cultural Consumer Profile: An Exploratory Investigation," in *Advances in Consumer Research*, edited by Scott Ward and Peter Wright, 136-144. Saint Louis: Association of Consumer Research.

Hair, F. Joseph (1971), "The Impact of the Acculturation Process on the Consumer Purchasing Patterns," PhD dissertation, University of Florida.

Hill, John S. and Richard Still (1980), "Cultural Effects of Technology Transfer by Multinational Corporations in Lesser Developed Countries," *Columbia Journal of World Business*, 15 (Summer), 40-51.

Hill, John S. (1984), "Targeting Promotions in Lesser-Developed Countries: A Study of Multinational Corporation Strategies," *Journal of Advertising Research*, 13(4), 39-48.

Hirschman, Elizabeth C. (1980), "Innovativeness, Novelty Seeking, and Consumer Creativity," *Journal of Consumer Research*, (December), 7, 283-295.

———— (1986), "Marketing as an Agent of Chance in Subsistence Cultures: Some Dysfunctional Consumption Consequences," in *Advances in Consumer Research*, 99-104. Saint Louis: Association for Consumer Research.

Inkeles, Alex and D. H. Smith (1974). *Becoming Modern: Individual Change in Six Developing Countries*. Cambridge: Harvard University Press.

James, Jeffrey and Francis Stewart (1981), "New Products: A Discussion of Welfare Effects of the Introduction of New Products in Developing Countries," *Oxford Economic Papers*, 33(1), 81-107.

Kahl, Joseph A. (1968), *The Measurement of Modernism: A Study of Values in Brazil and Mexico*. Austin: The University of Texas Press.

Kaynak, E. (1986), *Marketing and Economic Development*. New York: Random House.

Kish, Leslie (1965), *Survey Sampling*. New York: J. Wiley, Inc.

Korbin, Stephen J. (1979), "Multinational Corporations, Sociocultural Dependence, and the Industrialization: Need Satisfaction or Want Creation?" *Journal of Developing Areas*, 13(2) (January), 109-125.

Midgley, David F. and Graham R. Dowling (1978), "Innovativeness: The Concept and Its Measurement," *Journal of Consumer Research*, (March), 4, 229-242.

Nunnally, Jim C. (1978), *Psychometric Theory*, 2nd ed. New York: McGraw-Hill, Inc.

Nurske, Ragnar (1953), *Problems of Capital Formation in Underdeveloped Countries*. New York: Oxford University Press.

Parsons, Leonard and Randall Schultz (1976), *Marketing Models and Econometric Research*. New York: North-Holland.

Price, Linda, Lawrence Feick, and Daniel Smith (1986), "A Reexamination of Communication Channel Usage by Adopter Categories," in *Advances in Consumer Research*, 13, edited by Richard Lutz, 409-412.

Robertson, Thomas S. and James H. Myers (1969), "Personality Correlates of Opinion Leadership and Innovative Buying Behavior," *Journal of Marketing Research*, 6, (May), 164-178.

Rogers, Everett M. (1983), *Diffusion of Innovations*, New York: The Free Press.

Rostow, Walt W. (1967), *The Stages of Economic Growth: A Non-Communist Manifesto*. New York: Cambridge University Press.

Schiffman, Leon G., William R. Dillon, and Festus E. Ngumah (1981), "The

Influence of Subcultural and Personality Factors on Consumer Acculturation," *Journal of International Business Studies*, 2 (Fall), 137-143.

Sorokin, Pitrim A. (1962), *Society, Culture and Personality, Their Structure and Dynamics, A System of General Sociology*. New York: Cooper Square Publishers.

Summers, John O. (1972), "Media Exposure Patterns of Consumer Innovators," *Journal of Marketing*, 36 (January), 43-49.

Uusitalo, Liisa (1979), "Consumption Style and Way of Life–An Empirical Identification and Explanation of Consumption Style Dimensions," in *Acta Academiae Oeconomicae Helsingiensis*. Helsinki: The Helsinki School of Economics.

Chapter 7

Consumer Involvement in Services: An International Evaluation

Lee D. Dahringer
Charles D. Frame
Oliver Yau
Janet McColl-Kennedy

SUMMARY. Research was undertaken in Australia and the U.S. to evaluate whether the construct of consumer involvement in services is an empirically valid construct across nations. Preliminary findings in Australia and the U.S. suggest that it is. Managerially, although Australians and American consumers are involved at different levels in the same service, a standardized marketing campaign across the two national markets may still be appropriate.

GLOBALIZATION OF MARKETING

Without question, today's marketers operate in a global environment. World trade increases faster than domestic, "Triad Power" is increasing in popularity as a basis for strategy, worldwide investment is rapidly increasing, and strategic alliances are the corporate strategy of choice.[1]

The Emory Business School, Emory University, Atlanta, GA, and the Graduate School of Management, St. Lucia, Australia provided research funds for the findings reported in this chapter. Appreciation is also expressed to Henry Johns, Emory Business School, and Susan Dann, Graduate School of Management, for their assistance in data coding and analysis.

The consumer world is becoming smaller, as consumers are increasingly exposed to global media, international travel, new products, consumption patterns, and technologies. Some analysts argue that consumer tastes and needs are increasingly similar as a result (Levitt, 1983).

Global marketers have a potentially strong competitive advantage: their ability to seek out and exploit market similarities across nation markets. These global product markets allow the globally oriented firm to take advantage of coordination of marketing management plans and concentration of management talent, gaining economies of scale of production, and experience curve effects (Porter, 1986).

The most powerful and most appealing argument in favor of a global marketing orientation is based on the "experience curve effect," similar to the economic principle of economies of scale. If a company follows a global approach, two sources of the experience curve effect exist: production and marketing. The argument for achieving economies of scale through standardized production is well known. When a company produces more, up to a point the average cost of that product declines.

The second source of experience curve effects, the marketing mix, is potentially of even greater importance than production economies. Viewing the marketing mix as an asset base similar to productive facilities, managers may consider standardizing marketing mixes across national markets to achieve greater economies. Just as for production economies, when a company coordinates its marketing mix across countries, making only necessary adjustments, the per unit average cost of marketing declines.

There are more opportunities for the global marketer to coordinate activities across national markets than to use concentration. Concentration occurs when management and strategy are centralized, taking place in a "headquarters" environment and then communicated to other parts of the organization. Concurrent with centralization, a high level of standardization of the marketing mix occurs. In order for concentration to be successfully implemented, a highly homogeneous market across nations must exist. A high level of concentration elements is quite rare and difficult to achieve.

But concentration is not necessary to have a global marketing orientation in place. A global orientation also exists when an organization coordinates marketing activities across national markets to the extent possible. Gains in the experience curve effect from coordination permit savings on costs of advertising production and media placement, employing successful marketing promotions, positioning strategies, and sharing "good ideas" across national boundaries.

SERVICES MARKETING

It is important to study services separately from consumer goods and industrial goods in the global marketing context for several reasons. First, services continue to increase in importance within national economies. Second, the opportunities for growth at the world market level are considerable.[2] Third, unique barriers to trade in services exist. Finally, services have particular "product" dimensions that make global service marketing management different from that of physical goods.

Globally, services make up from 20 to 30% of world trade, with an estimated growth rate of up to 20%. Individually, the 24 most highly economically developed economies average 60% of their GDP in service sectors. Even Lesser Developed Economies (LDCs) average close to 30% of their GDP from services (Aronson and Cowhey, 1984).

Recently, GATT talks were expanded to include ways to make the international trade of services more efficient.[3] These trends signal an increasingly important role of services in world trade in the future. But marketers have been slow to systematically examine global services trading issues, especially in light of their increased importance.

Service Characteristics

Every product is a combination of physical or tangible, and non-physical or intangible attributes. Those products which are by and large non-physical or intangible are classified as services. A *service* is an intangible product that provides benefits to satisfy customer needs. The major difference between goods and services is that while goods are produced, services are performed (Rushton and Carson, 1985). Other differences between services and goods are that services are activities, not things, and production and consumption of services are relatively simultaneous (Gronross, 1982). Services, compared to physical goods, also possess other characteristics that influence their marketing.[4]

The marketing of services, as a field of study, has attracted considerable interest and activity. At its base, marketers have been interested in the characteristics of services, that is, how they differ from physical goods. These characteristics have various descriptions, the most popular of which are: intangible, inseparable, perishable, and heterogeneous (Zeithaml, Parasuraman, and Berry 1985; Lovelock 1983). Also of considerable interest is service quality, a multifaceted construct operationalized along the dimensions of tangibility, reliability, responsiveness, assurance, and empathy (Parasuraman, Berry, and Zeithaml 1986).

Considerable attention has also been paid to specific target consumer groups in terms of service marketing (Bush and Ortinau, 1988; Gilly and Zeithaml, 1987). From a management perspective, much discussion has centered around the intangibility dimension of service, and how it might be more efficiently and effectively managed (Rushton and Carson, 1985; Levitt, 1983). Others have explored personalization strategies for services (Surprenant and Solomon, 1987). The issue of structural change and its impact on service positioning has also been explored (Shostack, 1987). Despite the considerable amount of work that has been done, due to the relatively new attention of marketing scholars to the marketing of services and the increasing importance of services in the global economy, the call for research and "empirical study that transcends specific industries and tests service marketing concepts" is truer today than ever before (Zeithaml, Parasuraman, and Berry 1985).

Services–Global Marketing Activity

Already contributing some 30% of world trade, the next great battle for global corporations will be in the service industries. In particular, telecommunications, business services, entertainment, banking and finance, insurance, tourism, and education are experiencing significant global expansion. For example, advertising agencies span the world to service their globalizing clients better. Even education is growing in its global dimension, especially business education, as corporations demand the best-educated managers possible for the 1990s.

A global marketing manager of a service organization must be prepared to do global battle in the 1990s, just as her manufacturing counterpart had to learn to do so during the late 1980s. Additionally, managers within manufacturing will learn to take advantage of global service organizations that offer quality worldwide service at highly competitive prices.

Each of the four major characteristics of a service (intangible, inseparable, heterogenous, and perishable) suggests certain marketing approaches, leading to particular marketing strategies for dealing with such characteristics. Table 7.1 illustrates these as a review of service marketing strategy. Each characteristic is further discussed in this section from the perspective of marketing services across national boundaries.

Services are, by definition, *intangible*. This means they cannot be stored or transported in the same way goods can be. It also means that it is more difficult to protect services through the registration of industrial property rights. The inability to transport, store, or protect services in the same manner as physical goods also presents special problems. Firms providing global legal or consulting services, for example, must take special care that they present a physical environment such as well-dressed consultants based in a prestigious office building as a tangible cue to high quality. They must do so because quality assessment is more difficult for an intangible product than for a physical one. But internationally it is likely that cues which symbolize product quality are not the same in different cultures.

Since services cannot be stored or transported, service providers must deal directly with service customers. In fact, a service is consumed as it is produced. This gives services an *inseparable* quality and makes mass production difficult. Indirect channels of distribution are rare for service marketing. While agents may provide title transfer assistance, the actual service is provided directly by the provider to the customer. While indirect channels may serve as

TABLE 7.1. Service Characteristics, Marketing Problems, and Marketing Strategies

Unique Charc.	Service Features	Marketing Strategies
Intangibility	1. Services cannot be stored.	1. Stress tangible cues.
	2. Cannot protect services through patents.	2. Use personal sources more than nonpersonal sources.
	3. Cannot readily communicate services.	3. Stimulate word-of-mouth communications.
	4. Prices are difficult to set.	4. Create strong organizational image.
		5. Use cost accounting to help set prices.
		6. Engage in post-purchase communications.
Inseparability	1. Consumer involved in production.	1. Emphasize selection and training of public contact personnel.
	2. Other consumers involved.	2. Manage consumers.
	3. Centralized mass production of services difficult.	3. Use multisite facilities.
Heterogeneity	1. Standardization and quality control difficult to achieve.	1. Industrialize service.
		2. Customize service.
Perishability	1. Services cannot be inventoried.	1. Use strategies to cope with fluctuating demand.
		2. Make simultaneous adjustments in demand and capacity to achieve a closer match between the two.

Adapted from: Zeithaml, V., A. Parasuraman, and L. L. Berry, (1985), "Problems and Strategies in Services Marketing," *Journal of Marketing*, Spring, p. 35.

multisite locations for access to the service, the buyer must go to the producer for a service. Internationally, however, buyer/supplier mobility may constrain service marketing organizations. For example, quotas on the number of tourists who may leave or enter a nation constrain the tourism industry for that country.

Heterogeneous characteristics mean that services are virtually unique each time they are produced and consumed. The interaction between producer and consumer alone guarantees this. Since they are difficult to standardize (for example, every tourist trip to India is different from all others) they are also difficult to produce in mass quantities, and quality control is difficult.

Because services must be used at the time they are produced, and thus cannot be carried in inventory, they are *perishable*. Perishability means the marketing manager must devise ways to deal with fluctuating demand. Internationally, for example, ski tour packagers may gain coordination effects through bundling packages together to take advantage of the seasonal differences between the northern and southern hemisphere. Other global service providers may be able to manage personnel more readily if they are able to spread their costs over multiple markets that help counterbalance fluctuating demand in a given national market.

As service industries continue to develop, they are increasingly looking internationally for new markets much the same way goods marketers have. As mature economies face pressure to increase their services exports and trade, the management of global service activities will continue to increase in importance. For example, the U.S. has been interested in establishing free trade in services, as it sees high value-added services (computing, information services, and telecommunications, for example) as an area where U.S-based companies continue to have a comparative advantage. (Goods and services with a low value-added component shift to countries of production with lower labor costs. In order for the U.S. to generate exports, it should, the argument goes, concentrate on areas where its firms still have a comparative advantage.) A large, well-educated labor force such as that found in the U.S. should provide a base for competitive advantage in the more technically complex and therefore higher value-added services, for example financial or information services (McCullouch, 1987; Deardorff, 1984).

Another reason services are increasing in importance to world trade is the increased importance of service (product) lines to multinational corporations (MNCs). Service organizations that specialize in providing highly technical services, for example, are finding that they need to invest in research and development or training, a service organization's form of R & D, at increasing rates to maintain competitiveness. Just as consumer and industrial goods marketers need larger markets to justify such increased expenditures, so too do service companies (Dunning and McQueen, 1986).

Governments also are increasingly interested in services, both for comparative advantage reasons just discussed and to gain greater control of their domestic economies. Service MNCs, even more than those which produce goods, operate beyond the control of any individual country. Governmental concerns include national security, (e.g., telecommunications or information transmittal industries) and protection of infant industries, (e.g., providing market protection to computer software companies until they achieve world market capability). And just as governments buy goods, they are also major markets for services leading to improving global markets for marketers who sell to governments. Finally, governments provide services, often in competition with domestic or global organizations.

The preceding discussion of increasing interest in, and reliance upon, services by MNCs and governments combined with the unique characteristics of services raises important questions for the marketing of services in a multinational setting. The service characteristics discussed above, particularly inseparability and heterogeneity, depend upon provider/customer interaction. An initial question for the MNC is, therefore, whether customers have similar attitudes toward, and reactions to, a given service across cultures. This research addresses an aspect of the service encounter, consumer involvement with the service, and whether service involvement differs across two cultures.

SERVICES–CONSUMER INVOLVEMENT

Involvement, frequently expressed as the degree of interest in a product, has long been explored by consumer behavior researchers. The range of involvement research includes: high versus low product involvement, information processing and choice behavior, types of involvement, brand loyalty, attitudes held and their measurement, cognitive structure, and implications for marketing and advertising (Antil, 1984).

An ongoing problem with the involvement concept has been the direct measure of a consumer involvement profile. Researchers' attention has been more recently focusing on that issue (Zaichkowsky, 1985; Laurent and Kapferer, 1985; McQuarrie and Munson, 1987). But no matter what measurement instrument has been applied, no it validation of the concept as applied to services exists (see Table 7.2 for a listing of the studies and goods examined).

Zaichkowsky, for example, included several product categories in her study that validated her Personal Involvement Inventory scale (PII), but all were physical goods. However, one product, red wine, had two different involvement scenarios (special versus regular occasion), which at least implicitly involves high intangibility in the special occasion description.

Laurent and Kapferer's research, employing a different measurement instrument, also focused exclusively on physical goods. McQuarrie and Munson, in their revision of the Zaichkowsky Personal Involvement Inventory, measured involvement primarily on physical goods, but included a "pure" service, haircuts. Zaichkowsky and Sood applied the PII across subjects in 15 countries focusing largely on goods. They did include three services, air travel, cinema, and eating at a restaurant (Zaichkowsky and Sood, 1988). As with goods, services may also vary considerably by situational, physical, and personal factors that are proposed to lead to different levels of involvement. For example, eating at a restaurant may be potentially a low involvement activity such as in an everyday meal. Or it may potentially be of higher involvement, for example, a special occasion such as a birthday or anniversary. In addition, other consumers may be involved in the consumption situation, impacting involvement. Therefore, this research, in choosing services to examine, included two usage situation variants within two service categories to determine whether involvement varies between types of usage occasion and situation within a service category.

TABLE 7.2. Product Categories of Previous Selected Involvement Research

Researcher	Products
Zaichkowsky (1985)	Instant coffee, bubble bath, breakfast cereal, mouthwash, red wine (everyday and special occasion), facial tissues, headache remedy, 35 mm camera, color TV, jeans, laundry detergent, calculator, automobiles.
Laurent and Kapferer (1985)	dresses, bras, washing machines, TV sets, vacuum cleaners, irons, champagne, oil, yogurt, chocolate, shampoo, toothpaste, facial soap, detergents.
McQuarrie and Munson (1985)	canned corn, potato chips, laundry detergent, motor oil, soft drinks, toothpaste, cologne/perfume, records & tapes, business suits, credit cards, automobiles, hair cut/styled.
Zaichkowsky and Sood (1988)	beer, blue jeans, hair shampoo, soft drinks, stereo sets, air travel, going to the cinema, and eating at a restaurant.

For both practitioners and academics, a problem still exists with the current state of knowledge regarding services and involvement. Extension of the involvement construct to services and across national boundaries has been performed by Zaichkowsky and Sood. But no involvement study reported to date has empirically validated either the construct of involvement as applied to services, nor its appropriateness across nations. It would seem prudent to examine both issues before pursuing the managerial implications of such studies much further.

THE STUDY

The research reported in this study was conducted jointly in the United States and in Australia. The Zaichkowsky PII instrument was used to examine the appropriateness of involvement as applied to services. Services were selected for the study that were familiar to the respondent groups, and that included a potential range of involvement for the "same" service, e.g., fancy restaurant meal and everyday restaurant meal. Other services included: auto repair (minor and major), haircuts, and dental checkups.

Zaichkowsky used five questions in her research to validate the involvement measures. Except for income range (the U.S. has a higher salary range than Australia) and some minor changes designed to insure comparability (for example, *Choice* magazine was substituted in Australia for the U.S. *Consumer Reports* in the construct validity statement), the questionnaires were identical.

A pretest of the revised questionnaire was conducted in the United States using a convenience sample of 50 graduate students (MBA) at a major southern university. An overall ANOVA indicated a highly statistically significant relationship between the PII and the validation questions (P < .000). An initial factor analysis was performed which indicated a similar factor pattern to the pattern found in the Zaichkowsky study with one major factor explaining more than 50% of the variance. Usually one minor factor was also discovered, also consistent with the physical good research.

Based on the supportive results from this pretest, a mail survey of graduates of a small, private university in the Southeast was undertaken. Three hundred questionnaires were mailed out, along with a cover letter explaining the research project. A total of 210 usable questionnaires were returned. A supplemental sample of all entering MBAs in the same university was taken, resulting in an additional 152 usable questionnaires for a total U.S. sample of 362. In Australia, 500 undergraduate business majors were sampled, resulting in 305 usable questionnaires.

RESULTS OF THE STUDY

The full analysis of the data is reported elsewhere (Dahringer et al., 1989). While it is beyond the scope of this chapter to fully report that analysis, a short summary should serve to demonstrate the viability of involvement as applied to services.

In sum, the research indicates that the involvement construct is appropriate to apply to services. Tests of internal reliability (Cronbach alpha, factor analysis), discriminant validity (ANOVA), and construct validity (grouped mean comparison and T-tests, Pearson correlation analysis) all proved statistically significant for the measurement instrument's application to service situations.

The nominal rankings and tests of significant differences for ratings across services for each nation are presented in Figure 7.1. As that figure indicates, for both countries the nominal rankings of services are quite similar. For example, highly intangible services (i.e., services to people) such as haircuts, dental services, and special restaurant meals are more involving than less intangible services (i.e., service-to-product) in both nations. Interestingly, U.S. respondents reported a higher mean level of involvement for each of the services than did the Australians. Implications of this finding are discussed in the following section.

GLOBAL MANAGERIAL IMPLICATIONS

Given that global marketing should be viewed as the search for opportunities to exploit cross-national market similarities to the extent possible (not "sell the same thing the same way everywhere"), the management question of interest is whether service marketers can achieve coordination effects from marketing services in Australia and the U.S. in a reasonably global, standardized manner. Within the limitations of this research, the answer would seem to be yes.

The argument may be raised that Americans are more involved in services than are Australians. The results presented in Figure 7.1 would seem to indicate this is so. However, the similarity in nominal ranking between the two countries is of considerable importance. That is, in both nations, consumers are more highly involved in similar sets of services. Thus, a marketer of haircuts–an international franchiser, for example–should consider a somewhat standardized marketing campaign across both nations.

As illustrated in the similarly ranked involvement scores for special restaurant meals, dental services, and haircuts, consumers of these types of highly inseparable and intangible services hold a shared involvement set toward these services, i.e., relatively high involvement. The validity questions in the research indicate a shared behavior set common to consumers in both nations. Other research has argued that when behavior and attitudes are both

FIGURE 7.1. Involvement Domain

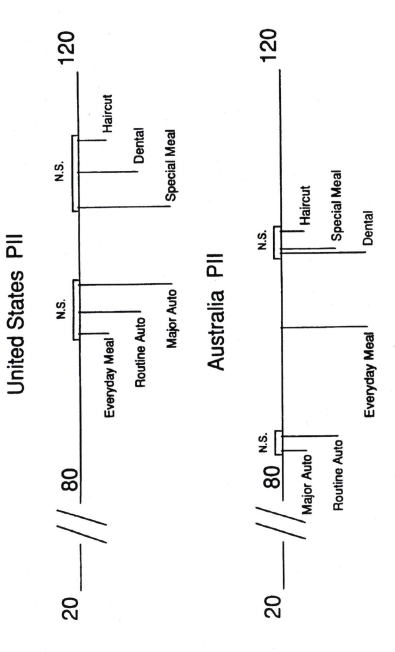

shared across cultures, a globally standardized marketing campaign is feasible (Verhage, Dahringer, and Cundiff, 1989; Sheth, 1986). Similar findings in this research argue that consumers could be successfully appealed to by a standardized marketing campaign.

For example, cues are often offered by service marketers to provide tangible evidence of product quality. Surrogate cues such as well-decorated shops and well-dressed and groomed stylists, and personalized attention such as mail follow-ups provide reassurance of correct product provider choice, in a similar manner, in both Australia and the U.S. Admittedly, the specific implementation of what constitutes an appropriately decorated shop may vary somewhat across the two cultures. But such differences are not sufficiently important distinctions to warrant individualized marketing campaigns.

LIMITATIONS/SUGGESTIONS
FOR FUTURE RESEARCH

The exploratory nature of this study presents some limitations. The range of services chosen was intended to aid in assessing consumer involvement across a range of encounters. The services studied, however, were for the most part of a localized, personal service nature. A useful follow-up study would entail analysis of consumer involvement with services offered by multinational firms (e.g., financial services, air travel). The cross-cultural managerial implications of consumer service involvement for multinational service firms could be more clearly defined with this additional research.

SUMMARY

Service marketers increasingly must be active in global marketing activities. Competitive pressures, global suppliers, strategic partnerships, and global markets all combine to imply that, like their physical marketing counterparts, service marketers must globalize or pay the consequences. In fact, there are strong signals that services are the international business battleground for the 1990s.

It is more widely accepted today that marketing concepts and models which were developed by physical goods marketers do indeed need adaptation, and verification, before they can be optimally applied by service marketers. This paper reports the first research designed to empirically validate that the consumer behavior construct of involvement may be appropriately applied to services. Further, since service marketers must also be concerned with global marketing strategies, it examines the validity of the service involvement construct in two different nations. In fact, the construct does hold up across at least two nations, Australia and the U.S. Finally, the marketing management implications of these findings are developed. In the case of services grouped similarly, and ranked nominally consistently across cultures, the argument is developed that a highly standardized marketing campaign is appropriate.

NOTES

1. For a discussion of these issues, see: Simson, Stuart (1988). New World–New Markets, *Business Review Weekly*, February 12, 38-41; Bolt, James F. (1988). Global Competitors: Some Criteria for Success, *Business Horizons*, January-February, 34-41; and Ohmae, Kemichi (1989). Managing in a Borderless World, *Harvard Business Review*, May-June, 152-161.

2. In an interesting example of evolving competitive advantage for banking services, Hungary is now considered the leading country for safe banking accounts; see: Hot Money Haven, *Fortune*, November 10, 1988, 8; for a detailed analysis of the future of international banking, see International Banking–Survival of the Fittest, *The Economist*, March 26, 1988, 6-76; and for a discussion on the global potential for software and computer services, see Arossa, Lydia (1988). Software and Computer Services, *OECD Observer*, April-May, Paris, 13-16.

3. For a thorough discussion on the issue of deregulation of services trade and the GATT system, see Chapter 3 in Aronson, Jonathan David and Cowhey, Peter F. (1984). *Trade in Services: A Case for Open Markets*, American Enterprise Institute, Washington, D.C.

4. For an annotated bibliography of articles discussing services marketing, see: Fisk, Raymond P. and Tansuhaj, Patricia S. (1985). *Services Marketing: An Annotated Bibliography*. Chicago: American Marketing Association.

REFERENCES

Antil, J. (1984). Conceptualization and Operationalization of Involvement, *Advances in Consumer Research*, 11, 203-209.

Aronson, J. and Cowhey, P. (1984). *Trade in Services: A Case for Open Markets*, Chapter 3, American Enterprise Institute, Washington, D.C.

Arossa, L. (1988). Software and Computer Services, *OECD Observer* April-May, Paris, 13-16.

Bolt, J. (1988). Global Competitors: Some Criteria for Success, *Business Horizons*, January-February, 34-41.

Bush, A. and Ortinau, D. (1988). Service Marketing to Yuppies, *The Journal of Services Marketing*, (Spring) 2(2), 19-28.

Dahringer, L., Frame, C., McColl-Kennedy, J., and Yau. (1989). Product Involvement: A Viable Concept for Services?, Working Paper Series, Emory Business School, Emory University, Atlanta, GA.

Deardorff, A. (1984). *Comparative Advantage and International Trade and Investment in Services*, paper presented at the Third Annual Workshop on U.S.-Canadian Relations, October.

Dunning, J. and McQueen, M. (1986). The Eclectic Theory of Multinational Enterprise and the International Hotel Industry, in *New Theories of the Multinational Enterprise*, edited by A.M. Rugman, 103. New York: St. Martin's Press, as referred to in Boddewyn, J.J., Halbrich, Marsha Baldwin and Perry, A. C. Service Multinationals: Conceptualization, Measurement, and Theory, *Journal of International Business Studies*, Fall, 1986, 51.

Fisk, R. and Tansuhaj, P. (1985). *Services Marketing: An Annotated Bibliography*. Chicago: American Marketing Association.

Gilly, M. and Zeithaml, V. (1987). Characteristics Affecting the Acceptance of Retailing Technologies: A Comparison of Elderly and Nonelderly Consumers, *Journal of Retailing*, Spring, 49-68.

Gronross, C., (1982). An Applied Service Marketing Theory, *European Journal of Marketing*, 16(7), 31.

Hot Money Haven, *Fortune*, November 10, 1988, 8.

International Banking–Survival of the Fittest, *The Economist*, March 26, 1988, 6–76.

Laurent, G. and Kapferer, J. (1985). Measuring Consumer Involvement Profiles, *Journal of Marketing Research*, (Feb.) XXII, 41-53.

Levitt, T. (1983). The Globalization of Markets, *Harvard Business Review*, May-June, 92-102.

Lovelock, C. (1983). Classifying Services to Gain Strategic Marketing Insights, *Journal of Marketing*, Summer, 9-20.

McCullouch, R. (1987). International Competition in Services, NBER Working Paper No. 2235, National Bureau of Economic Research, Cambridge, MA, 25.

McQuarrie, E. and Munson, M. (1987). The Zaichkowsky Personal Involvement Inventory: Modification and Extension, *Advances in Consumer Research*, 14, 36-40.

Ohmae, K. (1989). Managing in a Borderless World, *Harvard Business Review*, May-June, 152-161.

Parasuraman, A., Berry, L., and Zeithaml, V. (1986). SERVQUAL: A Multiple-Item Scale for Measuring Customer Perceptions of Service Quality Research, Report No. 86-108, Marketing Science Institute, August.

Porter, M. (1986). The Strategic Role of International Marketing, *The Journal of Consumer Marketing*, (Spring) 3(2), 17-21.

Rushton, A. and Carson, D. (1985). The Marketing of Services: Managing the Intangibles, *European Journal of Marketing*, 19(3), 19-40.

Sheth, J. (1986). Global Markets or Global Competition?, *The Journal of Consumer Marketing*, Spring, 9-11.

Shostack, G.L. (1987). Service Positioning Through Structural Change, *Journal of Marketing*, January, 34-43.

Simson, S. (1988). New World–New Markets, *Business Review Weekly*, February 12, 38-41.

Surprenant, C. and Solomon, M. (1987). Predictability and Personalization in the Service Encounter, *Journal of Marketing*, (April) 51, 86-96.

Verhage, B., Dahringer, L., and Cundiff, E. (1989). Will a Global Marketing Strategy Work? An Energy Conservation Perspective, *Journal of the Academy of Marketing Science*, Spring, 131.

Zaichkowsky, J. (1985). Measuring the Involvement Construct, *Journal of Consumer Research*, 12, December, 341-352.

Zaichkowsky, J. and Sood, J. (1988). A Global Look at Consumer Involvement and Use of Products, *International Marketing Review*, 6(1), 20-34.

Zeithaml, V., Parasuraman, A., and Berry, L. (1985). Problems and Strategies in Services Marketing, *Journal of Marketing*, Spring, 33-46.

Chapter 8

Conceptualization of India's Emerging Rural Consuming Systems

V. Mukunda Das
C. P. Rao

SUMMARY. While the literature dealing with marketing and development process is extensive and growing, there is very little research attention paid to the rural sectors of developing countries. However, major consumption system changes are taking place in rural sectors of many of the developing countries, which in turn may be significant for marketers in these countries. In this chapter we attempt to conceptualize the emerging rural consumption system in the second most populous country, India. The critical factors shaping the emerging rural consuming system are identified. The marketing implications of these emerging trends are identified and discussed.

INTRODUCTION

The interrelationship between marketing and distribution efficiency and the process of socio-economic development of developing countries has been of considerable interest both to developmental economists and marketing scholars in the post-second world war years. One observes extensive and growing literature on this topic. In recent years, periodic conferences were devoted to marketing and development processes. Early writings in this area have emphasized the importance of marketing for economic development (Holton, 1957; Galbraith and Holton, 1955; Emlen, 1958). As early as 1958, Emlen, emphasizing the relevance of marketing for economic development, cryptically remarked that "production may be the door to economic growth of the underdeveloped countries, but marketing is

161

the key that turns the lock" (Emlen, 1958). Following these initial writings, most of the subsequent writings dealt with the linkage between marketing and economic development at the macro level (Bretherton, 1977; Cundiff, 1982; Dholakia and Dholakia, 1982; Kingsley, 1982; Mentzer and Salmi, 1981). Some authors emphasized the social marketing aspects as the proper role for marketing in the context of developing countries (Rao and Oumlil, 1984). Others have advocated active state involvement in the development of marketing process in developing countries (Varadarajan, 1984; Taimni, 1981). Some authors explored the problems of transferring the marketing technology from the developed to developing countries (Etgar, 1983). Although the literature on this topic has been continuously growing in recent years, one area of significance seems to receive very little research attention. That topic area is the rural consumers in developing countries. In most of the developing countries, the rural sectors represent the largest proportions of their populations. Typically, the urban sectors, though growing, are still limited, which results in the classical problems of narrow markets in the developing countries. Hence, what happens in rural sectors of the developing countries will be critical for accelerating the market and marketing development in these countries. The rural sectors of developing countries, though traditionally considered to be primitive, backward, and undeveloped, have also been changing in recent years. The nature of these changes in the socio-economic and behavioral environment needs to be understood to find clues as to how to develop and expand these potentially large markets in the developing countries. From these perspectives, this chapter attempts to conceptualize India's emerging rural consumption systems. The major objectives of this chapter are: (1) to identify the major socio-economic and behavioral forces impacting on the rural consumption systems in India; (2) to contrast the emerging rural consumption systems with traditional patterns, and (3) to explore the market development and marketing management implications of such emerging consumption systems.

BACKGROUND

A significant development over the last decade in the Indian marketing milieu was the awareness of the dichotomy between urban and rural markets (Baig, 1980). Much research attention is now being focused on the studies of rural markets and consumers, as the urban marketing issues in India have long been addressed in literature (Rao, 1977). Because of the differing environmental conditions between the urban and rural consumers, the impact of material prosperity in the country generates different scenarios in the consuming systems. Changes in the Indian urban consuming systems were found to be more or less similar to the developed countries because of the urban ecology and patterns of life. In recent years, much emphasis has been placed on a growing urban middle class as the core of the Indian marketing system. However, the rural consuming systems and their evolution are considered to be different. Moreover, while in terms of size, the urban consumers constituted only 30% of the total Indian consumers, the rural consumers constituted about 70%. Ignoring the rural sectors in India is tantamount to ignoring more than two-thirds of the potential market. This could be detrimental to the development of markets in India, as the rural markets are becoming more important due to the rapid pace of material prosperity resulting from improved agricultural productivity, improved transportation and communications facilities, and ever increasing rural development investments. Therefore, it becomes very important to understand the rural consuming systems, the direction of changes, facilitating factors, and the critical conditions contributing to their evolutionary process.

Considerable research in marketing studies is devoted to the behavioral complexities of consumers in post-industrial societies of the west. Some limited research is devoted to marketing and development interrelationships in developing countries. In the latter category, as pointed out earlier, very little attention is paid to the complexities of the agrarian sectors of developing countries such as India. Nicosia and Mayer (1976) observed: "the social and economic processes that lead to the development of western societies no longer seem to work. In particular the visibility of consumption styles in western societies affects the kind and the intensity of consumption in developing societies, so that the old cycle of saving-investment-production and *then* consumption no longer seems applicable to these societies." However, so far very little research has gone into these aspects of developing societies.

In a related context, Kaynak (1982) observed: "Marketing systems are not static. They evolve over a period of time and are closely associated with overall conditions in a given LDC (less developed country) and its stage of socio-economic and technological development. . . . These marketing systems evolve as part of the overall socio-economic, cultural, and technological development of an LDC." Schultz (1964), while studying marketing in traditional subsistence economies, mentioned that "changes in the production system (of these economies) are taking place slowly, and marketing services, practices, and facilities are likely to accommodate themselves to needs as they emerge." This shows that the analysis and elucidation of various elements of the marketing environment acts only as a trace of the background. On the other hand, the consuming systems emerge as a result of the continuous interaction of the socio-economic, technological, and political parameters that are only individually dealt with in the analysis of marketing environment. Therefore, the study of the evolution of consuming systems shows the *process*, which from an operations viewpoint, is more important to a marketer in a developing country like India. In India, the conclusions about growing rural markets (Ganguly, 1984; Gupta, 1972; Srivastava, 1981) only focused on the macro-economic environmental aspects of market potential and not on how the rural consumer market is changing and evolving.

To explain the two dominant shifts in the consuming systems in India's rural sectors, we attempted to outline a conceptual framework. The purpose of this conceptualization is to explain the direction of changes in the rural consuming systems in India. In identifying the two facilitating factors and one critical condition, out of probably many, we have observed and analyzed the effects of these factors in relation to the rural consuming systems.

CONCEPTUAL BASES

The conceptual framework is based on three types of studies. First, the study on rural consumers (Das, 1986) made continuously over the last five years in Kaira district of Gujarat state in India with a view to know the factors affecting consumer choice behavior. This district is typical in terms of the prosperity in the agrarian sector and the faster pace of its occurrence (Rutten, 1986). Many other districts in different parts of the country similar to Kaira in terms of quicker agrarian prosperity have been documented (Bhalla and Alagh, 1979). Hence, conceptualization that is developed based on Kaira district can be generalized to some extent to the whole of rural India. Second, the research studies by National Council of Applied Economic Research (NCAER, 1975) on rural income and disposition also were considered for deriving certain salient features of the rural consumption patterns. Third, supporting evidence on the changes in the consumption profile was drawn from the studies on rural consumption by the Agro Economic Research Center (AERC, 1970). The research studies by the Agro Economic Research Center documented the quantitative differences between two periods in the consumption of items and did not go into the socio-cultural processes that were instrumental in such changes in consumption. In addition, in the Kaira district studies, Mass Observation Approach was utilized to verify the main tenets of these studies through visits to villages in some states in India.

DIRECTION OF RURAL CONSUMPTION SYSTEM CHANGES

There are two dominant changes or shifts that were discerned in the rural consuming system. These two changes are identified by comparing the situation in the pre-agrarian prosperity time period to that of the post-agrarian prosperity in the past decade. The first major change in spending is manifested in the form of an increasing proportion of incremental income being spent for buying consumer durables from a previous state of buying more land, in the affluent segments of rural consumers. The second change is from a situation of buying locally made (mostly within the village) goods to one of buying urban-made consumer goods and/or manufactured goods.

Change from More Land to More Consumer Durables

The emergence of this trend has been due more to the innate development within the rural consumption system than the result of marketing efforts as is usually the case in the developed western societies. Needless to say, the emergence of this trend has tremendously increased the potential demand for consumer durables. The market for consumer durables was mostly confined to urban India until recently, when this surge in demand in rural sectors emerged. This trend has also been supported by the data on consumption expenditures on consumer durables conducted by the National Statistical Surveys. The extent of rural spending previous to agricultural prosperity has been found to be lower than urban expenditure levels.

A combination of interacting factors resulted in the evolution of the above stated trend in the rural consuming system. These factors are: (a) spurt in agrarian prosperity, (b) the perception of reduction in risk in agriculture, and (c) changes in the conception of ideal consumption basket. The first two factors may be treated as facilitating factors and the third as a critical condition for the evolution of the rural consumption system that is taking place in India. A brief discussion of these factors follows.

The spurt in agrarian prosperity had enabled the rural consumers to reach higher levels of income. This income increase was caused by agricultural technological development and innovative behaviors inducing higher production levels (Hanumantha Rao, 1975). The higher production levels increased income levels especially of those rural segments that had higher marketable surplus. Converted into monetary terms, this spurt in agricultural income in rural India contributed to increased material base for some rural segments, and such enhanced agricultural incomes are considered to be very significant. However, if the old consumption patterns had continued, the incremental income would have been spent on land and/or gold at an increasing rate. On the contrary, this recent spurt in agrarian prosperity has induced considerable changes in the perception of certain consumer segments toward durables. This resulted in the change-over, or evolution, to purchase of consumer durables, which showed a significant departure from the past in the rural consuming system.

The increased productivity in agriculture changed the agricultural operations from a state of subsistence and primitivism to one of commercialized operation. Therefore, concomitant with the increased income from agriculture was the perception among the rural consumer segments with surplus income about the reduced risk in agriculture. The perceived risk in agricultural production was very high before the period of agrarian prosperity. The uncertainty in income received from agriculture because of its total dependence on natural conditions and low technology has now been changed. This has changed the "psyche" of the segments of rural consumers resulting in, simultaneously, induced changes from buying more land and/or gold to buying consumer durables. The perception of reduced risk could generate an atmosphere for increased potential for change (Rogers, 1969) in the consuming system.

Changes in the conception of "ideal" consumption basket is the critical condition for the direction of change in the rural consuming system. It has been stated that urban consumers in general are more impulsive in purchase decisions than are rural consumers. Unlike the urban consumers, consumers in rural India follow a concept of ideal consumption defined in the context of economic and social classes. The concept of ideal consumption is thus related to the material conditions and consumption values. Therefore, as material conditions change, changes could occur in the conception of ideal consumption. The concept of the ideal consumption basket is derived by the rural consumers from the conception of desired consumption basket. Whereas the desired consumption basket is basically an individual consumer's psychological disposition, the ideal consumption basket is one validated by social norms. While the desired consumption basket is defined by individual consumers, the ideal consumption tends to be socially desirable. Any change in income, especially when it is sudden, can impact on the ideal consumption system. Therefore, depending on the change in the economic conditions, individual consumers usually tend to change the ideal consumption basket. Before the recent agrarian prosperity, the concept of ideal consumption basket was significantly different for the rural consumer segments in India. The consumption basket included land and gold as the most important elements. However, after the agrarian prosperity in recent years, the changed ideal consumption basket consisted of consumer durables as important elements.

The evolution of a consuming system is thus a result of a changed consumption choice. This evolution is brought in by the mutual reinforcement of the two factors and the critical condition that are shown in Figures 8.1 and 8.2. Figure 8.1 is related to a durables goods situation and Figure 8.2 reflects the nondurable goods. The blackened area in the diagrams shows the mutually reinforced juncture for changed choice highlighting the evolutionary process.

MARKETING IMPLICATIONS

The implications of this to the marketers are self-evident. In the context of the Indian rural markets, the marketers of consumer durables seem to understand the first two factors. However, they failed to understand the third, the critical condition. In the absence of this understanding, the marketing efforts are not developed appropriately to influence and persuade the potential rural consumers. Therefore, the increased purchases of consumer durables such as tractors, agricultural implements, radios, televisions, etc., were more because of the "pull" by the consuming system than any deliberately planned and implemented efforts by the marketers in the country.

The change from locally made goods to urban-made consumer goods is typically caused by a different set of factors. The facilitating factors in this change are different from the change related to durable goods consumption. While an economic improvement due to rural development investment contributed as a facilitating factor (instead of the low risk perception factor in the durables consumption case), it is the influence of filtered urban consumption values that transcends the facilitating context in this trend. These two trends are presented in Figure 8.3.

In the durables consumption case, the changing trend can be attributed to higher agricultural productivity and marketable surplus through commercial agriculture, which in turn limited this change to the land-owning segment of the rural population. However, the shift in rural consumer preference for urban-made brand goods as opposed to locally made goods seems to permeate all segments of the rural population, including the agricultural and other working

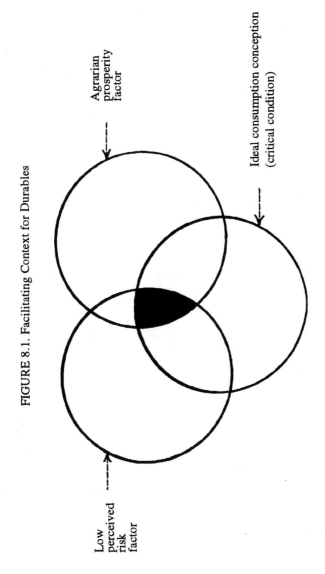

FIGURE 8.1. Facilitating Context for Durables

Agrarian
prosperity
factor

Ideal consumption conception
(critical condition)

Low
perceived
risk
factor

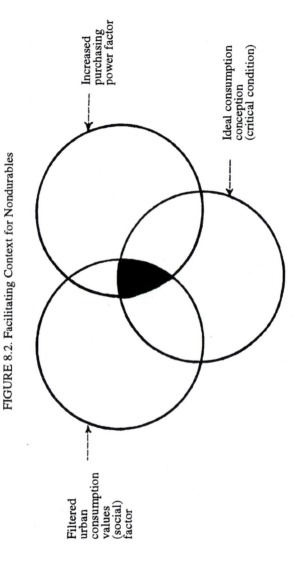

FIGURE 8.2. Facilitating Context for Nondurables

Increased
purchasing
power factor

Ideal consumption
conception
(critical condition)

Filtered
urban
consumption
values
(social)
factor

FIGURE 8.3. Change from Locally Made Goods to Urban-Made Consumer Goods

Sources of income	Purchase Effect	
	Durables	Nondurables
Agrarian source	High	Low
Public rural development source	Low	High

class segments in rural areas. This is partly because of the relatively low unit price of consumer nondurables compared to consumer durables. For example, from locally made coir ropes, rural consumers are shifting to urban-manufactured and -branded plastic ropes. Similar trends can be observed in a number of other consumer nondurables goods.

However, it should be noted that elements in the ideal consumption basket in the case of consumer nondurables are subjected to social scrutiny and therefore purchased selectively because of the high social involvement associated with some of these consumer nondurable goods. For example, buying and using more transparent dresses by females is taboo, although buying and using polyester dresses is not objected to in most rural areas. This phenomenon is similar to the findings of Witt and Bruce studies (1970) which "showed that products high in social involvement are those which are frequently used in the presence of other people and which have certain images which are transferred to the user."

The filtering of consumption choices of individuals in rural society especially relating to personal effects, mostly coming under consumer nondurables, have high social implications. The cultural mediation in the Indian rural society is different from that of the urban society. It is in this context that a good understanding of the rural consuming system and direction of change is important for the marketers in India whose experience is mostly confined to the urban sectors. Therefore, attempts to extend and replicate such urban marketing experiences and assumptions would be inappropriate in cultivating rural markets. The rural social context that determines the elements in ideal consumption basket need to be clearly understood.

LIMITATIONS

The conceptualization of the changing rural consuming system presented in this chapter has certain limitations. First, the conceptualization is based on research studies in a limited geographic area in India. Hence, the conceptualization cannot, perhaps, be generalized to all developing countries, as the factors influencing the agrarian sectors in different developing countries could be different from those in India. Even within India, the conceptualization is more appropriate to those rural sectors that are relatively more prosperous and where agriculture has advanced significantly in the recent past. However, one finds many pockets of agricultural backwardness in India and the trends identified in this chapter may not be applicable to the entire country. In spite of these limitations, the general trends and the consumption patterns identified and conceptualized in this chapter seem to be spreading across the country in India. Given the vast potential the rural markets offer to marketers both in India and in other developing countries, more research dealing with rural marketing issues is needed. For effective marketing in rural sectors of developing countries, marketers' knowledge and experience based on either developed countries' contexts or urban contexts of the developing countries may not be appropriate. The dynamic and complex nature of fast-changing rural market sectors in a developing country needs greater research attention.

CONCLUSIONS

In developing countries like India, the study of the evolution of rural consuming systems is highly relevant, especially in the context of economic prosperity occurring through agricultural and rural development. Such systematic study can reveal how the consuming systems adjust to material prosperity and the traditional value orientations typical of rural sectors. The facilitating context of the evolution of such consuming systems is not always provided by marketing efforts but by the interaction of certain socio-economic and behavioral factors and conditions.

In order to clearly understand the marketing implications of agrarian material prosperity in a country like India, the classified parameters of marketing environment such as economic, social, or technological do not help. What is required is the detailed understanding of the dynamic processes behind the evolution of rural consuming systems.

We have identified two dominant trends in India's rural consuming system and the conceptual basis of how these trends are emerging. These two trends in the consuming system were found in relation to consumer durables and consumer nondurables. While attempting to explain the evolution in India's rural consuming system, we found that the rural market for consumer durables and nondurables is developing not because of the initiatives of Indian marketers but by the "pull" from the consuming system itself. Additionally, we found that, especially in the case of nondurables, the marketing expertise based on urban marketing experiences may not be relevant in rural markets, as the latter are very much influenced by complex social and cultural norms.

REFERENCES AND RECOMMENDED READINGS

Agro Economic Research Center (AERC). (1970). *Change in Economic Life of a Tobacco Village in Resurvey of Indian Villages*. Vallabh Vidyanagar, Gujarat, India.

Baig, M. A. (1980). Guidelines for Urban and Rural Marketing. *Indian Journal of Marketing*, Vol. 10, No. 5, January, 3-8.

Bhalla, C. S. and Y. K. Alagh. (1979). *Performance of Indian Agriculture: A District-Wide Study*. New Delhi: Sterling Publishers Pvt. Ltd.

Bretherton, I. S. (1977). Does Marketing Activity in Mexico Help the Country's Development? In *Macromarketing Distributive Processes from a Societal Perspective: An Elaboration of Issues*, edited by P. D. White and C. C. Slatter, 351-364. Boulder: University of Colorado.

Chinoy, E. (1952). The Tradition of Opportunity and the Aspirations of Automobile Workers. *American Journal of Sociology*, 57, 453-459.

Cundiff, E. (1982). A Macromarketing Approach to Economic Development. *Journal of Macromarketing*, II (Spring), 47-56.

Das, M. V. (1985). Consumer Goods Flow into Rural India: Evidence from Some Villages in Gujarat. Anand, Gujarat, India: Institute of Rural Management.

Das, M. V. (1986). Rural Marketing Research in India: Some Aspects of Environmental Influence on Respondent Bias. Paper presented at the Special Session on Marketing in Asian Countries at the Academy of Marketing Science Annual Conference, Anaheim, California.

Dawson, J. A. (1979). *The Marketing Environment*. NY: St. Martin's Press.

Dholakia, N. and R. R. Dholakia. (1982). Marketing in the Emerging World Order. *Journal of Macromarketing*, II, Spring.

Douglas, S. P. and Y. Wind. (1974). Environmental Factors and Marketing Practices. *European Journal of Marketing*, Vol. 7, No. 3.

Emlen, W. J. (1958). Let's Export Marketing Know-How. *Harvard Business Review*, Vol. 36, No. 6, November-December, 4770-4776.

Etgar, M. (1983). A Failure in Marketing Technology Transfer: The Case of Rice Distribution in the Ivory Coast. *Journal of Macromarketing*, Spring, 59-68.

Galbraith, J. K. and R. H. Holton. (1955). *Marketing Efficiency in Puerto Rico*, Cambridge, MA: Harvard University Press.

Ganguly, A. S. (1984). The Growing Rural Market in India. Chairman's Speech. Bombay: Hindustan Lever Ltd.

Government of India, Department of Statistics (NSS). (1986). Quinquennial Survey of Consumer Expenditure, 38th Round. *Journal of the National Sample Survey Organization*, Vol. IX, No. 4.

Gupta, V. K. (1972). Changing Agriculture and the Market of Consumer Goods. In *New Opportunities in Changing Agriculture*. Ahmedabad, India: Indian Institute of Management.

Holton, R. H. (1957). Marketing Structure and Economic Development. *Quarterly Journal of Economics*, Vol. LXVIII, No. 3, August, 344-361.

Kaynak, E. (1982). *Marketing in the Third World*. NY: Praeger.

Kingsley, J. (1982). The Role of Marketing in Economic Development. *European Journal of Marketing*, Vol. 16, No. 6, 64-77.

Lande, I. K. (1967). Consumer Marketing Development in Emerging Economies. In *Marketing for Tomorrow . . . Today*, edited by N. Moyer and R. Vosburgh. Chicago: American Marketing Association.

Mentzer, J. T. and A. Coskum Samli. (1981). A Model for Marketing in Economic Development. *Columbia Journal of World Business*, Fall.

Murray, C. A. (1977). *A Behavioral Study of Rural Modernization: Social and Economic Change in Their Villages*. NY: Praeger.

National Council of Applied Economic Research (NCAER). (1980). *Household Income and its Disposition*. New Delhi: NCAER.

_____. (1975). *Changes in Rural Income in India*. New Delhi: NCAER.

Nicosia, F. M. and R. N. Mayer. (1976). Toward a Sociology of Consumption. *Journal of Consumer Research*, Vol. 3, September, 65-75.

Patel, R. M. (1982). *Glimpses of Change and Development in Borsad Taluka*. Vallab Vidyanagar, Gujarat, India: Agro-Economic Research Center.

Rao, C. P. (1977). A Survey of Research on Marketing in India: A Trend Report. In *Survey of Research in Management*, Vol. 2. New Delhi: Vikas Publishers.

Rao, C. P. and A. B. Oumlil. (1984). Proper Role of Marketing in a Developing Country. Paper Presented at the Ninth Annual Macromarketing Seminar, August, 16-19.

Rao, Hanumantha CH. (1975). *Technological Change and Distribution of Grains in Indian Agriculture*. New Delhi: Institute of Economic Growth.

Rogers, E. M. (1969). *Modernization Among Peasants*. NY: Holt, Rinehart and Winston.

Rutten, M. (1986). Social Profile of Agricultural Entrepreneurs: Economic Behavior and Life Style of Middle-Large Farmers in Central Gujarat. *Review of Agriculture, Economic and Political Weekly*, Vol. XXI, No. 13.

Schultz, T. W. (1964). *Transforming Traditional Agriculture*. New Haven, CT: Yale University Press.

Smelser, N. J. (1963). *The Sociology of Economic Life*. Englewood Cliffs, NJ: Prentice Hall.

Srivastava, V. D. (1981). Rural Marketing Environment in India, *Productivity*, Vol. XXII, No. 3, 81-83.

Taimni, K. K. (1981). Employment Generation Through Handicraft Cooperatives: The Experience. *International Labor Review*, Vol. 120, July-August, 505-517.

Varadarajan, R. P. (1984). Marketing in Developing Countries: The New Frontier. *Long Range Planning*, Vol. 17, No. 6, December, 118-126.

Witt, R. E. and G. D. Bruce. (1970). Group Influence and Brand Choice Congruence. *Journal of Marketing Research*, Vol. 9, November, 440-443.

Zaltman G. and R. P. Bagozzi. (1975). Structural Analysis and the Sociology of Consumption. Paper presented at the 70th Annual Meeting of the American Sociological Association, San Francisco, CA.

SECTION IV.

STANDARDIZATION OF MARKETING PROGRAMS AND PROCESS

Chapter 9

Consumer Nondurable Products: Prospects for Global Advertising

John S. Hill
William L. James

SUMMARY. This 15 MNC-120 subsidiary study of multinational advertising practices shows that there are few differences between various types of consumer nondurable products in their transfer and adaptation of international advertising messages. Food/drink and pharmaceutical products are more likely to adapt sales platforms than cosmetics or general consumer goods, but there were no significant differences among creative context adaptations. Reasons for standardizing messages were classified into external and internal factors, with corporate factors accounting for about one-third of standardized messages.

Compared to consumer durable and industrial products, nondurable consumer goods have acquired reputations over the years for being sensitive to change when transferred into foreign cultures. This sensitivity has also been noted in the international advertising arena. Killough (1978) reported that messages promoting food/drink and other "personal" products were more susceptible to having their sales platforms and creative contexts changed than other types of goods.

But can consumer nondurable products be treated as a group and generalizations made about them? The products that make up the nondurable category–food/drink, cosmetics, pharmaceutical, and general consumer goods (e.g., laundry detergents, household cleaners)–all have varying characteristics. For example, food/drink and general consumer goods are household products, whereas cosmetics and pharmaceutical products appeal to particular individuals (those wishing to be beautiful and those wishing to be healthy).

179

There are also some empirically charted differences among non-durable products. In a study of adaptations made to consumer goods in lesser-developed markets, Still and Hill (1984) noted significant differences in nondurable adaptation strategies. They found food/drink and general consumer goods to be more sensitive to environmental differences than cosmetics or pharmaceutical products.

The problem is that there has been very little empirical evidence about transnational advertising. There is even less about differences in transnational advertising strategies within particular industries. The aim of this chapter is to shed light on standardization-adaptation issues within the consumer nondurable industry, using information from a 15 MNC-120 subsidiary study of international advertising practices.

LITERATURE REVIEW

The international advertising area has attracted many academic commentaries over the years. Jain (1989) noted 14 studies between 1963 and 1988, over half of which had been conceptual. The few empirical studies that have been done generally suggest that adaptation tends to be a more prevalent strategy than is standardization (Walters, 1986; Douglas and Wind, 1987).

From a practitioner's viewpoint, the ability to transfer advertising messages virtually unchanged between markets has been a topic that has long intrigued international managers. The emergence of the European Economic Community in 1958 prompted marketing scholars to begin the search for a "European consumer" that would be receptive to pan-European advertising. Elinder (1965) and Fatt (1967) looked for evidence of commonalities among Europeans upon which standardized campaigns could be based. There were also many who were skeptical about uniform advertising in foreign markets. Lenormand (1964) and Green, Cunningham, and Cunningham (1975) were equally adamant that individualized approaches to country campaigns were best.

Evidence that standardized campaigns can work was unearthed by Ryans (1969), who cited Esso's "Put a Tiger in Your Tank" as a campaign that travelled the globe virtually unchanged. He also speculated that all countries had groups of "international sophisticates"–

high income, well-educated consumers with high profile lifestyles–who might be susceptible to standardized campaigns. His conclusion, however, was that it was premature for most companies to contemplate uniform advertising campaigns.

The focus shifted briefly during the 1970s from end-result (i.e., adaptation or standardization of marketing mix elements) to planning processes. Sorenson and Wiechmann (1975), in a study of executive opinions, found that the process of evaluating marketing mix transfers between markets was illuminating, as it opened up opportunities for standardization. Peebles, Ryans, and Vernon (1978), in their profile of Goodyear's international advertising efforts, reached similar conclusions, i.e., that whether companies could standardize campaigns across numerous markets was not as important as the interactive processes between head offices and subsidiaries in making those decisions. They differentiated between prototype and pattern advertising, which gave subsidiaries lesser and greater degrees of flexibility respectively in adapting GHQ-supplied campaigns to local tastes. In many cases, significant quantities of research were necessary to evaluate which alternative platforms were the most effective in individual markets (Colvin, Heeler, and Thorpe, 1980). Some commentators (e.g., Ryans and Fry, 1976; Dunn, 1976; Alsop, 1984) suggested that customer resistance was not the only factor acting against uniform campaigns. They all concluded that adverse managerial attitudes, especially at the local level, also played a part.

Only a few studies have reported empirical evidence on the extent of promotion transfers and tendencies to standardize and adapt. Of these, Killough's (1978) opinion-based study of senior executives has been the most important. He made the important distinction between buying proposals (i.e., sales platforms) and creative presentations (i.e., creative contexts). His results showed that executives thought that sales platforms could be transferred to new markets without substantial change more than half of the time. Creative contexts however, could be standardized less than 30% of the time.

With regard to sales platforms, there is no direct evidence of standardization and adaptation tendencies, especially within the consumer nondurable industry. However, within the developing market context, the Still and Hill (1984) study showed that product feature change (which would relate at least partially to sales platform adaptation) varied significantly among types of nondurables. While the study mean for feature change was 33%, food/drink, pharmaceutical, cosmetic, and general consumer goods averaged 51%, 11%, 19%, and 33% respectively, suggesting that food/drink products might be more susceptible to sales platform changes and that pharmaceutical and cosmetic goods were better candidates for standardized platforms.

While the aforementioned studies provide a number of valuable insights into the complexities of promotion standardization and adaptations, a number of key issues remain unresolved. Among them are:

1. Does the incidence of sales platform and creative context change vary across different types of nondurable products?
2. With regard to the factors responsible for standardization and adaptation, are there noticeable differences among factors cited as causing change and those enabling uniformity to occur over the four kinds of nondurables?

This chapter addresses those questions.

RESEARCH METHODOLOGY

Sample Frame

Thirty-three consumer nondurable MNCs were randomly selected from the *Directory of American Companies Operating in Foreign Countries* (1979). Each had a minimum of seven subsidiaries outside of the U.S. Fifteen agreed to participate, with responses coming from 117 overseas subsidiaries and three international divisions in the U.S. MNCs had the choice of responding from the head office or allowing their subsidiaries to fill out mail questionnaires. Most elected to have their subsidiaries respond. In all cases, permission to approach subsidiaries had first been obtained from head office personnel (often the V-P International or equivalent). Copies of letters requesting cooperation were sent to the Head Office executive giving permission. The fifteen cooperating MNCs were: Shulton International, Kellogg's, Warner-Lambert, Johnson & Johnson, Quaker Oats, Kraft, General Foods, Procter and Gamble, Pillsbury, Chesebrough-Pond's, Nabisco-Brands, Beatrice, Libby's, General Mills, and Bristol-Myers.

Responses were received from the following countries: (number in parentheses where more than one): Argentina (2), Australia (7), Belgium (2), Brazil (5), Canada (4), Colombia (5), Denmark (6), Dominican Republic, France (3), Germany (Federal Republic) (10), Guatemala (2), Indonesia (2), Ireland (3), Italy (3), Jamaica, Japan (5), Malaysia (3), Mexico (6), Morocco, Netherlands (3), New Zealand, Pakistan, Peru, Philippines (5), Singapore (2), South Africa (3), Spain (5), Switzerland, Taiwan, Thailand, Trinidad, United Kingdom (7), Uruguay, Venezuela (6), and Zambia.

Nine responses could not be coded by country. Three came from MNC international divisions in the U.S.A. Five were generalized by continent (e.g., South America, Western Europe, etc.) and one came from a company's international division headquartered outside of the U.S.A. In all, therefore, 117 responses came from outside the U.S.A.

Information Gathered

Respondents were to select any two recent product transfers and to respond to a series of questions about the promotional materials accompanying them if any. First, they were asked about the type of nondurable good promoted. Then, following up on Killough's (1978) distinction between buying proposals and creatives, respondents were asked to indicate for each of the two recent transfers whether the sales platform and/or the creative context of the message had been changed. The sales platform was defined in the questionnaire as "the product feature advertised or emphasized"; and the creative context as "the context of the message or the way the message was expressed." In the analyses that follow, the results of both examples are combined as though they were independent observations. While this is obviously not the case, independent analysis of both examples across variables of interest showed similar results both to each other and to the aggregated sample. Because of this, we combined them for ease of presentation. They were asked to identify for each transfer those factors contributing to the decision either to standardize or adapt. The factors listed were taken from the literature (Cateora, 1983; Britt, 1974; Keegan, 1980; Sorenson and Wiechmann, 1975; Killough, 1978; and Dunn, 1976). Many respondents listed more than one factor as causing adaptation or as reasons to standardize. In the post-survey analysis, we differentiated between internal reasons for standardizing (e.g., maintain product images, Peebles, 1989) and external factors (e.g., same customer use for product, Britt, 1974). This distinction was used to shed light on the relative importances of internal and external factors contributing to standardization decisions.

RESULTS

One problem with our results was a disappointing inequality in sample sizes among our four nondurable types of goods. Campaign details were obtained for 175 products, of which 99 were food and drink (56%). The remainder were split between pharmaceutical (22 campaigns, or 13%), cosmetics (also 22 campaigns) and general consumer goods (32 campaigns, or 18%). Given our four product classes, the divisions between standardization and adaptation of platforms and contexts, and our listings of factors causing such decisions, it was not surprising to have low frequencies in some categories. Nevertheless, there were some interesting results.

SALES PLATFORMS

Adaptation and Reasons to Change

It is evident from Table 9.1 that there are significant differences (at the 0.05 level) among consumer nondurable rates of platform change. Food and drink messages led the way with a 69% adaptation rate, followed by pharmaceuticals at 64%. Then there is a drop-off down to the 45 and 41% rates of change for cosmetics and general consumer goods. The high rate of adaptation for food and drink messages is not too surprising, since Killough (1978), and Still and Hill (1984) had previously noted the cultural sensitivity of this product class. Surprisingly, however, pharmaceuticals, the least sensitive category in the Still and Hill study, was the second-most-adapted at 64%. This probably relates to restrictions on pharmaceutical advertising outside of the United States, which by world standards is the least regulated with respect to pharmaceutical promotions (Dunn, 1982).

TABLE 9.1. Sales Platform Rates of Adaptation and Principal Reasons to Change and Standardize

%Platform adapted*	Food/Drink 69%		Pharmaceutical 64%		Cosmetic 45%		General Consumer 41%	
	n	%	n	%	n	%	n	%
Reasons to adapt								
Company policy	0	0	0	0	0	0	0	0
Consumer buying patterns	40	23.7	3	12	5	15.6	3	14.3
Brand name change	18	10.7	1	4	1	3.1	1	4.8
Change in consumer use	15	8.9	1	4	4	12.5	1	4.8
Consumer education differences	22	13.0	1	4	3	9.4	5	23.8
Legal factors	22	13.0	4	16	3	9.4	0	0
Cultural/social factors	24	14.2	7	28	7	21.9	5	23.8
Consumer preferences	21	12.4	6	24	7	21.9	5	23.8
Other	7	4.1	2	8	2	6.3	1	4.8
TOTAL	169	100%	25	100%	21	100%	21	100%

%Platforms standardized*	31%		36%		55%		59%	
	n	%	n	%	n	%	n	%
Reasons:								
Internal								
Company policy	3	5.6	0	0	1	3.1	0	0
Maintain product image worldwide	12	22.2	7	43.8	6	18.8	4	13.8
Manufacturing equipment limitations	1	1.9	0	0	0	0	1	3.4
Make use of transferred promotional materials	4	7.4	0	0	7	21.9	3	10.3
Total Internal Factors	20	37.1	7	43.8	14	43.8	8	27.5

TABLE 9.1 (continued)

%Platforms standardized*	31%		36%		55%		59%	
	n	%	n	%	n	%	n	%
Reasons:								
External								
Same product use by consumers	17	31.5	4	25	9	28.1	7	24.1
Retain American product image	2	3.7	0	0	0	0	1	3.4
Similar target market	13	24.1	5	31.3	9	28.1	10	34.5
Total External Factors	32	59.3	9	56.3	18	56.2	18	62.0
Other	2	3.7	0	0	0	0	3	10.3
TOTAL	54	100	16	100	32	100	29	100

*Differences significant at p < 0.05

Cosmetics and general consumer goods messages had their platforms changed less than half the time. While there were limited observations in both categories, some tentative conclusions may be drawn. First, it may be that the American images exuded by cosmetics MNCs such as Max Factor, Helena Rubinstein, and Revlon are promotion-worthy in the international marketplace, enabling greater degrees of standardization between countries. Perhaps the "Hollywood" influence of American-made movies does indeed encourage non-U.S. consumers to adopt American cosmetics and beauty standards.

In the case of general consumer goods, since laundry detergents, household cleaners, and the like are used for pretty much the same reasons worldwide (e.g., cleanliness, hygiene) it is likely that there are few reasons to change platforms noticeably. Indeed, platforms such as household cleanliness and hygiene are probably as close as marketers may come to universal appeals. This would be so in affluent markets whose consumers enjoy sufficient discretionary income to pursue lofty standards of household cleanliness.

With regard to factors causing change and contributing to standardization, there are some interesting contrasts among the product categories. Consumer buying patterns, not surprisingly, are relatively important elements causing platform changes for food and drink products. More frequent shopping expeditions, fewer working women, fewer cars, and smaller refrigeration units would all contribute to this finding. It is equally apparent that buying patterns are less likely to affect specialty purchases such as pharmaceuticals or non-essentials such as cosmetics.

Consumer education differences seem to affect general consumer goods more than other product types. This is probably because while food/drink, pharmaceutical, and cosmetic product applications are obvious, how to use detergents and household cleaners effectively is perhaps less apparent, especially goods that are chemically based. Under-use, over-use, and misuse of such products can have unfortunate consequences. Ensuring that consumers fully understand product features and usage is therefore an imperative, especially for MNCs in the developing world. Educational movies, demonstrations, and verbal promotions are typical methods used to prepare developing country consumers to use these types of products satisfactorily.

Food and drink products have reputations for being culturally sensitive (Killough, 1978; Still and Hill, 1984). However, in this study, they were also least affected by cultural and social factors compared to the non-food and drink sectors. It may be that while marketers can easily communicate food and drink benefits to consumers, the benefits and effects of new pharmaceutical, cosmetic, and general consumer products are more formidable communication tasks within the context of a magazine layout or 30-second commercial. This would certainly be the case in developing country circumstances, where deep-seated cultural idiosyncrasies abound, especially outside of urban centers. A similar finding is that consumer preferences are also prominent factors in pharmaceutical, cosmetic, and general consumer platform changes. Clearly, if non-food and drink messages are more susceptible to cultural and social factors, rigorous pretests would also reveal different sets of consumers' expectations about the products. It may be also that if these findings hold over larger samples, then non-food and drink products may be as insensitive to cultural and consumer differences than has been taught.

Reasons to Standardize

It can be seen in Table 9.1 that all other things being equal (e.g., that all MNCs test and screen imported messages), cosmetics and general consumer platforms are easier to maintain than those of food-drink and pharmaceutical products. However, despite our small sample sizes, there were few differences between internal versus external factors promoting standardization among the product groupings. On average, external elements such as same product use and similar target markets outnumbered internal factors by almost 2 to 1. This finding puts into perspective various viewpoints in the literature. For example, Britt (1974) cataloged those external factors causing changes in international marketing strategies. At the other end of the spectrum, Peebles (1989) suggests that a major reason MNCs standardize promotions is because they want uniform images for certain brands. The one-third internal factors also dovetails with Hill and Still's (1984) finding that about 30% of consumer nondurable lines are deliberately standardized to give companies commonalities among subsidiary product mixes. This premeditated standardization is particularly noticeable in pharmaceutical products. Some platform standardization is also encouraged by the physical transference of promotional materials among markets. This seems to be the case in the cosmetics industry, where elaborate point-of-purchase materials and image-oriented television commercials are important elements in promotional strategies.

External factors show remarkable consistency among the four product types, despite small sample problems. About a third of all factors are equally attributed to same product use and to similar target markets. This suggests that MNCs are aware of global consumer segments, such as babies and teenagers, that enable them to maintain similar platforms over a number of different markets.

CREATIVE CONTEXTS

Reasons to Change

Creative context showed few variations (none of them significant) among the four product types (see Table 9.2). This suggests that context changes occur for non-product-type-related reasons. For example, the desire to use locally appealing backgrounds and actors in advertisements may occur to avoid being associated with the product's country of origin (e.g., anti-American feelings in some parts of Europe and Central America); or because target audiences can more easily empathize with locally oriented commercials. Of course, the opposite is also true. In developing markets, Western-style actors and settings add prestige to brand images. This is so, for example, in South America, where European contexts and lighter-skinned actors are popular.

Reasons for context change also showed some uniformity over the four nondurable categories, despite a few deviations. Product feature changes cause more creative adaptations for pharmaceutical than other types of goods, for example. Given the importance of the basic product appeal for pharmaceuticals (its primary health-related benefit), it is perhaps not surprising that when it changes, so must its surrounding context. Because of the substantial restrictions on pharmaceutical advertisements outside of the U.S., there is probably greater emphasis placed on effective creative executions. This is reinforced by the finding that 25.8% of context changes occur because of the "need for greater impact in consumers." The effects of legal factors would also contribute to the extra attention paid to creatives.

Creative contexts were also uniformly affected by "existing context not meaningful" and "consumer preferences." This suggests that some degree of care is taken by MNCs to ensure that imported messages are suitable for their target markets. Consumer education differences also have consistent impacts, except for pharmaceutical goods, but since pharmaceutical companies must conform to extensive legal guidelines in foreign markets, it is likely that by the time messages are seen or heard, they would have been screened both inside and outside the company so thoroughly that additional clarification is not necessary.

Creative contexts were also uniformly affected by "existing context not meaningful" and "consumer preferences." This suggests that some degree of care is taken by MNCs to ensure that imported messages are suitable for their target markets. Consumer education differences also have consistent impacts, except for pharmaceutical goods, but since pharmaceutical companies must conform to exten-

TABLE 9.2. Creative Contexts: Rate of Adaptation and Principal Reasons to Adapt and Standardize

Consumer % Creatives adapted	Food/Drink 65%		Pharmaceutial 64%		Cosmetic 50%		General 63%	
	n	%	n	%	n	%	n	%
<u>Reasons</u>								
Change in the product feature promoted	9	7.1	5	16.1	3	9.7	3	9.1
Difference in consumer product use	16	12.6	2	6.5	5	16.1	5	15.2
Existing context of promotion not meaningful	18	14.2	3	9.7	3	9.7	4	12.1
Need for greater impact on consumers	14	11.0	8	25.8	5	16.1	3	9.1
Legal factors	19	15	6	19.4	3	9.7	4	12.1
Consumer preferences	19	15	5	16.1	5	16.1	5	15.2
Consumer education differences	31	24.4	2	6.5	7	22.6	6	18.2
Company policy	1	20.8	0	0	0	0	1	3.0
Other	0	0	0	0	0	0	2	6.1
Totals	127	100	31	100	31	100	33	100
<u>% Creatives standardized</u>	35%		36%		50%		37%	
<u>Reasons:</u> <u>Internal</u>								
Problems producing new promotions/ commercials	8	20.5	0	0	1	4.8	2	12.5
Company policy	1	2.6	0	0	3	14.3	0	0

% Creatives standardized	35%		36%		50%		37%	
	n	%	n	%	n	%	n	%
Maintain worldwide image	6	15.4	5	45.5	5	23.8	4	25
	15	38.5	5	45.5	9	42.9	6	37.5
External								
Preserve western/ modern image	3	7.7	0	0	1	4.8	0	0
Target market similarities	18	46.2	6	54.5	9	42.9	8	50
	21	53.9	6	54.5	10	47.7	8	50
Other	3	7.7	0	0	2	9.5	2	12.5
TOTAL	39	100	11	100	21	100	16	100

sive legal guidelines in foreign markets, it is likely that by the time messages are seen or heard, they would have been screened both inside and outside the company so thoroughly that additional clarification is not necessary.

Reasons to Standardize

The relative effects of internal versus external factors on creative standardization were again consistent over the four product types. Internal factors varied between 37.5% and 45.5%, with external elements uniformly contributing around 50% standardization reasons.

Within these groupings there were a few deviations. Food and drink creatives were more likely to be maintained in light of problems producing new promotions or commercials. They were also less concerned (along with general consumer and cosmetics goods) with maintaining brand images worldwide. Global uniformity was important (as it was with their platforms) in standardizing pharmaceutical creatives.

External factors centered around target market similarities, which, in spite of small cell size limitations, all accounted for between 42.9% (cosmetics) to 54.5% of factors (pharmaceuticals).

Even within a culturally sensitive industry like consumer nondurables, it seems that marketers recognize intercultural similarities as a marketplace force enabling them to maintain even the creative executions of transferred messages. This was interesting in view of Killough's (1978) finding that creatives were more changeable internationally. Perhaps surprisingly, preserving western or modern images were not significant factors, affecting only four creatives out of 175 campaigns.

CONCLUSIONS

As noted earlier, the conclusions from these analyses should be treated with caution because of the small sample sizes in pharmaceutical, cosmetic, and general consumer industries. Also, since we do not know how representative our sample of the nondurable industry was generally, we hesitate in extending these conclusions to all nondurables, even though our sample included many blue-chip MNCs.

Overall we found surprisingly little evidence suggesting that within-industry differences are critical in consumer nondurable advertising abroad. This is the opposite of what Still and Hill (1984) found in product adaptation strategies in LDC situations. It is true that sales platform changes were more frequent in food, drink, and pharmaceutical product categories, but by contrast, no significant differences were found among creative contexts. This was surprising given the culturally loaded nature of creative contexts. However, despite small sample sizes, there was some degree of consistency as to factors influencing message adaptation and standardization.

Despite our hesitancy in extrapolating our results, we would suggest that the factors noted in this study might form a suitable basis for screening transnational promotions. Only in 28 instances out of 687 did respondents list factors other than those identified in the literature.

Regarding sales platforms, we would suggest that food and drink MNCs pay particularly close attention to consumer buying patterns, and that pharmaceutical, cosmetic, and general consumer goods managers be vigilant with regard to cultural/social factors and consumer preference differences. All nondurable products standardized platforms and creatives for internal and external reasons. However, pharmaceutical MNCs do appear to have specific guidelines with respect to maintaining brand images worldwide, a finding that dove-tails with the pharmaceutical product standardization findings of Still and Hill (1984). All sectors recognized similarities in target markets and consumer end-uses and were able to maintain sales platforms and creative contexts across at least some national markets. Consumer educational differences were also important influences on platform and creative decisions.

We realize that this study needs to be replicated over more MNCs and subsidiaries to obtain the sorts of sample sizes over which better statistical techniques can be used. Based on these results, about 40 MNCs would need to be polled with promotional strategy details being obtained from over 300 subsidiaries. We would also urge refinement of the factors that cause platforms and creatives to be maintained and changed. For example, consumer buying patterns could be defined further, as could consumer education differences, legal factors, and social/cultural differences. Standardization elements needing clarification would be target market similarities (e.g., similarities in age, education, sex, or lifestyle factors) and why companies wish to standardize some brands worldwide and not others. All in all, however, we would hope that this study and its results stimulate further interest in the area, and that sufficient research be carried out to answer the many questions remaining in the transnational advertising field.

REFERENCES

Alsop, Ronald (1984), "Efficacy of Global Ad Projects is Questioned in Firm's Survey," *Wall Street Journal*, September 13, 31.

Britt, S. Henderson (1974), "Standardizing Products in Overseas Markets," *Columbia Journal of World Business*, 9 (Winter), 30-45.

Cateora, Philip R. (1983), *International Marketing*, 4th ed. Englewood Cliffs, NJ: Richard D. Irwin.

Colvin, Michael, Roger Heeler, and Jim Thorpe (1980), "Developing International Advertising Strategy," *Journal of Marketing*, 44 (Fall), 73-79.

Douglas, Susan P., and Yoram Wind (1987), "The Myth of Globalization," *Columbia Journal of World Business*, 22 (Winter), 19-31.

Dunn, S. Watson (1976), "Effects of National Identity on Multinational Promotional Strategy in Europe," *Journal of Marketing*, 40 (October), 50-57.

_____ (1982), "United Nations as a Regulator of International Advertising" in *Proceedings of the 1982 Conference of the American Academy of Advertising*, edited by Alan D. Fletcher. Knoxville, TN.

Elinder, Erik (1965), "How International Can European Advertising Be?" *Journal of Marketing*, 29 (April), 7-11.

Fatt, Arthur C. (1967), "The Danger of 'Local' International Advertising," *Journal of Marketing*, 31 (January), 60-62.

Green, Robert T., William H. Cunningham, and Isabella C.M. Cunningham (1975), "The Effectiveness of Standard Global Advertising," *Journal of Advertising*, 4 (Summer), 25-30.

Jain, Subhash C. (1989), "Standardization of International Marketing Strategy: Some Research Hypotheses," *Journal of Marketing*, 53 (January), 70-79.

Keegan, Warren J. (1980), *Multinational Marketing Management*, 2nd 3d. NJ: Prentice Hall.

Killough, James (1978), "Improved Payoffs from Transnational Advertising," *Harvard Business Review*, 56 (July), 102-114.

Lenormand, J. M. (1964), "Is Europe Ripe for the Integration of Advertising?" *The International Advertiser*, 5 (March), 12-14.

Levitt, Theodore (1983), "The Globalization of Markets, *Harvard Business Review*, 61 (May), 92-103.

Michel, Paul (1979), "Infrastructures and International Marketing Effectiveness," *Columbia Journal of World Business*, 14 (Spring), 91-98.

Peebles, Dean H., John K. Ryans, Jr., and Ivan R. Vernon (1978), "Coordinating International Advertising," *Journal of Marketing*, 42 (January), 28-34.

_____ (1989), "Don't Write Off Global Advertising: A Commentary," *International Marketing Review*, 6, 1, 73-78.

Ricks, David A. (1983), *Big Business Blunders: Mistakes in Multinational Marketing*. Columbus, OH: Grid, Inc.

Ryans, John K., Jr., and Claudia Fry (1976), "Some European Attitudes on the Advertising Transference Question: A Research Note," *Journal of Advertising*, 5 (Spring), 11-13.

Ryans, John K. Jr. (1969), "Is It Too Soon to Put a Tiger in Every Tank?" *Columbia Journal of World Business*, 4 (March), 69-75.

Still, Richard R., and John S. Hill (1984), "Adapting Consumer Products to Lesser-Developed Markets," *Journal of Business Research*, 12, (1), 51-62.

Sorenson, Ralph Z., and Ulrich E. Wiechmann (1975), "How Multinationals View Standardization," *Harvard Business Review*, 53 (May), 38-54, and 166-167.

Walters, Peter G. P. (1986), "International Marketing Policy: A Discussion of the Standardization Construct and its Relevance for Corporate Policy," *Journal of International Business Studies*, 17, (2), 55-69.

World Trade Academy Press (1979), *Directory of American Companies Operating in Foreign Countries*. NY: Simon & Schuster.

Chapter 10

Are Global Markets with Standardized Advertising Campaigns Feasible?

Alan T. Shao
Lawrence P. Shao
Dale H. Shao

SUMMARY. This empirical study examined whether or not it is feasible to promote products the same way everywhere. This concern has been heavily debated since Levitt's (1983) call for globalized markets. Information regarding environmental factors and advertising strategy was gathered from 344 affiliates of U.S. advertising agencies in six major world regions. It was concluded that environments were too different to capitalize on advertising standardization; this perspective was echoed by practitioners when only a small percentage indicated that they standardized their multi-country campaigns.

INTRODUCTION

Few articles today have created more unrest among both academicians and practitioners than Levitt's "The Globalization of Markets" (1983). His cry for global markets and standardized consumer products was based on his belief that "Gone are accustomed differences in national or regional preference" (p. 92). But marketers have yet to conclusively agree on which method (standardization, adaptation, or customization) is the best, although many researchers have indicated that adaptation strategy has gained increased support (Dunn and Lorimor, 1979; Peebles, Ryans, and Vernon, 1978; Quelch and Hoff, 1986; Meffert and Althans, 1986). What has been agreed upon is that standardized offerings can greatly benefit practitioners by lowering costs and increasing margins (Jain, 1989; Levitt, 1983; Peebles, Ryans, and Vernon, 1978).

While some standardized products are currently being offered worldwide (e.g., Coca Cola, McDonald's), the extent to which they can be promoted without making changes to their advertising campaigns is yet unresolved. While Levitt does not advocate the systematic disregard of local or national differences, he does strongly encourage companies to utilize the same promotional campaigns everywhere. But is this reasonable? Is he correct in asserting that "Different cultural preferences, national tastes and standards, and business institutions are vestiges of the past" (p. 96)? Levitt admitted that "barriers to globalization" (p. 97) exist and therefore left the door ajar so that some adaptation or customization may be implemented. But before deciding on which type of strategy they will use in their markets, advertisers must take into account some factors that may affect their campaign developments, such as cultural sensitivities, economic concerns, literacy rates, legal considerations, and the like in their markets. This research addresses these topics by examining various environmental factors (both general and industry-specific) in six world regions. If significant differences are found, it seems unlikely that global campaigns would be feasible and that the barriers to globalization are too large to overlook, necessitating adaptation or customization.

BACKGROUND INFORMATION

Advertising Standardization

The earliest mention of standardized advertising can be traced to Elinder (1961) who stated that since European consumers were becoming more alike, uniform advertising was both desirable and feasible. Similar reasoning supporting standardized advertising was offered by Roostal (1963) and Fatt (1964). However, opponents such as Lenormand (1964), Reed (1967), and Ryans (1969) questioned whether Europe was ready for advertising integration. They concluded that a common denominator that would enable standardization to occur had not yet been found.

In the 1970s, the debate continued with Britt (1974) suggesting that methodologies and conceptual frameworks needed improvement before meaningful research on cultural and psychological aspects of international advertising could be performed. He concluded that whether products and services could be standardized depended on consumption patterns, psychological characteristics, and generalized cultural criteria. Dunn and Lorimor (1979) suggested that the best approach to European markets was to preserve "some covert multinationalism in the campaign but to add a deft touch that is distinctively French or British or Italian . . ." (p. 57). Finally, Peebles, Ryans, and Vernon (1978) found that neither complete standardization nor adaptation was the best option and recommended a programmed management approach to coordinate multicountry campaigns. They also advocated "prototype standardization" where the same campaigns would be used by the multinational enterprise in multiple markets, with the only differences being appropriate translation and idiomatic changes (Peebles, Ryans, and Vernon, 1977).

There have been few empirical studies regarding international advertising. Killough's (1978) study involving 65 senior executives in more than 120 international advertising campaigns inquired about advertising resource transferability. He concluded that complete standardization was not feasible. Meffert and Althans (1986) surveyed the European headquarters of international advertising agencies to inquire about how far multinational corporations standardized their advertising activities in Europe. They found, similar to Sorenson and Wiechmann (1975), that many multinational companies standardized all or parts of advertising campaigns across borders. They also found that the major barriers to advertising standardization were media-related.

Environmental Factors

Environmental factors play key roles in determining how successful companies operate abroad. For example, those companies in Western Europe are mainly operating in developed nations where infrastructures are intact and advertising support devices are plentiful. But those existing throughout most of Asia are in newly industrialized countries (NIC) where advertising factors are not as sophisticated. Therefore, the regions where companies operate will likely influence their effectiveness. Some factors dependent on geographic region include cultural universals, economic conditions, literacy rates, and legal requirements.

General Environmental Factors

While marketers have substantial power over many of the factors that influence their market effectiveness (such as the marketing mix elements), several external factors are out of the marketing manager's control. These uncontrollable factors must be recognized by managers and considered in all aspects of their marketing strategies. Cateora (1990) noted that it is the environment, including cultural differences, within which marketing plans must be implemented that differentiates the domestic market from international markets. Although cultural differences are difficult to measure (Mesdag, 1987), there are many "cultural universals" (i.e., items common to all cultures) (Terpstra, 1990), where some elements of culture are widely accepted as key ingredients of culture including different languages and dialects (Whorf, 1956; Ricks, 1983), religious differences (Terpstra, 1990) and ethnic groups or races (Root, 1987).

But to pretend that understanding only culture will lead multinational advertising agencies to succeed in foreign markets is an oversimplification of what environments involve. Toyne and Walters (1989) stated that marketers must also examine economic, social, political, and technological factors to comprehend foreign environments. Therefore:

H1:   The extent environmental factors influence promotional strategy depends on the region where it operates.

Industry-Specific Factors

Besides the general environmental factors that may affect a firm's promotional strategy, there are also industry-specific concerns of which advertising agencies must be aware. Meffert and Althans (1986) noted that media-related restrictions oftentimes prohibit agencies from offering standardized campaigns. For example, in Germany, commercial television advertising is limited to 20 minutes per day in blocks of 5 to 7 minutes between 5:00 p.m. and 8:00 p.m.

Advertising-specific regulations also affect multinational advertising agencies since they aim to protect consumers from misleading advertising or protect advertisers from unfair competitive practices (United Nations, 1979). This reality is usually more evident in developed nations (e.g., EC members) than NICs or developing countries (like those found throughout Pacific Asia) since controls are better established. Therefore:

H2:   The availability and coverage of various types of media differs by region.

METHODOLOGY

Data

The population surveyed consisted of all foreign affiliates of U.S.-based advertising agencies. Sampling procedures involved a two-step process. The aim of the first part was to identify U.S. parent agencies with six or more active overseas affiliates so that they could qualify as "multinational" according to the terms laid out by Aharoni (1971). Twenty-one U.S. parent agencies met this criterion. Out of those, 15 agreed (71%) to allow their foreign affiliates to participate in the study.

The second part of the sampling procedure involved contacting affiliate agencies. A total of 755 questionnaires were mailed to foreign affiliates. Only one questionnaire was mailed per affiliate. Affiliate "managers" or "managing directors" were asked to complete the questionnaires. Twelve were returned to sender, as they were no longer in business as an agency. An additional 13 came back since these agencies were no longer affiliated with the parent company. But out of the remaining 730 questionnaires, 344 were returned by January 1989, a 47% response rate. To guard against geographic biases, a chi-square goodness-of-fit test was used to find if respondents were regionally representative of U.S. ad affiliates operating overseas. The test indicated that indeed questionnaire returns were regionally represented.

Results

To examine whether significant differences existed among the six world regions, chi-square tests were used. In Tables 10.1 and 10.2, only those environmental factors where significant differences were found are given, along with their p-values.

General Environmental Factors

Environmental factors can adversely affect all companies doing business in foreign markets. Out of the eleven market conditions examined in this study, nine proved to reveal significant differences among the regions (only "legal restrictions on claims advertisers can make" and "government bias against advertising" did not). Table 10.1 shows that the region where environmental factors posed the most severe problems was Africa. In fact, of the nine factors, only two (religious groups/factions and consumer groups) were not stated to have caused problems for at least half of the respondents. The Middle East, with five factors posing problems to at least half of the U.S. advertising affiliates, was also a difficult region to advertise in. Agencies operating in Europe were found to have the least number of environmental problems. In all nine cases, more than two-thirds of the respondents indicated that the factors were not problems for them. These findings support the hypothesis that environmental factors influence advertising strategy differently according to region. As one would expect, the two regions (Africa and the Middle East) where most problems occurred are considered developing areas and where few problems existed, the region was generally developed (Europe). Therefore, it seems that standardized ad campaigns may be possible in similar market development types.

Industry-Specific Factors

In most developed markets, choosing which type of media to use for promotional purposes is oftentimes up to individual advertising

TABLE 10.1. Environmental Factors' Effect on Promotion

Environmental Factor	Degree of Problem			P-value
	No Problem	Slight	Definite	
MULTIPLE LANGUAGES/ DIALECTS				
Africa	7 (44%)	2 (13%)	7 (44%)	.00013
Asia	71 (81%)	11 (13%)	6 (7%)	
Europe	132 (84%)	12 (8%)	14 (9%)	
Middle East	9 (53%)	3 (18%)	5 (29%)	
North America	22 (71%)	4 (13%)	5 (16%)	
South America	29 (94%)	1 (3%)	1 (3%)	
RELIGIOUS GROUPS/ FACTIONS				
Africa	10 (4%)	5 (11%)	1 (7%)	.00002
Asia	67 (75%)	16 (18%)	6 (7%)	
Europe	141 (89%)	15 (9%)	3 (2%)	
Middle East	9 (56%)	3 (19%)	4 (25%)	
North America	26 (84%)	5 (16%)	0 (0%)	
South America	31 (100%)	0 (0%)	0 (0%)	
DIFFERENT ETHNIC GROUPS/RACES				
Africa	8 (50%)	1 (6%)	7 (44%)	.00000
Asia	65 (73%)	16 (18%)	8 (9%)	
Europe	146 (92%)	9 (6%)	4 (3%)	
Middle East	10 (63%)	2 (13%)	4 (25%)	
North America	26 (84%)	4 (13%)	1 (3%)	
South America	29 (94%)	2 (7%)	0 (0%)	
INFLATION				
Africa	5 (31%)	3 (19%)	8 (50%)	.00000
Asia	63 (73%)	18 (21%)	5 (6%)	
Europe	146 (92%)	8 (5%)	4 (3%)	
Middle East	8 (47%)	5 (29%)	4 (24%)	
North America	16 (53%)	10 (33%)	4 (13%)	
South America	12 (39%)	2 (7%)	17 (55%)	
LITERACY PROBLEMS				
Africa	3 (19%)	5 (31%)	8 (50%)	.00000
Asia	73 (84%)	13 (15%)	1 (1%)	
Europe	139 (93%)	9 (6%)	1 (1%)	
Middle East	8 (47%)	2 (12%)	7 (41%)	
North America	24 (77%)	5 (16%)	2 (7%)	
South America	17 (59%)	8 (28%)	4 (14%)	

TABLE 10.1 (continued)

Environmental Factor	Degree of Problem			P-value
	No Problem	Slight	Definite	
RESTRICT ADVERTISING MATERIAL IMPORTS				
Africa	8 (50%)	4 (25%)	4 (25%)	.00000
Asia	48 (55%)	15 (17%)	25 (28%)	
Europe	132 (84%)	24 (15%)	2 (1%)	
Middle East	8 (47%)	6 (35%)	3 (18%)	
North America	14 (45%)	15 (48%)	2 (7%)	
South America	6 (19%)	5 (16%)	20 (65%)	
RESTRICTIONS ON HIRING FOREIGNERS				
Africa	7 (44%)	7 (44%)	2 (13%)	.00024
Asia	41 (47%)	33 (38%)	14 (16%)	
Europe	106 (67%)	39 (25%)	13 (8%)	
Middle East	4 (24%)	5 (29%)	8 (47%)	
North America	16 (52%)	10 (32%)	5 (16%)	
South America	18 (60%)	5 (17%)	7 (23%)	
FOREIGN CURRENCY EXCHANGE				
Africa	4 (25%)	4 (25%)	8 (50%)	.00000
Asia	80 (92%)	4 (5%)	3 (4%)	
Europe	134 (86%)	13 (8%)	9 (6%)	
Middle East	6 (38%)	1 (6%)	9 (56%)	
North America	24 (80%)	5 (17%)	1 (3%)	
South America	14 (50%)	5 (18%)	9 (32%)	
CONSUMER GROUPS				
Africa	13 (81%)	2 (13%)	1 (6%)	.01223
Asia	49 (56%)	26 (30%)	12 (14%)	
Europe	112 (71%)	42 (27%)	4 (3%)	
Middle East	10 (67%)	5 (33%)	0 (0%)	
North America	19 (63%)	9 (30%)	2 (7%)	
South America	24 (86%)	4 (14%)	0 (0%)	

TABLE 10.2. Media Availability by Region

Medium	Market Restrictions				
	None	**Limited Coverage**	**Limit some Product Ads**	**Cannot Use**	**P-value**
TELEVISION					
Africa	3 (21%)	2 (14%)	8 (57%)	1 (7%)	.00001
Asia	20 (23%)	6 (7%)	60 (70%)	1 (1%)	
Europe	11 (7%)	7 (5%)	128 (82%)	10 (6%)	
Middle East	1 (6%)	0 (0%)	16 (94%)	0 (0%)	
North America	8 (27%)	1 (3%)	21 (70%)	0 (0%)	
South America	15 (50%)	0 (0%)	15 (50%)	0 (0%)	
RADIO					
Africa	10 (71%)	0 (0%)	4 (29%)	0 (0%)	.00013
Asia	32 (37%)	5 (6%)	47 (55%)	2 (2%)	
Europe	30 (20%)	12 (8%)	96 (64%)	11 (7%)	
Middle East	4 (24%)	0 (0%)	11 (65%)	2 (12%)	
North America	9 (32%)	1 (4%)	18 (64%)	0 (0%)	
South America	19 (63%)	0 (0%)	11 (37%)	0 (0%)	
NEWSPAPER					
Africa	10 (71%)	1 (7%)	3 (21%)	0 (0%)	.05460
Asia	49 (61%)	6 (8%)	23 (29%)	2 (3%)	
Europe	107 (74%)	5 (3%)	33 (23%)	0 (0%)	
Middle East	8 (47%)	1 (6%)	8 (47%)	0 (0%)	
North America	16 (57%)	2 (7%)	10 (36%)	0 (0%)	
South America	28 (93%)	1 (3%)	1 (3%)	0 (0%)	
POSTER					
Africa	11 (79%)	1 (7%)	1 (7%)	1 (7%)	.07184
Asia	51 (61%)	5 (6%)	26 (31%)	2 (2%)	
Europe	103 (70%)	9 (6%)	35 (24%)	0 (0%)	
Middle East	9 (60%)	1 (7%)	4 (27%)	1 (7%)	
North America	17 (63%)	1 (4%)	9 (33%)	0 (0%)	
South America	26 (90%)	2 (7%)	1 (3%)	0 (0%)	
MAGAZINE					
Africa	10 (71%)	2 (14%)	1 (7%)	1 (7%)	.00024
Asia	55 (67%)	8 (10%)	17 (21%)	2 (2%)	
Europe	111 (77%)	2 (1%)	32 (22%)	0 (0%)	
Middle East	7 (41%)	2 (12%)	8 (47%)	0 (0%)	
North America	16 (59%)	2 (7%)	9 (33%)	0 (0%)	
South America	27 (90%)	1 (3%)	0 (0%)	2 (7%)	

TABLE 10.2 (continued)

Medium	None	Market Restrictions Limited Coverage	Limit some Product Ads	Cannot Use	P-value
DIRECT MAIL					
Africa	11 (79%)	0 (0%)	0 (0%)	3 (21%)	.00003
Asia	53 (70%)	7 (9%)	7 (9%)	9 (12%)	
Europe	107 (76%)	2 (1%)	30 (21%)	2 (1%)	
Middle East	9 (60%)	1 (7%)	3 (20%)	2 (13%)	
North America	18 (69%)	1 (4%)	7 (27%)	0 (0%)	
South America	22 (79%)	0 (0%)	0 (0%)	6 (21%)	

agencies or their clients. But in less sophisticated markets, media availability may be the deciding factor. Survey results involving industry-specific factors revealed some interesting findings (see Table 10.2). First, it was found that at least half of all agencies in South America stated that there were no restrictions on each of the media types, although at the same time several respondents indicated that some products could not be mass-advertised (specifically on television and radio). Second, the category with the greatest range differences was "certain products cannot be legally advertised on this medium." For example, 94% of the respondents in the Middle East indicated that some products could not be advertised on television, whereas only half of those in South America indicated specific product limitations. Finally, some media types were not available for commercial use. In Africa and Asia, for example, over 20% of the respondents indicated that direct mail could not be used.

These findings suggest that before advertisers formulate their promotional strategies, they must strongly consider the potential restrictions that may exist regarding the various types of media, including media availability, regulations, and market coverage. If agencies have used mass media types in their markets during the past but plan to enter some developing areas where these promotional devices are not as readily available, they may be forced to create new types of campaigns to accommodate the available media types.

What Percentage of Client Campaigns Are Standardized?

To gain a perspective of the extent to which advertising practitioners are standardizing their offerings (regardless of whether they were dictated by their clients to do so or not), respondents were asked to state the percentages of their clients' campaigns that they were able to standardize concerning both the sales platform and creative context. As shown in Table 10.3, of the 229 respondents who participated in multi-country campaigns, less than 10% standardized both the sales platform and its creative context. This finding indicates that apparently the accustomed differences in national or regional preferences are not gone, as Levitt indicated, and that practitioners believe that there is a strong need to adapt or customize advertising campaigns to local or regional markets.

SUMMARY AND CONCLUSIONS

This study attempted to address Levitt's (1983) call for globalized markets and standardized procedures by examining various environmental considerations that posed potential threats to the operations of U.S. advertising affiliates operating abroad. After having looked at how various world regions differed with respect to market environments, and considering what advertising practitioners have done regarding the standardization issue, the answer to the initial question "Are global markets with standardized advertising campaigns truly feasible?" is *usually not!* In a few cases it was found that this task was able to be performed. However, for the

TABLE 10.3. Percentage of Client Campaigns that are Standardized

Categories	Frequency	Percentage of Total
0%	12	5%
1 - 20%	68	31%
21 - 40%	28	13%
41 - 60%	38	17%
61 - 80%	36	16%
81 - 99%	19	9%
100%	19	9%

most part it was revealed that the environments in different regions of the world created difficulties for advertisers. Whether the problems were media-specific, legal, cultural, economic, or social in nature, it is safe to say that the world is different enough to discourage attempts at advertising standardization. This view was echoed by the majority of advertising practitioners sampled. Of those agencies that participated in multi-country campaigns, it was discovered that only 10% standardized both the sales platform and creative context of their ad campaigns. This showed that while some attempts were being made to lower costs and increase margins through standardization, the majority of those "in the field" believed that customization or adaptation was a necessity.

In conclusion, advertising agencies operating abroad are discouraged from any attempts at standardization. While the time may come when advertising the same way everywhere becomes feasible, for now, multinationals should adapt their ad campaigns to be in tune with their target markets.

Limitations

While this empirical study sheds some light on U.S. advertising affiliates' operations, a major limitation must be noted. This concern involves the key informants (affiliate managers) used in this survey. There are advantages and disadvantages to this method of obtaining information. Disadvantages include the possibilities that informant reporting may be judgmental, and that biases or ignorance may occur (Phillips, 1981). But since informants were carefully selected, and internally consistent scales were used, individual biases were likely negated and reliable and valid data were provided (John and Reve, 1982).

REFERENCES

Aharoni, Yair (1971), "On the Definition of a Multinational Corporation," *The Quarterly Review of Economics and Business*, 11(3), 27-37.

Britt, Steuart H. (1974), "Standardizing Marketing for the International Market," *Columbia Journal of World Business*, 9 (Winter), 39-45.

Cateora, Philip R. (1990), *International Marketing*. Homewood: Richard D. Irwin, Inc.

Dunn, S. Watson and E. S. Lorimor (1979), *International Advertising and Marketing*. Columbus, OH: Grid Publishing.

Elinder, Erik (1961), "How International Can Advertising Be?" *International Advertiser*, (December), 12-16.

Fatt, Arthur C. (1964), "A Multinational Approach to International Advertising," *International Advertiser*, (September), 17-20.

Jain, Subhash C. (1989), "Standardization of International Marketing Strategy: Some Research Hypotheses," *Journal of Marketing*, 53 (January), 70-79.

John, George and Torger Reve (1982), "The Reliability and Validity of Key Informant Data from Dyadic Relationships in Marketing Channels," *Journal of Marketing Research*, 19 (November), 517-524.

Killough, James (1978), "Improved Payoffs From Transnational Advertising," *Harvard Business Review*, 56 (July-August), 102-110.

Lenormand, J. M. (1964), "Is Europe Ripe for the Integration of Advertising?" *The International Advertiser*, (March), 21.

Levitt, Theodore (1983), "The Globalization of Markets," *Harvard Business Review*, 61 (May-June), 92-102.

Meffert, Heribert and Jurgen Althans (1986), "Global Advertising: Multinational vs. International," *International Advertiser*, (February), 34-37.

Mesdag, Martin van (1987), "Winging It in Foreign Markets," *Harvard Business Review*, 65 (January-February), 71-74.

Peebles, Dean, M., Jr., John K. Ryans, and Ivan R. Vernon (1977), "A New Perspective on Advertising Standardization," *European Journal of Marketing*, 11(8), 569-76.

_____ (1978), "Coordinating International Advertising," *Journal of Marketing*, 42 (January), 28-34.

Phillips, Lynn W. (1981), "Assessing Measurement Error in Key Informant Reports: A Methodological Note on Organizational Analysis in Marketing," *Journal of Marketing Research*, 18 (November), 395-415.

Quelch, John A. and Edward J. Hoff (1986), "Customizing Global Marketing," *Harvard Business Review*, 64 (May-June), 59-68.

Reed, Virgil D. (1967), "The International Consumer," in *Managerial Marketing: Perspectives and Viewpoint*, 3rd ed., edited by Eugene J. Kelley and William Lazer.

Ricks, David A. (1983), *Big Business Blunders: Mistakes in Multinational Marketing*. Homewood: Dow Jones-Irwin.

Roostal, I. (1963), "Standardization of Advertising for Western Europe," *Journal of Marketing*, 27 (October), 15-20.

Root, Franklin R. (1987), *Entry Strategies for International Markets*. Lexington, MA: Lexington Books.

Ryans, John K. (1969), "Is It Too Soon to Put a Tiger in Every Tank?" *Columbia Journal of World Business*, 4 (March-April), 69-75.

Sorenson, Ralph Z. and Ulrich E. Wiechmann (1975), "How Multinationals View Marketing Standardization," *Harvard Business Review*, 53 (May-June), 38.

Terpstra, Vern (1990), *International Marketing*. NY: The Dryden Press.

Toyne, Brian and Peter G. Walters (1989), *Global Marketing Management*. Needham: Allyn and Bacon.

United Nations (1979), *Transnational Corporations in Advertising*. NY: United Nations.

Whorf, Benjamin L. (1956), *Language, Thought, and Reality*. NY: John Wiley & Sons, Inc.

Chapter 11

Winning the Global Advertising Race: Planning Globally, Acting Locally

Roger D. Blackwell
Riad Ajami
Kristina Stephan

SUMMARY. This paper focuses on the ability to think globally about consumer marketing programs and to implement global advertising strategies. Analysis of global consumer behavior focuses on the structural analysis of markets and cross-cultural analysis of lifestyles as well as the traditional areas of individual decision making. Advertising strategies require a global approach but not necessarily a global agency. Acquisitions and mergers that have resulted in global mega agencies have many problems. A more efficient approach may be a network of domestic agencies with informal structures for sharing market information, creative ideas, and production costs.

Perhaps no manager should be promoted to a position of major responsibility in contemporary business organizations if that individual cannot "think globally." The globalization of marketing requires managers, especially those dealing with consumer products and services, to understand the broad forces that characterize contemporary markets.

The purpose of this chapter is to provide managers with a guide to the major conceptual contributions in the marketing literature toward understanding global consumer behavior. The focus is upon the application of these concepts to the development of global advertising strategies and the effective implementation of global advertising programs. Examples of this focus are drawn from companies currently involved in this process, especially on the issue of how advertising agencies are changing and how agencies may be effectively organized to provide a competitive edge to firms involved in global marketing.

WHAT IS GLOBAL MARKETING?

Thinking globally involves *the ability to understand markets beyond one's own country of origin, with respect to sources of demand, sources of supply, and methods of effective management and marketing.*

Globalization of Competition

The forces affecting globalization of markets and international competition have been identified by Michael Porter to include the following:

1. Growing similarity of countries in terms of available infrastructure, distribution channels, and marketing approaches;
2. Fluid global capital markets–national capital markets are growing into global capital markets because of the large flow of funds between countries;
3. Technological restructuring–the reshaping of competition globally as a result of technological revolutions such as in microelectronics;
4. The integrating role of technology–reduced cost and increased impact of products have made them accessible to more global consumers, and;
5. New global competitors–a shift in competitors from traditional country competitors to emerging global competitors (Porter, 1986).

Ford Motors is an example of a "global company" that has prospered in globalized markets, more at least than General Motors. When the U.S. auto market was under siege from Japanese imports, Chrysler and GM were in dismal shape. Ford had its troubles also but was "saved" by Ford of Europe, a subsidiary operating with considerable autonomy and innovation in developing cars with appeal that cuts across national boundaries. Ford developed "world class cars" such as the *Escort* and later the *Taurus/Sable* that could sell in multiple countries. Another such car was the *Scorpio*, developed by Ford of Europe but also sold in the United States.

Global Advertising Agencies

The changing business environment has created an urgency among many corporations to develop global thinking in their marketing and advertising strategies. Some firms have turned to global advertising agencies to promote their products in a variety of nations. The perceived need for a global mega advertising agency to represent the company on a worldwide basis has caused some agencies to merge to satisfy their customers. Are the new mega agencies really satisfying their customers? Are such agencies suited for the environment of increased international business activities in North America, in the New Europe, in the emerging markets of the Pacific Rim, Eastern Europe, the Third World, Latin America and other markets? These are a few of the issues raised and addressed in the following text.

Importance of Global Thinking in Marketing

Emergence of the Multi-National Enterprise (MNE) makes it essential that managers have the ability to "think globally." Corporations such as Coca-Cola, IBM, Gillette, Nestlé, Sony, Phillips, and Unilever derive over 50% of their sales outside their country of domicile. So do many small, relatively obscure companies with specialized "niches" that transcend national boundaries. A small wood products company in Boring, Oregon now gets 70% of its business from Japan because it made the effort to master the Japanese grading system for wood and the Japanese cultural preference for vertical grain stacking instead of the manner ordinarily employed in the U.S.

Today's consumers choose not only from products made in many countries, but also from ideas, advertisements, and friends representing a diversity of nations and cultures. Consumer analysts need to be global thinkers to design strategies to reach today's consumers.

Global Managers

The corporate cultures of today's successful organizations also are increasingly global. Volkswagen in Germany and Procter & Gamble recently appointed new presidents, based partly on their experiences across cultures. The president of Coca-Cola came from Cuba, and the president of Procter & Gamble gained his position because of his international experience. For the first time, IBM recently appointed an American to head its far-flung European Division, which includes Africa and the Middle East. Caterpillar in the U.S. recruited its head of manufacturing from Austria.

Global managers must be able to learn a new language quickly. They must understand the structure and culture of any country in the world. They must work effectively with people from any country. Consumer analysts can play a key role in this process. Growth in global marketing is one reason McDonald's has prospered while its competitors have stagnated in their attempt to grow. McDonald's now sells more hamburgers in Japan alone than major competitors do in the U.S. and reportedly serves 30,000 customers a day in Moscow.

STRUCTURE OF GLOBAL MARKETS

Formulating global consumer marketing strategies requires careful consideration of the structure of global markets. The study of consumer behavior has traditionally focused on individual decision making of consumers, but strategic planning involves committing corporate resources to the most promising areas of the world. Thus, one of the most important areas of consumer analysis involves the study of global market structure. This requires accurate projection of world population trends over the next few decades.

Population Trends

The important trends in global population can be summarized as follows:

1. Prolonged below-replacement levels of fertility in developed nations.
2. Rapid growth despite falling fertility in developing nations.
3. Rapid urbanization in less developed countries, with unprecedented migration from poor LDCs to more affluent industrialized nations.

Economic Resources and Market Attractiveness

The most attractive markets are countries that are growing in economic resources as well as population. Economic resources, or ability to buy, is measured by consumer analysts in various ways. Per capita income is an important indicator, although there are problems such as the currency with which it will be measured and the purchasing power of income within a country. One of the most valid indicators is "hours required to purchase" standard consumer goods. For example, consumers might require 11 hours at an average wage to purchase a standard television receiver in the United States but as much as 11 months in some developing countries. Unfortunately, such data are not readily available for market analysis purposes.

A useful indicator of "ability to buy" is Gross National Product (GNP) per capita in a country. Even though the statistic does not reflect variations in distribution between countries, per capita GNP is a commonly accepted indicator of market attractiveness. Three other indicators of market attractiveness are: *Natural increase* (percentage increase in population each year considering births and deaths), *life expectancy*, and *urban population* (as a percentage of total population). Data for most countries of the world are available from the Population Reference Bureau (World Population Data Sheet, 1987).

Market Growth

Where will the growth be in future markets? Using a combination of demographic factors and technological structure of economies, Bouvier (1984) estimated that global markets will be of the following types and size:

1. Service/information societies (4% of global population) where immigration balances low fertility to prevent population decline.

2. Industrialized nations (38% of population) with fertility close to or at replacement level and growth slowing.
3. Developing nations (43%) in sight of replacement-level fertility.
4. Least developed nations (15%) with still-critical demographic problems.

The challenge for MNE's is to develop a portfolio of products, marketing programs, and advertising agencies that will be effective in reaching a global portfolio of markets. In North America, many firms have formulated a strategy based upon the lifestyles of consumers rather than the traditional "supply side" approach to developing marketing programs (Blackwell and Talarzyk, 1983). The challenge lies in determining which products and retail offerings in a domestic portfolio lend themselves to adaptation to the lifestyles of other countries. Markets may be identified as attractive and a suitable portfolio of products and retail offerings may be developed, but ultimately global analysis must also focus upon the issue of what types of activities will effectively communicate to consumers concerning these strategies and what form of advertising agency organization can accomplish such activities.

CULTURAL ANALYSIS OF GLOBAL MARKETS

After structure of markets is examined, the next major area of understanding global markets involves cultural analysis. This involves the ability to understand and be effective in communicating with the core values of a society. Ethnographic analysis of marketing, such as that of Prus, focuses on the interactive processes of exchange with particular attention to the subtle nuances and orderliness of the selling process (Prus, 1989).

Developing Cultural Empathy

Marketing practitioners need *cultural empathy*, defined as *the ability to understand the inner logic and coherence of other ways of life*. Cultural empathy includes restraint from judging the value of other ways of life. Consumer analysis focuses on the "meaning systems" of consumers in a nation that are intelligible within the cultural context of that country. Analysis of what type of advertising agencies should be employed should include criteria that determine whether or not the agency has cultural empathy with the markets with which the agency intends to communicate.

Global strategies usually need to be adapted to meaning systems of the market rather than attempting to change the market to the customary marketing programs of the firm. This includes interenvironmental considerations (Griffin, 1987), or the characteristic ways a culture responds to marketing.

Cultural analysis provides an approach to understanding the consumer behavior not only of diverse nations, but of diverse groups within a nation. In Africa, for example, tribal cultures within countries such as Zambia, Nigeria, Zimbabwe, and South Africa may be far more influential than differences that exist between countries. Many of the tribal influences cut across national boundaries established by white colonists with little regard to cultural or tribal boundaries. In Europe, people in the south of Switzerland may have more cultural similarity to France than in the north of Switzerland. Cross-cultural analysis provides an approach for understanding such situations.

Cross-Cultural Analysis

Cross-cultural analysis is the *systematic comparison of similarities and differences in the material and behavioral aspects of cultures*. Cross-cultural studies in anthropology often focus upon social organization, child rearing, belief systems, and similar topics. In marketing, the elements studied are more likely to be distribution systems, beliefs about sales and pricing activities, and communications channels.

Cross-cultural studies often involve collection of attitudinal data from several countries, permitting statistical description. As an example, Plummer considered the role of hygiene across cultures. It appears that Americans may be obsessed with cleanliness from the percentages found in each nation agreeing with the statement, "Everyone should use a deodorant" (Plumber, 1977).

United States	89%
French Canada	81%
English Canada	77%
United Kingdom	71%
Italy	69%
France	59%
Australia	53%

An alternative interpretation of these data, however, might be that Americans simply need a deodorant more than do people in other countries! Or at least that Americans believe they need a deodorant.

This leads us to an interesting issue that increases in complexity as we move toward global thinking and advertising strategy. When marketing to the needs of its consumers, should the MNE market to the real needs or the perceived needs of the consumer? How does the determination of this strategy differ in the global portfolio of markets? The resolution of this issue has caused one of the greatest controversies in global advertising, discussed in the following section.

CAN MARKETING BE STANDARDIZED?

Can one marketing program be used in all or at least many countries? Or must marketing programs be modified for each country? If marketing programs must be modified to each culture, firms will fail if they do not develop specific products, promotions, and organizations for each country. Yet enormous economies are achieved if the marketing program is standardized.

Many corporations have chosen to adopt a global marketing strategy. However, the question that must be asked concerns whether adopting such a strategy implies stringent adherence, or is it possible and advisable to adapt a global strategy locally through advertising efforts or a portfolio of strategies?

Is consumer behavior subject to cultural universals? Erik Elinder answered this question affirmatively many years ago and advanced the position that advertising can be standardized (Elinder, 1965). Elinder's question and the validity of his answer has intrigued marketers since he first raised the issue.

The issue of standardization has become more important because of increased global competition facing marketers. The debate was intensified by a controversial article written by Ted Levitt describing the globalization of the marketplace (Levitt, 1983).

The need for globalized marketing strategies arises not only from market characteristics but also from technological and organizational characteristics. To compete, a firm must use technology that is not limited to national borders and people operating in worldwide organizations. Measures of marketing efficiency must now include global market share, requiring firms to understand their market niche in terms of customer types, not geodemographic segments (Leontiades, 1986). Firms are increasingly defining market segments to consist of similar types of customers and cultures throughout the New Europe rather than groups within a specific country.

Global Market Segmentation

Global market segmentation is already used by many European firms. Global segmentation involves defining market targets in multiple countries on some basis other than national boundaries. Frequently the variable is lifestyle or value systems.

With the unification of Europe, some U.S. firms have recently developed new strategies that respond to the new dramatic changes in the European market. Many European firms, however, have been adapting their strategies and business functions for years. Does this put U.S. firms at a disadvantage in formulating and implementing effective global strategies? How will European firms capitalize on their head start? Have they been better able to assess the effectiveness of global advertising agencies, and can we learn from their conclusions?

Standardization Based on Similarities

Standardization should be based on a solid understanding of the similarities as well as the differences between countries. Marketing organizations now seek such standardization in international marketing programs (Buzzell, 1986). A study of 27 MNE's, including companies such as General Foods, Nestlé, Coca-Cola, Procter & Gamble, Unilever, and Revlon, found that 63% of the total marketing programs could be rated as "highly standardized." The authors of that study describe the need for cross-cultural (or "cross-border") analysis:

> Management of multi-nationals should give high priority to developing the ability to conduct systematic cross-border analysis, if they are not already doing so. Such analysis can help management avoid the mistake of standardizing when markets are significantly different. At the same time, systematic cross-border analysis can help avoid the mistake of excessive custom-tailoring when markets are sufficiently similar to make standardized programs feasible. (Sorenson & Wiechmann, 1975)

People are basically the same around the globe. They vary in specific traits, often influenced by structural elements such as economic resources, urbanization, age of the population, and other variables. The challenge is to build the core of the marketing strategy on the *universals*, and the goal is to construct a detailed plan of action that considers the underlying differences.

An example of standardization based on universals is the desire to be beautiful. In a sense, young women in Tokyo and those on either side of the now fallen Wall in Berlin are sisters not only "under the skin," but on their skin, lips, fingernails, and even in their hairstyles. Consequently, Fatt states, they are likely to buy similar cosmetics with similar appeals. If they could, Fatt believes, the women of Moscow would follow suit, and some of them do (Fatt, 1967). Appeals such as mother and child, freedom from pain, glow of health, and so forth may cut across many boundaries. Avon found, for example, that its program of selling cosmetics door-to-door in the U.S. could be extended to countries such as Japan, where affluent women with high usage of beauty products are typically still at home during the day.

Another example of successful international standardization is Coke. Armed with essentially the same universal packaging, logo, taste, and advertising, Coke has carried its carbonated beverages to over 160 countries and accounts for almost 50% of all soda pop consumed worldwide. Recently, Coke's success overseas has been emphasized as operating profits in 1989 were 80% from overseas markets as compared to 50% only four years ago (McCarthy, 1989).

The Globalization Continuum

A realistic approach to the issue of standardization-localization is that some elements must be localized and some can be standardized. The more a marketing manager can learn about the cultures, the more likely the standardized approach can be used by avoiding elements that would be ineffective in one or more of the target countries. Some firms, such as Nestlé are highly decentralized. Other firms, such as Coca-Cola, are highly standardized (still maintaining variations between countries, however) and this diversity of approaches forms a continuum of effective global strategies.

While cultural differences can sometimes account for product acceptance, it is not always prudent to make elaborate changes to otherwise "generic" products. Despite perceived differences in culture, the tailoring of various products to each market can prove costly. Several years ago Quaker Oats tried several different packaging and promotional approaches to one dog food product and found profits elusive; recent dog food strategies by Quaker are much more consolidated and standard (McCarthy, 1989).

Success at any part of this globalization continuum requires certain basic elements. Gordon Link describes four key rules:

1. There is no one ideal approach to global marketing and advertising. It must be tailored to the specific needs of each product category. Flexibility is the name of the game.
2. Globalization is best approached as an evolutionary process. A revolutionary approach is often too disruptive to local marketing personnel. Time and patience are of the essence. There are no overnight successes in global branding.
3. Companies can begin the process at quite different points on a broad spectrum. The process can be visualized as a continuum from left to right. On the left are companies with highly decentralized, multi-domestic operations and products. Toward the middle are companies that have increasingly centralized product and brand positionings, adapted to local differences. On the right are totally integrated, global markets and advertised brands or companies. Global firms must consider whether their own company and/or its brands already fit or might find a point of entry along this broad range of possibilities.

4. Whatever the company's stage of brand development, the move toward global advertising is greatly abetted by the right kind of agency structure: This means strong local agencies working in concert with the centralized creative, account, and media management resources of a major global advertising agency (Link, 1988).

While Coke maintains a highly standardized worldwide focus, there is still room for some fine-tuning in approaching various markets. For example, Spanish Coke enthusiasts see the soft drink as an excellent mixer, Italians replace wine with Coke as a dinner drink, and the Chinese view Coke as a refined luxury drink for only the most fortunate (McCarthy, 1989).

THE GLOBAL ADVERTISING CONTROVERSY

Business without borders will not become reality, but global relationships between MNE's and their new markets will. In this rapidly changing environment, the advertising agency will continue to serve as the primary link between the MNE and its consumer. And with the diversity of consumers within these markets and the global vision of these MNE's, the agency's role may become more important than ever. Global corporations are looking more and more to advertising agencies for guidance in penetrating markets in which they have no prior business experience.

Global Advertising Agencies

The desired outcome expected from advertising agencies is usually well understood. The controversy about how agencies can achieve such results on a global basis, however, is a hot topic among corporate leaders, agency directors, and academicians. Marcio M. Moreira, executive vice president and international creative director of McCann-Erickson Worldwide, attributes the continued controversy to the following factors:

1. There exist many interests and interested parties involved that have much at stake.

2. Most of the successful global brands that exist today were successful before it became fashionable to be global.
3. Most advertisers who have decided to become global recently have yet to succeed.
4. Most people's understanding of global advertising is either too rigid or too literal for it to succeed. The key to success is flexibility.
5. There are still enormous misconceptions about what being global really means and what tangible results can be expected from it.
6. And most companies try to become global overnight (Moreira, 1986).

The key to evaluating effective agency approaches lies in an agency's ability to link effective communications to consumers. The strength of this link depends directly on how well a firm and its agency understand their markets. A global environment makes this more challenging than before due to cultural diversity.

This raises the questions: Is it a necessity for corporations with a globally competitive vision to contract with an advertising agency with this same vision? Do these firms need to adopt a global/standardized advertising plan, or can they still use a local/customized approach? Is it size or competitive scope of the firm that matters? Or is it the nature of the product and the nature of its consumer markets that matters?

Finding a Basis for Global Market Segmentation

Market segmentation must be re-examined to determine the best basis for segmentation with the emergence of global marketing. Global consumer markets are best understood as groups of buyers that share the need and desire for a product and the ability to pay for it rather than those who share a national border.

Buyers in a segment seek similar benefits from and exhibit similar behavior in buying a product. Although these consumers may live in different areas of the world and come from very different backgrounds and value systems, they do have commonalities. Many of these similarities exist in lifestyle. By targeting to consumer markets, firms are able to address all consumers while spanning national boundaries.

Nestlé has globalized its Nescafé brand of coffee. "What coffee means to a culture, when it is consumed and how often it is consumed, varies throughout different cultures" (Moreira, 1986). Although coffee is a part of almost every culture, its capacity varies in each part of the world. In coffee cultures such as the U.S. and West Germany, instant coffee is not an automatically accepted product. In some countries, Nescafé has to prove that its coffee was made from real coffee as opposed to synthetic materials.

Nestlé made Nescafé a global brand by overcoming all of these various differences. By having a brand or product available for whatever kind of coffee drinker exists and for every occasion in which coffee is consumed, global appeal prevailed. Nescafé has successfully sold "coffeeness" in order to compete with European leaders such as Jacobs and Tschibo. This theme associates aroma, warmth, and the ritual of coffee drinking which can apply to any consumer in the world (Moreira, 1986).

The forecast by some academics that there will be eventually one world market is heard less today than it once was. However, there has been an increase in the number of homogeneous consumer groups. Ted Levitt refers to this as segment simultaneity (Pickholz, 1986). This concept describes a world made of market segments appearing in different countries or regions at the same time. The sharing of needs and wants and the existence of these homogeneous consumer groups is exemplified by the acceptance of brands such as Levis, Pepsi, Coca-Cola, and Sony.

Global Positioning Strategies

Marketing to consumer groups requires positioning. Does a firm want its product to be positioned the same in all markets? Should uniform positions be a goal of MNE's in their efforts to market globally (Pickholz, 1986)? What portfolio of global advertising agencies and local agencies is best able to meet the needs of these MNE's?

Many European firms have chosen to position their products the same in all markets. Mercedes Benz, B.M.W., and Miele Company, all domiciled in West Germany, have positioned their products as high quality, expensive, prestige products. In a survey of five European countries, consumers named these three brand names as the most recognized brand names in Europe (Blackwell and Talarzyk, 1990). All are associated with quality and represent the top of the line in their respective product categories, whether it be automobiles or appliances. All three companies have positioned their products similarly in all markets.

Yet some firms have chosen to position their products differently in different markets. A firm may choose to position itself as a low price competitor in one market and as a high quality product in another market. But if the brand is truly a global brand, inconsistency may create image problems and confusion in the minds of the consumer.

Ford of Europe has positioned its cars differently in various European countries. For example, in England, Ford automobiles are considered to be a top of the line, prestige car; whereas in Germany, the Ford is viewed as an average to lower end automobile. Ford is positioned as luxury in England, but transportation in Germany, two different positions in two different markets (Engel, Blackwell, and Miniard, 1990).

THINKING GLOBALLY, ACTING LOCALLY

Many firms find it profitable to market globally, using global advertising in their efforts. Global advertising "assumes that modern communication and rapid travel have homogenized the world and that the ads that work well in one place will work equally well anywhere else" (*Marketing News*, 1988). Yet, very few truly global brands exist.

Many mega agencies are promoting the idea of a global approach for global brands to all of their clients. Yet this uniform concept for every product in every market around the world seems rather narrow. The benefits of cost efficiency and economies of scale sway many agencies to promote this idea. These advantages can only be recognized, however, if the advertising is equally relevant in each market. If ads are not effective in certain markets, then the efficiency is diluted (Jordan, 1989).

Planning Globally

John Deere promotes its products with a globalized, single-strategy advertising campaign because the message to be communicated to each market is primarily the same throughout the world. The nature of the product, the tractor, is such that it is used and perceived similarly in nearly all markets (Jordan, 1989). This lends itself well to a global strategy. The result is a uniform image worldwide.

Acting Locally

The key is to think globally but act locally. For some products, acting locally may result in the same strategy in all markets as it has for John Deere. But just as it is not safe to say that all the world is one marketplace, it is also not safe to say that all groups of people are the same. Consumers are beginning to adopt some of the same lifestyles, but culture and traditional values do not disappear. Marketers must consider these differences when creating effective ads and relevant messages.

McDonald's is considered to be a global brand, yet it practices a local plan of attack when operating in foreign countries. Although McDonald's utilizes a global strategy by offering its basic product line to all markets and consumers, it has modified its line to suit tastes and preferences as required. For example, McSpaghetti is offered in the Philippines because it was discovered that Filipinos consider this a treat (Engel, Blackwell, and Miniard, 1990).

Coca-Cola, a name recognized all around the world, represents yet another global brand. However, a commercial for Coke that features 1,000 singing children was edited 21 different ways for broadcast overseas, because "most products cannot be successfully advertised through a single, uniform campaign without generating 'culture clash'" (*Marketing News*, 1988), not even Coca-Cola.

The appeals used in an advertisement may be appropriate in one country and not in another. For example, a Nivea print advertisement was published in the United States and was ultimately banned from further publication due to what in the U.S. is considered indecent exposure. The same message and image had been used in Germany, however, without any controversy. The advertisers failed to consider that what is appropriate, accepted, and allowed in one country may not be in another.

Winning with Global Advertising

What conclusions can be drawn from the study of case examples and the application of marketing theory? We suggest that certain advertising messages and specific product characteristics tend to be suited better than others for a globalized advertising approach. These characteristics are summarized as follows:

1. The communications message is based on similar lifestyles.
2. The appeal of the ad is to basic human needs and emotions.
3. The product satisfies universal needs and desires.
4. Company personnel should have a globalized perspective.

The emergence of unified Europe has caused critics to speculate on the degree of homogeneity in this new market. It is important to realize how rapidly the world is changing in its attitudes about many aspects of life, thanks to "the accelerating spiral of global information" (Earle, 1986). Television, films, and music are being shared by people all around the world, enhancing global convergence in the areas of culture, demographics, and habits. The Berlin Wall probably came down more because of telephones and television than debates over the economic philosophies of Marx or Lenin.

One argument suggests that universal marketing will work in the cases where media type and media level of penetration are parallel between home and host country. For example, Belgium and the U.K. have 468 radios and 993 radios per 1000 people respectively (Loyola College, Maryland, 1989). With the levels of media growing and the media itself becoming globally universal, there is a greater likelihood of international marketing and advertising succeeding through these channels.

Many observers believe that the cultural barriers between countries will continue to weaken with the increased use of "high-power, direct broadcast TV satellites throughout Europe" (Loyola College, Maryland, 1989). Cultural convergence will be enhanced by the freer access to international television and the absence of language barriers. It is not uncommon to hear a television ad in Europe that includes a direct response phone number for each of a large number of countries.

We propose, however, that neither Europe nor the world can be considered one marketplace. In spite of the tendency of some to treat them as such, Europe consist of distinct countries with cultures, values, and traditions of their own. Consumers in Europe and much of the rest of the world are becoming more receptive to foreign products and lifestyles, but still retain unique value systems that require communication and marketing programs to be localized in many ways.

It has been observed that when individuals begin to travel and experience other ways of life and then return to their native country, their perception of the home country is far more favorable than before. A renewed cultural identity and reinforcement takes place when the person realizes that life in an admired country isn't really that wonderful and that life at home really isn't that bad.

In the past decade, Americans have begun to discover something about themselves that foreign visitors have always known: "We are a nation of culturally diverse regions. It may be that brand loyalty, like patriotism, begins at home–or pretty close to home" (Fenn, 1987). American consumers continue to take pride in their local communities by supporting local brands, such as Cape Cod Potato Chips, Soho Natural Soda, and Ben & Jerry's Homemade Ice Cream. These local brands have become national because of an increased desire to adopt other region's products.

This rediscovery of local color has increased the shared interest in regional products. Marilyn Block, vice president of the Naisbitt Group, a Washington, D.C.-based research firm, states that although regional pride may have always existed, it is becoming more evident now (Fenn, 1987).

If French, British, Germans, Italians, and Swedes are all treated the same and viewed as EUROPE instead of separate countries, there will be a tendency to polarize as each seeks identity in its traditional cultures and values. Perhaps the regional product in the U.S. can be equated with products produced in France or Spain. Forecasts in future trends in the European market will be fraught with great difficulty if Europe is treated as a generic market. Advertisers must be sensitive to these possibilities. Global advertisers directing efforts to the masses may alienate potential consumers if not sensitive to a peoples' cultural identity and pride. Ray Higgs, marketing director for Rothman's International, states that national pride is rising rather than declining and when developing new campaigns, advertising agencies will ignore this at their peril (Higgs, 1984).

MERGER MANIA AND THE EMERGENCE OF MEGA AGENCIES

Mega agencies have emerged in recent years as a response to the global marketing needs and activities of MNE's. Global mega agencies are defined as advertising and public relations agencies operating on a worldwide basis through a portfolio of institutions with a local, regional, and international scope.

Why have so many advertising agencies merged to become mega agencies? Ted Levitt attributes the phenomenon to the basic idea that "you want to be close enough to the client, whether their headquarters are in Chicago, Stuttgart or Tokyo. There are certain kinds of local adaptations that you may have to have, and to have the local presence to do some of that becomes important. The idea is to have a kind of similarity" (Chakravarty, 1986).

One of the first agencies to act on this trend of perceived global marketing needs was Saatchi & Saatchi Compton Worldwide. For the Saatchis, it was no longer good enough to grow by expanding client lists. Rather, growth was facilitated by acquisition. The recent move by Saatchi & Saatchi to consolidate, restructure, and strengthen its offices in the west with regional headquarters in San Francisco was a globally minded measure aimed at positioning itself for Pacific Rim business. A Saatchi official comments that "clients have [are] looking to the Far East and clients on the Far East [are] looking to market here" *(The Economist,* December, 1989).

Some industry leaders see the race to grow simply as one for the sake of growth. The Saatchis seemed to create a phobia among agencies of "acquire or be acquired." Agencies did not want to be the leftovers as mega agencies were choosing team members, being forced to merge with mismatched agencies simply for survival.

With the globalization of business and the presence of acquisition phobia, advertising agencies recognized the significance of global advertising and its potential effects on the industry. Backer & Spiel-vogel was excluded from the competition for the United Technolo-gies, Chase Manhattan Bank, Merrill Lynch, and Hasbro toy ac-counts because of a lack of international marketing capabilities, says agency Chairman Carl Spielvogel. He had also watched as McCann-Erickson launched a Brazilian Coca-Cola campaign and ultimately won the account because of its international advertising success (Reed, 1986).

Has bigger been better for advertising's mega agencies? Saatchi & Saatchi announced 1989 profits significantly lower than in 1988. After a reorganization charge, it reported a post-tax loss of $24 million in 1989 against a 1988 profit of $139 million *(The Econo-mist,* May 1989). Since its acquisition spree, Saatchi & Saatchi has lost the Colgate-Palmolive account with billings estimated at $110 million, and Procter & Gamble later announced that it would be pulling $85 million worth of accounts, notably Luvs diapers, Bounty paper towels, and Crisco oil (Koepp, 1986).

Not all acquisitions lead to problems merely in areas of creativi-ty, client conflicts of interest, and loss of accounts. WPP's acquisi-tion of J. Walter Thompson created problems in management, prov-ing to be just as challenging to remedy as the traditional consequences of acquisition *(The Economist,* May 1989). Quality consistency and control are areas that continue to challenge the success of mega agencies.

A different strategic approach was exhibited by Interpublic Group of Companies. Interpublic permitted its advertising agencies to remain separate, while combining such activities as media buy-ing to create economies of scale through combined purchasing power *(Advertising Age,* 1988). This strategy permits diversifica-tion and specialized client services, while minimizing client confi-dentiality concerns. The disadvantage of this strategy is less control for the parent and the potential for a lack of global perspective within the individual agencies. The parent must be able to pool the talents of the organization and use them across the international borders, but the structures depend more on informal interactions than formal organization and control.

The consolidation of corporations spanning international bound-aries is based on a shaky set of premises, argues futurist and author

Alvin Toffler. He explains that it is based on two basic ideas: economies of scale and synergy. Both are increasingly dubious, if not obsolete economically, Toffler argues. By getting big, you get slow. Toffler adds that it is too easily assumed that one message can cross all cultural borders (Cox, 1989).

Winning the Global Advertising Race

So how do we characterize the true winners of this race? Is the race won simply on profitability? If so, then mega agencies, as a whole, have not fared so well. Or is it won on size? If so, Saatchi & Saatchi is one of the largest and, therefore, a winner.

From the perspective of the client, globalization appears best-suited to products that can be standardized from country to country. However, many products must be specialized to adapt to differing international markets and their advertising must reflect this specialization. The best advertising agencies to meet specialized requirements are those that are located in the market area and that have the greatest understanding of the target market.

Finally, perhaps another definition of winning is meeting the needs of the MNE's without the traditional problems that plague the mega agencies. The merger game may turn out to benefit the supposedly endangered mid-sized agencies the most (Kovach, 1986). Smaller agencies have a greater chance of landing domestic accounts as the mega agencies focus on international accounts. Because of the conflict of interest existing in many of the mega agencies, clients transfer accounts to smaller agencies where representation of competing brands is rare. If a client represents the largest account for a mid-sized agency, a greater amount of bargaining power is ensured as well. It may be the mid-sized agencies that are the true winners of the race.

SOLUTION: GLOBAL AGENCY NETWORKS

The solution to the advertising agency controversy for many global marketers will probably be the development of or linkage with a global agency network. The nature of the network may vary considerably but often will consist of a portfolio of advertising agencies (and public relations agencies, as well).

The nature and structure of global communications agencies should and most probably will follow the nature and structure of global markets and marketing strategies. As the first part of this chapter described, markets exhibit increasing similarities. Similarities in lifestyles and buying behavior allow some MNE's to adopt globalized communications efforts, with an attendant need to project similar messages to all or many of their consumers. While the strategy may be global, the implementation often requires a localized approach that places emphasis on the differences among segments within these cross-cultural consumer groups.

The cross-cultural analysis involves both a global and localized reality of marketing. Agency selection and use will require the same. Thus, our prediction is that mega agencies will require a portfolio of institutions, with a major component of the portfolio agencies that can provide the cultural empathy and knowledge of local market structures necessary to implement global strategies on a local basis.

Marketers with a global vision may select a domestic or localized advertising agency, but increasingly it will probably be one that maintains a global network of agencies available to the agency and its client. This network decreases the probability of marketing mistakes occurring due to a lack of knowledge or misinterpretation of a culture. Franchising offers a potential approach to a controlled network of agencies while retaining the advantages of individual ownership and local expertise.

Global clients will often require a portfolio of agencies. For some clients, the portfolio will be satisfied by one relationship to a mega agency and its portfolio. Other clients will find it more effective to relate to a portfolio of their own creation to achieve a network of agencies that will allow the client to plan globally and act locally.

REFERENCES

Advertising Age. (1988). Mega-Shops Set Global Media Test, (March), 2.

Blackwell, R. and Talarzyk, W. (1990). *Contemporary Cases in Consumer Behavior.* Chicago: The Dryden Press.

Blackwell, R. and Talarzyk, W. (1983). Lifestyle Retailing, *Journal of Retailing*, 59(4), 7-27.

Bouvier, L. (1984). Planet Earth 1984-2034: A Demographic Vision, *Population Bulletin*, (February), 39.

Buzzell, R. (1986). Can You Standardize Multinational Marketing? *Harvard Business Review*, (November-December), 46, 102-113; Also see Levitt, T. (1983). The Globalization of Markets, *Harvard Business Review*, (May-June), 61, 92-102; Multinationals Tackle Global Marketing. (1984). *Advertising Age*, (June), 25, 50ff; and Marketers Turn Sour on Global Sales Pitch Harvard Guru Makes, (1988). *Wall Street Journal*, (May), 1.

Chakravarty, S. (1986). The Croissant Comes to Harvard Square, *Forbes*, (July), 69.

Cox, J. (1989). Media Giants Rush for "Global" Reach, *USA Today*, (April), 1A.

Earle, R. (1986). Global Advertising, *Madison Avenue*, 40-44.

The Economist. (May 1989). Bowtie versus Calculator, 64.

The Economist. (December 1989). The Saatchi Brothers Retreat, 54.

Elinder, E. (1965). How International Can European Advertising Be? *Journal of Marketing*, (April), 29, 7-11.

Engel, J., Blackwell, R. and Miniard, P. (1990). *Consumer Behavior*. Chicago: The Dryden Press.

Fatt, A. (1967). The Danger of "Local" International Advertising, *Journal of Marketing*, (January), 31, 60-62.

Fenn, D. (1987). The Rediscovery of Local Pizzazz, *Working Woman*, (July), 66-70.

Griffin, T. (1987). *International Marketing Communication Planning–A Focus on Substructure*, International Conference of the Academy of Marketing Sciences, Barcelona.

Higgs, R. (1984). Not Yet a Global Village, *Marketing*, (September), 40-45.

Jordan, J. (1989). Translating the Human Touch, *Madison Avenue*, 46.

Koepp, S. (1986). The Not-So-Jolly Advertising Giants, *Time*, (November), 73.

Kovach, J. (1986). More Mega-Mergers, *Industry Week*, (August).

Leontiades, J. (1986). Going Global–Global Strategies vs. National Strategies, *Long Range Planning*, 19, 96-104.

Levitt, T. (1983). The Globalization of Markets, *Harvard Business Review*, (May-June), 61, 91-201. For the contrasting perspective see Wind, Y. (1986). The Myth of Globalization, *Journal of Consumer Marketing*, (Spring) 3, 23-26.

Link, G. (1988). Global Advertising: An Update, *Journal of Consumer Marketing*, (Spring), 5, 69-74.

Marketing News. (1988). Ad Exec: Going Global Is Not Always the Best Choice an Agency Can Make, (August 1).

McCarthy, M. (1989). As Global Marketer, Coke Excels by Being Tough and Consistent, *Wall Street Journal*, (December).

Moreira, M. (1986). Global Advertising, *Review of Business*, (Fall), 26-27.

Pickholz, J. (1986). The End of the World: Market Segmentation Is Changing the Way the World Turns, *Direct Marketing*, (September), 42-45.

Plumber, J. (1977). Consumer Focus in Cross-National Research, *Journal of Marketing*, (November), 5-15.

Porter, M., ed. (1986). *Competition in Global Industries*. Cambridge, MA: Harvard Business School Press.

Potential for International Advertising Standardization: An Empirical Investigation of the Role of Media. (1989). AI 13 Northwest Chapter Annual Meeting, Loyola College in Maryland, (June 5-6).

Prus, R. (1989). *Pursuing Customers: An Ethnography of Marketing Activities.* Newbury Park, CA: Sage Publications.

Reed, J. (1986). Selling Soap on a Global Stage, U.S. *News & World Report,* (May), 49-50.

Sorenson, R. and Wiechmann, U. (1975). How Multinationals View Marketing Standardization, *Harvard Business Review,* (May-June), 53, 38-56. Also see Davidson, W. and Haspeslagh, P. (1982). Shaping a Global Product Organization, *Harvard Business Review,* (July-August), 60, 125-132.

World Population Data Sheet. (1987). Population Reference Bureau, Inc.

Chapter 12

Toward an Understanding of the Use of Foreign Words in Print Advertising

Nina M. Ray
Mary Ellen Ryder
Stanley V. Scott

SUMMARY. This chapter addresses the possible effects on consumers of words from a foreign language in print advertisement. With the emergence of the unified Europe, much attention is focused on "pan-European" advertising strategies that attempt to make a product appear as "European" as possible rather than be perceived as Spanish, French, or Italian. We investigate the possible linguistic rationales for and against the use of foreign language words and phrases in ads aimed primarily at a monolingual audience. We also discuss implications for further research and possible effects marketers should consider when combining languages in an advertisement.

INTRODUCTION

As the European Community (EC) emerges more unified, most internal trade barriers are being dismantled and common external trade rules are ideally in effect. The United States, too, is being strongly affected by the unification, and must find new ways to become "Europeanized" itself. In one sense, such Europeanization has been ongoing in advertisements for some time. Marketers have been using foreign languages, especially European languages, in more and more advertising campaigns.

English names for products and businesses are quite common in ads throughout Europe and Latin America (Harris, Sturm, Klassen, and Bechtold, 1986). Here we offer several examples from Spanish publications. One is a jeans advertisement in English with the main information in Spanish (Figure 12.1); others are a Burberrys advertisement in English, with information on how to obtain the product in Spanish (Figure 12.2) and a Winston cigarette ad (Figure 12.3) that keeps the American name, but tells the reader in Spanish that the product is American (El genio sabor Americano), and presents the imagery in Spanish. There are also examples of ads with the combining of two languages in one line: the ad for "Solares Waterproof," with the remaining text completely in Spanish (Figure 12.4) and another for Ermenegildo Zegna, an Italian product, where English is used in combination with Spanish (Figure 12.5).

One can find similar cases where languages other than English are drawn on, in ads and for product names in the United States. These examples are not always grammatically correct. Harris et al. (1986) report on examples such as Le Tigré shirts (correct spelling is le tigre, without an accent). Mexican restaurants may be named El Casa, even though the correct spelling would be *la casa*. Since English contains no accents or gender markings, these names are marked as foreign, and thus "classy." Sometimes foreign words are also included, even when it is extremely unlikely that the American public will understand their meaning. For example, we have the recent campaigns of Volkswagen extolling *Fahrvergnügen* and of Mazda making claims about *Kansei* engineering. Another American example is Yoplait's campaign a few years ago. In various commercials, famous Americans were speaking *French* in the ads promoting Yoplait. While the surprise of a famous American speaking French must have served as an attention-getting device, it is almost certainly the case that most of the viewers understood little or nothing of what was being said.

Volkswagen, in its promotional brochures, describes Fahrvergnügen as "Description of a pleasurable sensation experienced when a car and its driver are in mutual harmony; A unique driving experience; Pleasure; Satisfaction; A feeling experienced by Volkswagen drivers." This description is certainly close to official translations of the German words involved. *Fahren* means to drive a

FIGURE 12.1. Advertisement for Pepe Jeanswear (*Marie Claire 1990b*)

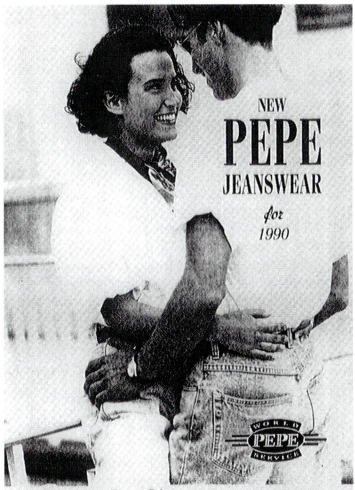

car or train, and *vergnügen* means pleasure, enjoyment, and entertainment (Langenscheidt, 1969). While Mazda makes little attempt
to translate Kansei engineering in its promotion, Koyima and Takebayashi (1984) define *kansei* as "to finish," "to complete," "per-
fection," "shout of joy," or "nice, quiet."

FIGURE 12.2. Advertisement for Burberrys (*Marie Claire* 1990a)

The mixture of foreign languages with the native one is often found in Italian ads as well. The words and phrases used are not exclusively drawn from English. For example, Figure 12.6 incorporates the French word "Parfum" in an ad appearing in an Italian magazine. However, English seems to be by far the most popular language used in Italian advertising. Note that even in the "Parfum" ad, the French word is embedded in a text written completely in English; the headline reads "The sun is high enough to start the day" and the bottom text says "The Parfum."

Even a casual tourist in Italy will notice the extensive use of English language expressions and words in Italian advertising. Examples of commercial phrases written completely in English abound. For example, one of the authors of this chapter remembers the recent appearance in Italy of billboards with "Dr. Pepper: Welcome from America" and "Merry Christmas from Marlboro Country." Even more interesting are the phrases in "Itangliano" (Dunlop, 1989), "Englotalian" (Mewshaw, 1988) or "Italiese" (Titone, 1988). These are slogans or names of products that make use of both Italian and English. One example containing such slogans is shown in Figure 12.7. Here, the ad is for an Italian product (Benetton), with its headline in English, but text containing information as to where one can find the product is in Italian. Figure 12.8 is an example of an English product advertising in an Italian publication. Again, while the headline is in English, Italian is used to help the consumer locate the product. Italian ads have also used American logos, even in places where they seem completely inappropriate to an outsider. Mewshaw (1988) reports that one cigarette company uses an American stop sign as its logo. Dunlop (1989, p. 33) mentions an extremely interesting example of a mixture of the two languages in a lingerie show window in Parma:

> Printed decoratively across the front of the nightie was the apparently nonsense legend: "Happiness in estate." The perpetrator had no idea that *estate* is an English word, but was using the Italian word *estate* (three syllables), meaning "summer."

A few (Dunlop, 1989; Mewshaw, 1988) have hypothesized about the reasons for this influx of English into Italian advertising, but no one has come to any sound conclusions as to why it is done, especially in places where it seems that the message will be inappropriate or even meaningless to the Italian consumer. Mewshaw (1988) suggests, perhaps only half seriously, that the use of the stop sign to advertise cigarettes could only happen in a country like Italy, where the people always attempt to do the opposite of what they are told,

FIGURE 12.3. Advertisement for Winston (*El Europeo* 1990c)

FIGURE 12.4. Advertisement for Solares Waterproof (*Marie Claire* 1990c)

but this explanation will hardly suffice for the general phenomenon of English intrusion into Italian advertising.

O'Shaughnessy and Holbrook (1988, p. 197) report a "linguistic turn" in social science that has forced "thinkers in a wide range of disciplines to recognize the manner in which language shapes the course and meaning of the human condition." If language plays

FIGURE 12.5. Advertisement for Ermenegildo Zegna (*El Europeo* 1990a)

such an important role in behavior, the linguistic analysis of marketing and, in particular, advertising, should not be overlooked.

The objective of this chapter is to provide possible explanations of the use of foreign words in print advertising that is aimed primarily at monolingual audiences. We feel that reviewing both linguistic

FIGURE 12.6. Advertisement for Charro Perfume (*Panorama* 1989b)

FIGURE 12.7. Advertisement for Benetton (*Panorama* 1989a)

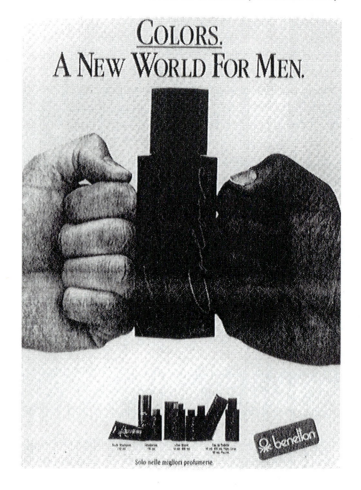

FIGURE 12.8. Advertisement for Chesterman (*Panorama* 1989c)

literature as well as the advertising literature will help to formulate a conceptual basis so that future researchers will have an underlying foundation on which to draw.

CONCEPTUAL FRAMEWORK

Advertising Explanations

Past research has shown that the misunderstanding of monolingual print ads is widespread; in some cases, up to 40% of print and television ads are misunderstood (Jacoby and Hoyer, 1987). It seems likely that using two languages in the same ad would increase the rate of misunderstanding. While two-language ads may attract the attention that the sponsor desires, they could be very confusing and might cause the readers to wonder which language they are reading and lead them to misunderstand the intended meaning of the ad. Given the fact that the average ad is viewed for only five to seven seconds, the consumer's confusion could be exacerbated by a two-language technique. If it is true that reading is a "psycholinguistic guessing game" (Suhor, 1984, p. 249), how much more of a random event is the interpretation of these ads? How much effort is the consumer really ready to exert deciphering the text? On the other hand, if he or she does exert the effort, the ad could be rehearsed just enough to remember the sponsor later (Schachter, 1989).

What we do know from the advertising literature (Stern, 1988) is that ungrammatical ads are thought to attract attention. They may just break through the advertising clutter. However, progressing along the advertising hierarchy of effects model (awareness, interest, evaluation, trial, adoption) certainly cannot be assured simply by attracting attention. How these ads are interpreted must be considered as well.

Also, concrete words appear to be more desirable than abstract terms, unless the abstract phrase evokes a sensory experience such as a mental visual image or sound. Past studies have found that the words "fantasy" or "dream" have a high imagery value (Percy, 1981). It is possible that understanding the English ad in the Italian shop window as "happiness in summer" could evoke many mental images equivalent to those produced by the word "fantasy. " However, it is very unlikely that the majority of people seeing the ad know enough English to even comprehend the words "happiness in." This would seem to indicate that the *epistemic* context (background knowledge shared by participants) (Harris et al., 1986) is almost nonexistent between the advertiser and the consumer.

One theory in favor of the use of two languages is that of script interruption. In both linguistic and advertising literature (Harris et al., 1986), examples abound of how, when various scenarios are interrupted by an unrelated set of events, the interruptions were remembered better than the main scenario itself. They report that advertisers may improve consumers' memory for key points in advertisements by inserting these key points as interruptions. With these interruptions, entirely new meaning or implications can be attached to the ad and this new implication might be the most memorable. Harris et al. (1986, p. 7) describe the process as follows:

> For example, the idea of script interruption may be applied to ads which use slogans, such as "Get Lucky." Suppose the advertiser wanted to suggest that Lucky Cola will not only increase one's luck in general but also with the opposite sex specifically. This may be accomplished by inserting a small picture in the corner of the ad showing one of the couples in the beach scene being amorous with each other in a dimly-lit apartment. The revised ad interrupts the reader's beach party script with a "sexual fantasy script." The result is that an entirely new meaning is attached to the slogan, and, according to some research, it is this new meaning which will be most memorable. In addition, the script may have guided the inference of a causal relationship between the cola and the love.

While studies concerning script interruption have not involved foreign languages in advertising, the insertion of a foreign word would most likely force a mental interruption in processing.

Linguistic Explanations

Code-Switching. At first glance, it seems possible that ads containing two languages are intended to be understood as examples of *code-switching*. Bilingual speakers often *code-switch*, that is, use two languages within a single utterance or discourse (Grosjean, 1982). While anyone learning a second language will occasionally resort to his or her first language when at a loss for a word, this is not true code-switching (Jacobson, 1982). Code-switching occurs only in the conversation of *balanced bilinguals*, people who speak both languages equally and fluently (Hakuta, 1986).

There are some characteristics of code-switching that might be relevant to its use in advertising. Although speakers are often unaware that they are code-switching, when they are aware, they report a variety of reasons for doing so. Most code-switching occurs in informal, even intimate situations, in conversations between friends and close relatives (Jacobson, 1982). Such an impression of intimacy could be exploited by marketers in selling a product. Speakers may switch a word or phrase because that element carries a different social or affective meaning in the two languages. Thus, a Mexican-American may choose to use the Spanish phrase "en México" rather than "in Mexico" because the connotations and set of associations for the "Mexico" in Spanish are quite different from those in English, in terms of affection and respect for the country, for example (Jacobson, 1982). In the same way, advertisers could use the associations of a word or phrase in a particular language to enhance their product. Bilingual speakers may do more extensive code-switching to identify themselves and those who can understand them as different and (in this context) superior to others who cannot understand such discourse or understand it only poorly. Thus, extensive use of code-switching was used by certain members of a Chicano student organization on the University of Texas campus whenever they wished their ideas to be adopted. The implication was that those using it were in some sense more truly Chicano than those whose Spanish was not as good, and therefore they had more right to dictate the activities of the organization (Limón, 1982). Thus, code-switching can be used to create solidarity between speaker and listener and influence the listener to take the speaker's views. The creation of this feeling of solidarity between the producers of a product and the consumer could conceivably have the same type of influence.

The possibility that ads with two languages are meant to be processed as code-switching discourse is strengthened by the fact that the ads' creators did not switch from one language to the other at random places in the text. Code-switching is governed by strict linguistic constraints. Speakers switch at natural constituent boundaries such as between a noun phrase and verb phrase, and the words in the less-used language within the text (e.g., the English words in a predominantly Spanish discourse) usually involve content words (nouns, adjectives, verbs) instead of function words (articles, prepositions, and conjunctions). In addition, the word order before and after a switching point must be possible in both languages (Poplack, 1982). The ads we have collected show the same linguistic constraints found in code-switching.

If these ads are intended for a bilingual audience, they may suffer from some disadvantages. While it is still an open question as to whether code-switching always makes language processing more difficult (Grosjean, 1982), there has been some research done that seems to show that it takes longer to read passages with code-switching than equivalent monolingual ones (Grosjean and Soares, 1986). One reason for this may be a priming effect created by the first language used (Simpson, Peterson, Casteel, and Burgess, 1989). Grosjean and Soares (1986) found that more stimuli were categorized as French when the prior phrase was French and more were categorized as English when preceded by English words. Given the short amount of time generally given to processing ads, this would seem to be a serious disadvantage in an advertisement.

Code-switching can have another negative connotation. Many monolinguals consider it to be substandard language. For example, Gibbons (1987) found that in Hong Kong, switching between Cantonese and English among university students is quite common. However, student subjects who used the mixed code frequently themselves rated code-switching speakers to be less well mannered, more aggressive, and more inclined to show off than monolingual speakers. Therefore, advertisers do risk some negative consumer reactions with the use of mixed language advertising.

In short, the use of two languages in an advertisement might create positive feelings in bilingual speakers, through the affective aspects of the meanings of some of the words used, and through the creation of a feeling of solidarity between the presumably bilingual creator of the ad and the bilingual reader. However, such positive effects might be partially or completely negated by the greater length of processing time and chance of misidentification of words that is apparently inherent in texts with code-switching, as well as the possible negative emotional reactions to code-switching.

If these ads are meant for bilingual audiences, however, they are going to have much more serious problems than those just suggested. While it may be true that 26% of Italians and 21% of Spaniards read at least a little English (Mitchell, 1984), it is very unlikely that many of them are balanced bilinguals. Since only 1% of Italians and 3% of Spaniards claim to read English fluently, (Mitchell, 1984), it seems unlikely that these consumers will even understand many of the words in these ads, as the advertisers have made no effort to stick to a *basic vocabulary*, words that would have a high probability of being in the low-level English speaker's repertoire (Carter and McCarthy, 1988). Nor does it seem reasonable that the advertisers should want to give the impression of a beginning speaker who cannot get his or her message across in one language or the other and therefore must resort to a halting use of both.

Surely the creators of these ads containing foreign words and phrases are aware of the relatively small numbers of fluent, literate bilinguals in their market, and are aiming the ads primarily if not exclusively at the monolinguals, who form the great majority of their prospective buyers. Yet if these advertisers are targeting monolingual audiences, they may have a serious problem to consider. If few of the ad's readers are going to recognize the message as code-switching, or be able to interpret the foreign language portion, why are the advertisers using this format? The most likely answer is that the foreign words and phrases have a value in an ad that is independent of their meaning. Let us investigate this second hypothesis.

Borrowing. Linguists have long known that languages have varying degrees of prestige. Lambert's (1960) classic experiments with English and French in Canada showed this. He taped French/English bilinguals reading equivalent texts in each language. The tapes were then played for French and English speakers, who were asked to rate the speakers on such dimensions as good/bad or educated/ uneducated. Even though the same speaker was used for both the English and the French texts, the ratings of that speaker differed with the language used. Both English- and French-speaking subjects rated the speaker more positively when English was used than when French was. While it is true that the subjects understood the meaning of at least one of the tapes, clearly, meaning did not affect the results, since the same text was used in both cases.

While Lambert's experiment dealt with bilinguals, there is also evidence that a foreign language can have an effect on a speech community even when that community is essentially monolingual. This evidence comes from a study of *borrowing*, the permanent adoption of words or phrases from one language or dialect into another. There are two basic reasons for borrowing to take place (Hock, 1986). One is *need*. If a speech community adopts a new technological device, or a new religious or cultural concept, it may well adopt the originating culture's name for it at the same time. The second reason is *prestige*. By adopting terms from an appropriate foreign language into their own speech, people can show that they are cosmopolitan, educated, or up-to-date (Hock, 1986). What language is appropriate has depended in part on the period of history in which borrowing took place. Latin and secondarily Greek were the prestigious foreign languages throughout the Middle Ages, and to a certain extent have stayed prestigious through modern times. French and Italian achieved ascendancy during the late Middle Ages and the Renaissance, and then French became the language of court and nobility, and later of diplomacy, during the eighteenth and nineteenth centuries (Kahane, 1982). After World War II, English began to supersede French as the prestige foreign language in Europe (Fishman, 1982; Hock, 1986).

Partly due to their historical roles, different languages have contributed to different semantic areas in the vocabularies of borrowing groups. Since Latin was for centuries the language of scholarship, Latin words have been borrowed for educational, technological, and scientific terms. In modern times, German has joined Latin as a language of science, based on the worldwide respect for German engineering that began with their technological advancements made during World War II. The economic preeminence of Italy during the Renaissance caused a number of Italian financial terms to be borrowed, while an enduring admiration for Italy's music and art has caused many Italian aesthetic terms to be borrowed over several centuries. And as the language of the political and social center of Europe, French has contributed words to governmental and legal domains as well as those dealing with fashion and the arts (Pyles and Algeo, 1982). For example, Germany, following its defeat in the Thirty Years' War and World War I, borrowed an enormous amount of vocabulary from the languages of its conquerors, especially from French. The borrowed words had to do both with war (e.g., Schergeant" [sergeant]) and with culture and intellectuality (e.g., "Alamode-Cavalir" [fashionable gentleman]) (Hock, 1986).

Since World War II, America has played many of the roles just mentioned: military conqueror, technical innovator, economic force, and exporter of culture, at least the culture of American popular music and clothing styles. As a result, it is not surprising that words from English and especially American English are being borrowed into many European languages, even in the face of official discouragement (Kahane, 1982). Following is an Italian example (Dunlop, 1989) that shows clear evidence of borrowing of English words for business terms:

> collaborano con il loro *staff*, recepiscono ogni *input* per incrementare le proprie *skills* e acquirire nuovi *know-how* (collaborate with their staff, receive each input to increase their own skills and gain new know-how)

A more extensive example from Germany is given by Kahane (1982):

> One typical issue of the German weekly, *Der Spiegel* (April 29, 1974), contained more than 160 Americanisms, covering primarily American business organization, its cult of efficiency, and its hectic informal style of life, with a stress on both social relations and technology. Characteristic examples of business organization: *Team, Broker, Promoter, Service.* Terminology of efficiency: *Know-how, Trend, Test, Lobby.* Social

psychology: *Image, Fan, Stress, Backlash.* Fads: *Jogger, Jeans, Rock, Afro-look.* Technology: *Hifi, Instant-on, After-shave Lotion, Bulldozer.*

Recently, while visiting Spain, one of us saw advertisements for *The Madrid Business School: Master en Business Administration.* Even though this school was attempting to appeal to Spaniards, every word in this title is written in English, except for the preposition "en."

Unlike code-switching, borrowing is a phenomenon found among all speakers, both bilingual and monolingual, although the small bilingual population may supply the "bridge" by which the words pass into the vocabularies of the rest of the population.

What does this phenomenon of borrowing have to do with the use of foreign words in advertising? Foreign words from the different languages have a special force in those semantic domains to which they have contributed the most: Latin and Greek words represent science and therefore factuality and truth; French and Italian words represent beauty, culture, and cosmopolitanism. While advertisers are probably not trying to introduce foreign words into the consumer's language permanently, the same motivations that cause words to be borrowed may well make them effective in advertisements. For example, the connection of Latin and Greek with science has long been exploited by English-speaking advertisers. In Victorian times, pseudo-Latin and Greek terms appeared in hundreds of advertisements to impress a public who held the classical languages in high regard, even, or perhaps especially, when the readers were not familiar enough with them to understand the meanings of the invented terms. "Teeth were stopped with 'mineral marmoratum'; raincoats were 'siphonias'; hair cream was an 'aromatic regenerator'; hair dye was an 'atrapilatory'" (Hughes, 1988). Modern brand names take the same linguistic advantage; consider names such as the cold medicine NeoSynephrine, Acutrim Diet Formula, and Neosporin, which contains Polymixin B-Sulfate.

Due to their modern connotations, both German and Japanese can also be used to convey an impression of scientific and engineering excellence, as in the Mazda campaign promising *Kansei* engineering or the Volkswagen campaigns using *Fahrvergnügen.* One source (*Who's News*, 1990) reports that the latter campaign has been a success and Volkswagen plans to extend it. The linguistic interpretation is that "since the cars *sound* German, they are built with high-quality German engineering" (p. 2). Although the sales staff for both companies are well-briefed on the meanings of the foreign terms, a number of prospective Volkswagen and Mazda customers ask what *Fahrvergnügen* and *Kansei* mean (John Dowdle, Joe Sedillo, personal communication), which shows that it is not the actual meaning of the word that has brought them in, since that is still unknown at the time the people come to the dealership.

Cosmetic products, underwear, and cooking products often have French names that are generally not understood by the consumer, who only knows that French-sounding terms are associated with the best in fashion, cuisine, and the arts. After all, many of the most essential words in these areas, such as "chic," "lingerie" and "sauté" are French borrowings, whose "foreignness" and even "Frenchness" is still recognizable to many people who do not speak French (Hock, 1986). The use of French in the Yoplait ads already mentioned is an example of the *identification* rather than comprehension of French as an advertising device. In at least some cases, the advertisers seem quite aware that the public may partially or completely misunderstand the foreign words, since, if they are translated correctly, the result is either semantically or grammatically odd. For example, a U.S. fashion advertisement ran: "Go ahead. We derrière you to try the chic French look of our famous N'est ce pas French fit jeans . . ." (Hughes, 1988), where the noun "derrière" is used as a verb, capitalizing on its similarity to the English verb "dare." Notice, too, that the brand name, a phrase meaning "isn't that true?" has no meaningful connection to jeans.

What does English, perhaps especially American English, stand for in the minds of even monolingual European speakers? We can estimate its image by looking at English words already borrowed into European languages. The majority of "Americanisms" are terms in the areas of mass media, pop art, economics, business, the consumer society, technology, and the lifestyle of the young (Kahane, 1982). For example, the jeans ad mentioned earlier (Figure 12.1) could be an appeal specifically aimed at the young. In addition, as a result of its status as an international language, English is seen as the most suitable language for science, international diplomacy, industry/commerce, high oratory, and pop songs (Cooper and Fishman, 1977). This image of the English language is separate from the meanings of individual English words. Anecdotal evidence supporting this comes from an ex-student of one of the authors of this chapter. This Swiss student in an English-as-a-second-language program in San Diego stated that she loved American and English rock songs until she learned the words. Until then, they seemed glamorous and exciting, but the words, once understood, were really boring and trite. Clearly, the glamour and excitement resided in the language itself, not in the meaning.

An extreme example of the use of the English language as separate from its meaning is the name for a brand of Italian leisure-wear, Honky. The company even sponsors a professional basketball team and neither the team members nor Italian shoppers appear to know or care that "honky" is a derogatory racial term (Mewshaw, 1988). Perhaps it is simply a name or label that was chosen with no regard as to how it would translate in other languages. Examples experienced by American companies come to mind such as when Esso discovered that its name meant "stalled car" in Japanese, and the translation of the car name "Nova" to "it doesn't go" in Spanish-speaking countries.

In short, just as Latin and French words have been used to create reliable or glamorous images respectively even when the readers did not know what they meant, so English words may be included in ads for primarily monolingual audiences to suggest to the buyer that he or she is cosmopolitan, a part of the lifestyle of the young, conspicuous consumer that is so connected with Americans. To do this, the language need only be identified as English; no further message is necessary.

IMPLICATIONS FOR RESEARCH

As we have shown thus far in this chapter, the basic premise that use of a foreign language that has prestige value will enhance an ad can be supported by evidence in small part from code-switching and in much greater part from linguistic borrowing. Clearly, the advertisers who are using these foreign words believe that such enhancement takes place. However, controlled research into the effects on both monolingual and bilingual audiences from ads with and without foreign words would strengthen this claim. Are the English elements in Italian ads easily understood by the bilingual consumer, and, if so, do they create a good affect or a feeling of solidarity? Likewise, if these often rather trite English words and phrases were translated into Italian, would the ads' effectiveness decrease, as predicted by the literature on borrowing? A brief pilot project was done presenting ads we created using both English and Italian to fairly competent bilinguals.

A small group of volunteers (ten) in an industrial city of Northern Italy responded to possible advertising phrases. The phrases were constructed with words that could be interpreted as either Italian or English, but were used in conjunction with other English words in the phrase. The example "happiness in estate" mentioned earlier in this chapter was included. The respondents were asked to read each phrase and the interviewer recorded whether the "foreign" word was pronounced in Italian or English. Then, the respondent wrote some brief words describing what the phrase meant to him (all respondents were male).

The results seemed to show that interpretation of the ads was highly varied, with some interpretations seeming to be meaningless. For example, some interpretations of the "happiness in estate" ad were "the sea" and "happiness is everywhere." Moreover, there was no evidence that either the different nuances of the English words (as opposed to possible Italian counterparts) had an effect on the readers, or that they felt any intimacy or solidarity with the creator of the ads due to the code-switching. Further research needs to be conducted on advertisements using borrowed foreign words. Also, future researchers should include both monolinguals and bilinguals in any further studies.

Foster, Sullivan, and Perea (1989) advise avoiding colloquialisms and words with multiple meanings. Their study involved monolingual Hispanics in the United States and bilingual (Spanish/ English) speakers as well who were presented with advertisements completely in Spanish. No significant differences existed between the monolingual groups or bilingual groups on overall comprehension, fact comprehension, or inference comprehension. If these findings apply to the European environment, then both monolinguals and bilinguals would interpret ads written in the native language in similar ways. However, we do not know if their interpretations of two-language ads would differ.

An advertisement has many purposes, two of which are to attract the buyer's attention and to inform him or her of the product attributes. If English words and phrases are intended to catch the attention and create a receptive mood rather than to be understood, they will not carry the informative part of the ad. Instead, the important information will be in the native language, while the English words will mean relatively little. In the ads collected by the authors, this is the case; aside from the product name, the only other words in the foreign language contribute nothing significant to the meaning of the ad. For example, in the Spanish ad given in Figure 12.4, the phrase "High performance" could be deleted without even creating a gap in the ad's text. In fact, the text would be more coherent without it since its meaning seems somewhat irrelevant to the rest of the text: "un traje ligero, fresco y con tanta personalidad como el hombre que lo lleva" ('a light suit, fresh and with as much personality as the man who wears it'). More examples of such advertising would either strengthen or disconfirm this prediction.

Likewise, if the function of the use of English is to suggest the young, cosmopolitan, conspicuous consumer, the types of products in which it is used should be those designed for this kind of market. The products represented in our collection certainly support this. Many of them are luxury items: they are for men's cologne, jeans, quality leather products, watches, expensive suits, and video equipment. Two that are not luxury products are cigarettes and sun screen, both of which are connected in advertising primarily with the lifestyle of the young. Again, more research on this is needed, designing studies using either actual or hypothetical ads with English being paired with different types of products. For example, would advertisers use English in ads for household products, and if so, what would be the reaction of the prospective buyer?

In some of our collected ads, the only use of English is in the brand name. The use of English for brand names seems to be a subject of some disagreement. While Sony keeps its "handycam" name across cultures (Figure 12.9 shows a Handycam ad in Spanish), Unilever has a reputation for marketing its product under a variety of names. In the Netherlands, the brand is known as Radion, but in Spain it is Luzil and in Germany it is Omo. Its fabric softener is Cajoline in France, Coccolino in Italy, Kuschelweich in Germany, Mimosin in Spain, and Snuggle in the United States (Fraser, 1990). This change in name may be done in part to create a word that conforms to the sound patterns of the native language of the country, since English includes a number of sounds and sound combinations not found in other European languages. There are more motivations for the change than this, however. The intent in the various names for the fabric softener is to convey "cuddly softness" in each language. There appears to be a possible trade-off between native brand names, which can convey emotional meaning directly, and foreign brand names, which must do it indirectly with the affective value the language itself has. Further research is needed on which of these methods is more effective, and on whether relative effectiveness changes depending on the nature of the product.

Just as the use of English might have varying effects depending on the product, the same might be true for the type of consumer at which it is aimed. Since English appears to be a language with international prestige, it could influence an emotional response in the minds of the consumers. Stout and Leckenby (1988) recently reaffirmed the belief that consumers who have an emotional response to an ad have more favorable attitudes toward the ad and the brand. They also indicate a higher likelihood to purchase the product than those who show no emotional response.

Since it is clear that the value of borrowed words is often *solely* in their prestige, as the borrowing language already has adequate terms for items covered by the borrowings, introduction of words from a prestige language should enhance an advertisement, but will it do so for all socio-economic groups? It is often the middle and lower classes that are most receptive to foreign words. French words from the Middle Ages survived in the rustic Middle-Low German dialects; fashionable Italianisms spread from Venice's empire to Greek fishermen and farmers (Kahane, 1982). The greater adoption of foreign words by the least educated class may seem surprising at first, but there are at least two possible reasons for this phenomenon. First, there is the desire on the part of lower socioeconomic groups to appear to be higher in the social strata than they are. This is evidenced by such phenomena as the upgrading of dialect characteristics to a more prestigious variety under conditions that allow monitoring of speech (Fasold, 1984). If the lower socio-

FIGURE 12.9. Advertisement for Sony (*El Europeo* 1990b)

economic groups perceive use of foreign words as a sign of education as they do the use of more prestigious dialectal forms, they will
be eager to adopt them for that reason. A cause for distaste of
foreign words by some of the upper socio-economic groups is suggested by Hock (1986, p. 416):

> Linguistic nationalism has been embraced mainly by (a subset
> of) the elite, traditionally defined as the educated and those in
> political power. On the other hand, the general populace, as
> well as many sections of the elite, are less concerned with
> linguistic nationalism and more with the prestige of foreign,
> often international, culture and vocabulary.

In other words, some of the elite may see use of foreign words as
implying that the native language, and therefore the native culture
and society, are inferior to the foreign one, and will therefore fear
and resent the intrusion of foreign words into the native language.
This is clearly the case in the official stance of France on the use of
English words (Kahane, 1982). This would suggest that, while the
lower and middle classes might find the use of English words in an
ad attractive, some of the upper class would be offended. Are the
advertisers using English in their ads in Italy and Spain aiming at a
particular socio-economic group, and if so, is the use of English
helping or hurting them?

There are linguistic problems we have only briefly touched on in
borrowing words, even on a temporary basis, from one language
into another. One of the most obvious is that the sounds and sound
combinations in the words may be sufficiently different from those
in the borrowing language that the words are difficult to pronounce.
In the ads we have found, there has been no concession made to the
pronunciation differences between English and Italian. Certainly
the "Solares Waterproof" example in Figure 12.3 does not contain
a headline which would easily flow off the lips of a Spanish speaker. Is this because the words were never intended to be pronounced
in the first place, but merely recognized as English? Are English
words also appearing in *spoken* ads, and if so, do the kinds of words
chosen differ due to this problem? It is interesting to note in this
connection that of the two foreign slogans being used in the United
States, *Fahrvergnügen* and *Kansei*, the second is more in accord

with English pronunciation than the first. In fact, the former word when used in the television ads is pronounced without the umlauted u, making it sound somewhat more "English" without causing it to lose its German "flavor."

In short, much more research needs to be done on the interacting variables involved in the introduction of foreign words into ads, if we are to have a complete understanding of their positive or negative impact on the consumer.

CONCLUSION AND MANAGERIAL IMPLICATIONS

We have investigated the possible linguistic rationales for the use of foreign language words and phrases in print advertisements aimed primarily at a monolingual audience. While various aspects of both *code-switching* and *borrowing* theories are useful, we conclude that the use of the foreign language is mostly for prestige purposes. While advertisers may succeed in eliciting a feeling of eliteness and sophistication, some cautions are necessary. First, two-language ads could easily be misinterpreted. If important information crucial to the success of the product is contained in the foreign language, consumers may not perceive the information correctly. By using two languages, code-switching theory tells us that comprehension can be more difficult and some social ramifications could be exhibited. For instance, various groups of consumers could be insulted by the foreign "intrusions."

Until further research is conducted in this area, we recommend that advertisers proceed cautiously with two-language advertising. If a foreign language word or phrase is used, care should be taken that there is no evident "dual-meaning" (such as with the "happiness in estate" example). The important, information-loaded part of the ad should appear in the native language with the foreign phrases used only to attract attention and to indicate prestige. If the two languages are to be mixed together in the ad, changes from one to the other should occur at natural linguistic breaks, such as is done when bilingual speakers code-switch.

Naturally, no amount of speculation will take the place of valid testing of proposed ads with representative monolingual and bilingual consumers. Only they can shed light on the question of whether the two-language ads are having their intended effect.

REFERENCES

Carter, R. and McCarthy, M. (1988). *Vocabulary and Language Teaching*. London: Longman.

Cooper, R. L. and Fishman, J. A. (1977). English as a World Language: The Evidence. In *The Spread of English*, edited by J. A. Fishman, R. L. Cooper, A. W. Conrad et al. Rowley, MA: Newbury House.

Dowdle, J. Sales manager, Dennis Dillon Mazda. Boise, Idaho.

Dunlop, A. (1989). Parliamo Itangliano. *English Today*, 5(2), 32-35.

El Europeo (1990a, June). Advertisement for Ermenegildo Zegna, (24).

———— (1990b, June). Advertisement for Sony, (24).

———— (1990c, June). Advertisement for Winston, (24). Back cover.

Fasold, R. (1984). *The Sociolinguistics of Society*. Oxford, England: Basil Blackwell, Ltd.

Fishman, J. A. (1982). Sociology of English as an Additional Language. In *The Other Tongue: English Across Cultures*, edited by B. B. Kachru. NY: Pergamon Press.

Foster, J. R., Sullivan, G. L., and Perea, V. (1989). Comprehension of Spanish Language Ad Claims by Hispanic Consumers: A Comparison of Bilingual and Monolingual Performance, *Southwest Journal of Business and Economics*, 6 (2-3), 13-18.

Fraser, I. (1990, April). Now Only the Name's Not the Same, *Eurobusiness*, 2(7), 22-25.

Gibbons, J. (1987). *Code-Mixing and Code Choice: A Hong Kong Case Study*. Clevedon, England: Multilingual Matters.

Grosjean, F. (1982). *Life with Two Languages: An Introduction to Bilingualism*, 129-332. Cambridge, MA: Harvard University Press.

Grosjean, F. and Soares, C. (1986). Processing Mixed Language: Some Preliminary Findings. In *Language Processing in Bilinguals: Psycholinguistic and Neuro-psychological Perspectives*, edited by J. Vaid, 145-176. Hillsdale, NJ: Lawrence Erlbaum Associates, Publishers.

Hakuta, K. (1986). *Mirror of Language: The Debate on Bilingualism*. NY: Basic Books.

Harris, R. J., R. E. Sturm, M. L. Klassen, and J. I. Bechtold. (1986). Language in Advertising: A Psycholinguistic Approach, *Current Issues and Research in Advertising*, 9(1/2), 1-26.

Hock, H. H. (1986). *Principles of Historical Linguistics*. Berlin: Mouton de Gruyter.

Hughes, G. (1988). *Words in Time: A Social History of the English Vocabulary*. Oxford, England: Basil Blackwell, Ltd.

Jacobson, R. (1982). The Social Implications of Intra-Sentential Code-Switching.

In *Spanish in the United States: Sociolinguistic Aspects*, edited by J. Amastae and L. Elías-Olivares. Cambridge, England: Cambridge University Press.

Jacoby, J. and Hoyer, W. D. (1987). *The Comprehension and Miscomprehension of Print Communications*. Hillsdale, NJ: Lawrence Erlbaum Associates.

Kahane, H. (1982). American English: From a Colonial Substandard to a Prestige Language. In *The Other Tongue: English Across Cultures*, edited by B. B. Kachru. NY: Pergamon Press.

Koyima, Y. and Takebayashi, Y. (1984). *Light House Japanese-English Dictionary*. Kenkyusha Publishers.

Lambert, E. E. (1960). Evaluational Reactions to Spoken Languages, *Journal of Abnormal and Social Psychology*, 60, 44-51.

Langenscheidt's German-English, English-German Dictionary. (1969). Berlin and Munich: Langenscheidt KG.

Limón, J. E. (1982). El Meeting: History, Folk Spanish, and Ethnic Nationalism in a Chicano Student Community. In *Spanish in the United States: Sociolinguistic Aspects*, edited by J. Amastae and L. Elías-Olivares. Cambridge, England: Cambridge University Press.

Marie Claire (Spanish Language Version) (1990a, June). Advertisement for Burberrys.

_____ (1990b, June). Advertisement for Pepe Jeanswear, p. 86.

_____ (1990c, June). Advertisement for Solares Waterproof, p. 58.

Mewshaw, M. (1988, December). For Only in Italy, Where People Think "Go" Whenever They See "Stop," *European Travel & Life*, 4(10): Murdock Magazines, 12-13.

Mitchell, D. (1984). A European Researcher's View of European Business Marketing: Some Observations and Tips, *Business Marketing*, (April), 70-76.

O'Shaughnessy, J. and Holbrook, M. B. (1988). Understanding Consumer Behavior: The Linguistic Turn in Marketing Research, *Journal of the Market Research Society*, 30(2), 197-223.

Panorama (1989a, December 10). Advertisement for Benetton, 27 (1234): Arnjoldo Mondadori Editore, p. 170.

_____ (1989b, December 10). Advertisement for Charro Perfume, 27 (1234): Arnoldo Mondadori Editore, p. 2.

_____ (1989c, December 10). Advertisement for Chesterman, 27 (1234): Arnoldo Mondadori Editore, p. 294.

Percy, L. (1981). Psycholinguistic Guidelines for Advertising Copy. In *Advances in Consumer Research*, edited by A. A. Mitchell, 107-111. Conference held in St. Louis, Missouri, (October).

Poplack, S. (1982). "Sometimes I'll Start a Sentence in Spanish y Termino en Español ": Toward a Typology of Code-Switching. In *Spanish in the United States: Sociolinguistics*, edited by J. Amastae and L. Elías-Olivares. Cambridge, England: Cambridge University Press.

Pyles, T. and Algeo, J. (1982). *The Origins and Development of the English Language*, 3rd. ed. NY: Harcourt Brace Jovanovich, Inc.

Schachter, D. L. (1989). Memory. In *Foundations of Cognitive Science*, edited by M. I. Posner. Cambridge, MA: The MIT Press.

Sedillo, J. Sales manager, Treasure Valley Volkswagen, Incorporated. Boise, ID.

Simpson, G. B., R. R. Peterson, M. A. Casteel, and C. Burgess (1989). Lexical and Sentence Context Effects in Word Recognition, *Journal of Experimental Psychology*, 15(1), 88-97.

Stern, B. B. (1988). How Does an Ad Mean? Language in Services Advertising, *Journal of Advertising*, 17(2), 3-14.

Stout, P. A. and Leckenby, J. D. (1988). The Nature of Emotional Response to Advertising: A Further Examination, *Journal of Advertising*, 17(4), 53-57.

Suhor, C. (1984). Towards a Semiotics-Based Curriculum, *Journal of Curriculum Studies*, 16(3), 247-257.

Titone, R. (1988). From Bilingual to Mixtilingual Speech: "Code-Switching" Revisited. *Rassegna Italiania di Linguistica Applicata*, 20(2), 15-21.

Who's News. (1990, September 21-23). *USA WEEKEND*, p. 2.

Chapter 13

The Changing South Korean Marketplace: Perceptions of Consumer Goods

Linda J. Morris
John H. Hallaq

SUMMARY. As South Korea opens its trade doors, it becomes strategically important for marketers to gain some knowledge about the Korean consumer. This chapter examines the "country of origin" effect on consumer purchasing behavior for six familiar product categories. Comparative countries include Japan, Taiwan, the United States, and South Korea. Despite the similarities between Japan and the United States, the results show that U.S. products are preferred after removing South Korea from the list.

INTRODUCTION

Economists predict that by the year 2010 Japan will become a leading power in world politics, and following behind this superpower will be four smaller Asian Pacific countries–South Korea, Taiwan, Singapore, and Hong Kong (*Newsweek*, February 22, 1988). Of the four newly industrialized countries, South Korea has made the most rapid progress in its struggle to join the elite ranks of industrialized nations. Prior to hosting the 1988 Summer Olympics, South Korea was witnessing a 12% annual growth rate, although this rate has recently slowed to 7.8% (Simos and Triantis, 1989).

Overall, the U.S. is expected to become a prime benefactor of South Korean prosperity because of its strong economic and military support since 1946. Consequently, U.S. marketers need to understand how their products are viewed by South Korean consumers in comparison to other competing countries. International researchers (Bilkey and Nes, 1982; Morello, 1984; Wall and Heslop, 1986) have found that both industrial and consumer buyers develop stereotype images of countries and/or their outputs. Such images can impact consumption behavior, and can also color the image of other well-known products produced by a particular country (Hooley, Shipley, and Krieger, 1988).

These findings have important implications for U.S. industrial marketers, given the recent report by the Korean Trade Association. Based on a survey of 283 Korean businesses, it was reported that 59% consider American industrial goods to be more expensive than Japanese goods. In the non-price category, an average of 85% gave superior marks to Japan over the U.S. in meeting delivery schedules, providing services, knowing the Korean market, and accommodating small orders (*The Korean Herald*, 1987).

COUNTRY OF ORIGIN LITERATURE

Country of origin literature has taken two directions–a macro view and a micro view. General image studies (i.e., macro level) have used the "made in (name of country)" format to examine products in general. The micro, or product class level, has examined specific products, and is reported to be more relevant for marketing purposes (Halfhill, 1980; Khanna, 1986; Wall and Heslop, 1986).

From the macro perspective, researchers have concluded that the willingness of consumers to buy foreign-produced goods is partially determined by the economic, political, and cultural environments of the country of origin (Wang and Lamb, 1980, 1983; Wall and Heslop, 1986). Schooler and Wildt (1968) found that product perceptions can vary according to the prevailing attitudes toward people of the country, and its perceived cultural similarity to their own (Lillis and Narayana, 1974). These findings have important implications for the study of the South Korean marketplace because of the mixed emotions held by South Koreans. Older Koreans tend to have negative attitudes toward Japan due to government rule prior to 1946, and the younger generation hold similar attitudes toward the U.S. because of the current political turmoil.

Although general image studies have provided some guidelines for measuring country of origin effect, several authors (Kaynak and Cavusgil, 1983; Niffenberger, White, and Marmet, 1980) suggest that perceptions tend to be product-specific rather than country-specific, and contend that the use of general national stereotypes are likely to be misleading. There have also been numerous studies at the product class level (Bilkey and Nes, 1982) which report that strong patriotism can impact product and service preferences (Gaedeke, 1973; Nagashima, 1970, 1977; Wang and Lamb 1980, 1983).

Many of the earlier studies on the country of origin effects have somewhat mixed results possibly due to shortcomings in methodological approaches. In particular, many of the studies have viewed country of origin as a single cue, and many of the product comparisons used unfamiliar product classes (Bilkey and Nes, 1982). Bradley (1981) and Johansson, Douglas, and Nonaka (1985) contend that product images and perceptions are usually more clearly formed than country images as a result of direct experience with the brands. Thus, several researchers have proposed improved methodological approaches for country image studies (Johansson, 1989; Hooley, Shipley, and Krieger, 1988).

PURPOSE OF THE STUDY

Few researchers have examined the country of origin effect on South Korea's product perceptions during its current economic transition. This study is an attempt to increase our understanding of the South Korean marketplace by looking at the macro and micro levels separately. Specifically, this article investigates (1) the overall image of U.S.-made products relative to Japanese, South Korean, and Taiwanese products; (2) the importance of the country of origin cue compared to other salient attributes for familiar product classes; and (3) the likelihood of purchasing familiar products that are produced by competing countries.

METHODOLOGY

Sample

The data for this study were collected during the two summers preceding the 1988 Summer Olympics. Data gathered during the first summer were used in developing and refining this survey instrument. As with any cross-cultural research, there are problems gaining access to the culture, obtaining representative samples of the population in homogenous settings, and writing meaningful questions that are properly translated (Hansen, 1976; Brislin, Lonner, and Thorndike, 1973). In this study, access to the culture was made possible by two South Korean nationals who assisted in translating and transcribing the questionnaire into South Korean script. The students also administered the survey at a Seoul university. Of the 200 respondents, approximately 82% were under 25 years of age, 28% were female, and about 8% were married. The small number of females in this study is reflective of South Korea's male-dominated society which does not encourage females to attend higher education programs. Although the sample is more reflective of the youth market, it is often the more educated and affluent segment of a marketplace that stimulates economic changes and political reform. Education, age, and income all tend to correlate positively with a more open attitude toward foreign products, although it is not clear whether such individuals pay attention to or disregard "made in" labels (Wang, 1978). Other international studies relied on convenience samples of students as the relevancy of the population depends on the nature of the research issues under investigation (Hampton, 1979; Zaichkowsky and Sood, 1989). The value of this particular study lies in determining the existing attitudes toward U.S-made products among the Korean youth market, since this group will be the primary target market of affluent consumers in the next decade. As the South Korean economy flourishes, and as these students become full-fledged consumers and heads of households, their perceptions will be influential in designing marketing strategies.

Questionnaire Design

The survey instrument was a modified form of Nagashima's (1970, 1977) scale to measure general product perceptions of products produced in Japan, the United States, South Korea, and Taiwan. All of these countries are trading partners with South Korea. While the U.S. and Japan are highly industrialized nations, Taiwan is still a developing country. For our purpose, the 13 items analyzed in Jaffee and Nebenzahl's (1984) study were used because our intent was to use scale items that reflected more of the extrinsic cues relating to product/technology attributes and price attributes rather than marketing-related attributes. As stated by Malhotra (1988), most developing countries are oriented toward production rather than marketing; therefore, approaches for measuring consumer preferences used in more developed countries are not likely to be appropriate for use in less-developed countries. South Korea is still in the early stages of economic development and many of the marketing-related activities are not yet well enough established to justify using the remaining scale items.

In addition to measuring the overall product image (macro level), efforts were made to measure the country of origin effect on six familiar product categories (micro level) using multiple cues. Intuitively, country of origin effects would appear to be stronger for buyers with little or no product familiarity (Johansson, 1989), but some studies have found that a positive correlation exists between "knowledge about product class" and "importance of the country of origin" (Johansson, Douglas, and Nonaka, 1985; Johansson and Nebenzahl, 1986).

For data analysis purposes the product categories and the product attributes were categorized as follows:

Consumer Product Categories

Low Risk Items: Clothing/Clothing Accessories
                            Sporting Goods Equipment
                            Liquor, Wine, and Beer

High Risk Items: Automobiles
                            Medical and Pharmaceutical Items
                            Electronic Goods and Equipment

Product Attributes

Extrinsic Cues: Price
                    Country of Manufacture
                    Availability
                    Warranty/Guarantee

Intrinsic Cues: Quality
                    Styling
                    Prestige/Status Symbol
                    Good Value for the Money

The six product categories were selected based on the information gathered during the first summer of this project and trade information available from the Department of Commerce publications. Our justification for categorizing the products stems from prior research that indicates consumers' perceptions of products are formed by intrinsic (i.e., taste, performance, and quality) and extrinsic cues (price, brand, country of origin) (Olson and Jacoby, 1972; Szybillo and Jacoby, 1974). Extrinsic cues are particularly valuable in risk reduction when consumers have low self-confidence in a producer's intrinsic cues and when such cues have low predictive value (Cox, 1962). Extrinsic cues are often used as surrogate indicators of quality, while intrinsic cues are used as the basis for forming an overall evaluation (Olson and Jacoby, 1972).

Another measure of interest was the country of origin effect on the behavioral intentions of South Korean consumers with respect to these six familiar product categories. Prior studies have shown that a "home country" bias exists among most cultures (Gaedeke, 1973; Nagashima, 1970; Reierson, 1967; Baumgartner and Jolibert, 1978; Darling and Kraft, 1977; Wall and Heslop, 1986), and that there is a tendency for consumers to evaluate their own country's products relatively more favorably than do foreigners (Bilkey and Nes, 1982; Lillis and Narayana, 1974). The research on behavioral intentions, however, is not very extensive and suffers from methodological shortcomings (Wang, 1978; Johansson, 1989).

DATA ANALYSIS AND FINDINGS

General Products

General product comparisons among Japan, Taiwan, South Korea, and the United States were examined by an item analysis and a factor analysis of all 13 items. Table 13.1 shows a list of the product attributes used in the study and an item mean score for each of the countries investigated.

The table results indicate that South Korean respondents seem to have realistic perceptions about products manufactured in their country. Despite South Korean's nationalistic sentiments, many of the respondents realize that products of their country lag behind those of Japan and the U.S. on several key product characteristics. The critical features they perceive are that their products are most inexpensive and imitative. They see U.S and Japanese products as most expensive, but they rate Japan very low on inventiveness, a distinction they reserve for U.S. products. However, they still perceive Japanese products as having the following attributes: more technically advanced and reliable, mass produced, and of high quality. It is ironic that despite Japan's success in the U.S. and European markets it has not yet gained the distinction of being an innovator.

ANOVA Results

ANOVA tests were applied to each of the 13 product characteristics, using the four countries as independent variables and the mean scores of each attribute as the dependent variables. As shown in Table 13.1, all items were significant beyond the .0001 level.

Pairwise comparisons were made using the Scheffe and Sidak tests for each of the 13 product characteristics. In almost all instances, there appeared to be two clusters of similarities: the first, made up by South Korean and Taiwanese product characteristics; the second, by U.S. and Japanese product characteristics. The only two dimensions where South Koreans view their products distinctly different from Taiwanese products were on the dimensions of *Handmade Items-Mass Produced Items* and *Inventive-Imitative* products. South Koreans view their products as being more on the

TABLE 13.1. Mean Scores of Product Attributes for Each Country

Product Attributes	ANOVA Results				
	Country				P-Values
	Taiwan	Japan	USA	South Korea	
1. Inexpensive–Expensive	3.1	5.2	5.2	3.2	.0001
2. Luxury Items-Necessary Items	4.2	4.0	4.2	4.7	.0001
3. Technically Backward-Technically Advanced	3.6	6.0	5.9	3.6	.0001
4. Mostly Domestic Distribution-Worldwide Distribution	4.3	5.1	4.0	4.4	.0001
5. Heavy Industrial Products-Light Manufactured Products	4.7	3.6	3.2	4.5	.0001
6. Reasonably Priced-Unreasonably Priced	3.8	4.5	4.3	4.2	.0001
7. Unreliable-Reliable	3.8	5.5	5.3	3.4	.0001
8. High Status Items-Low Status Items	4.3	2.8	2.9	4.2	.0001
9. Contemporary Design-Conservative Design	3.9	1.9	3.4	3.9	.0001
10. Handmade Items-Mass Produced Items	3.2	5.5	5.8	3.8	.0001
11. High Quality-Low Quality	4.0	2.6	2.8	4.1	.0001
12. More Concerned with Appearance-More Concerned with Performance	3.7	3.7	5.1	3.4	.0001
13. Inventive-Imitative	4.6	4.3	2.5	5.4	.0001

mass production level than Taiwanese products, but not quite at the same level as Japan and the U.S. Also, South Koreans view their products as being more imitative than Taiwanese products. On both dimensions, there were also significant differences between South Korea-U.S. and South Korea-Japan. A feasible explanation for these differences is that South Koreans view their country as on the rise in terms of mass production and many of the items that are being mass produced are those items that are imitations from Japan and the U.S. For example, South Korea has recently increased its production in electronics, automobiles, and clothing made for Western countries (U.S. Department of Commerce, 1988). Taiwan, on the other hand, is still making handmade items that are less imitative of Western world products and more inventive from the aspect of creating products to meet their cultural preferences and tastes.

Three dimensions where Koreans view U.S and Japanese products as being significantly different are *inventiveness, performance,* and *design.* The U.S. is viewed as more inventive and more concerned with functional product performance rather than the stylistic appearance of a product. Japan is viewed as having more contemporary designs than the U.S.

Factor Analysis

Factor analysis has been used by several authors (Barker, 1987; Johansson, Douglas, and Nonaka, 1985) to identify sets of dimensions underlying a larger number of country of image measures. Principal component analysis, using varimax rotation, was performed on each of the individual countries to provide a sharper insight into the product perceptions of the respondents. Factor loadings indicate the presence of four factors for all countries except South Korea, which had five. These factors are shown in Table 13.2. It seems that respondents see more dimensions to the products of their own country. This phenomenon has been observed by the authors in a survey of British respondents (Hallaq and Denton, 1987).

It is interesting to note that South Korean respondents perceive their own products as inferior to those of other countries. This dominant factor in the analysis, *product inferiority,* represented 20% of the explained variance out of a total of 61.4%. The second factor, *backwardness* of Korean products, underlines a similar theme and explains 15% of the variance.

Taiwan fared no better, and its products were perceived very much like those of South Korea. In fact, *product inferiority* also explained 20% of the variance of a total of 52.5%, which was identical to that of South Korea. In contrast, Japanese products were perceived as most modern, of high quality, and luxurious. U.S. products were perceived to be very similar to Japanese products.

Specific Product Categories

The general product information indicated there were some overall product stereotypes assigned to each country. The next step in

TABLE 13.2. Factor Analysis

So. Korea	% of variance	Taiwan	% of variance	Japan	% of variance	U.S.	% of variance
Inferior	19.8	Inferior	19.6	Modern	19.5	Modern	15.7
Backward	15.1	Imitative	13.6	Quality	15.0	Quality	15.7
Low Priced	9.6	Backward	10.0	Luxury	9.7	Well designed	10.3
Imitative	9.0	Light industry	9.3	High Priced	9.2	Luxury	9.4
Basic	7.9						
Total	61.4		52.5		53.4		53.8

the analysis was to determine whether these images were related to specific product categories. In a separate question, respondents were asked to name three products that came to mind when they saw a "made-in" label of the countries listed in the study. All of the products mentioned were listed, a frequency distribution was formed, and a ranking for each product associated with a country was established. This information provides us with product commonalities among various countries. It was hypothesized that countries like South Korea and Taiwan, on the one hand, and the U.S. and Japan, on the other, would exhibit the highest correlation. Pairs of countries were matched using Spearman's Rank Correlation test. As expected, the correlation coefficient between Taiwan and South Korea was .73, significant at the p = .01, and .53 between U.S. and Japan, significant at p = .025. Major products listed for Taiwan and South Korea included food items and clothing, while primary products from Japan and the U.S. included electronics and automobiles. Although South Korea is predicted to be a prime challenger to Japanese production in the 1990s, respondents currently perceive a very low correlation between products of the two countries.

In another section of the study, respondents were presented with a list of nine product attributes that are likely to play a role in the selection of six familiar product categories. The importance of these attributes in product selection was measured using a 1 (not important) to 7 (very important) scale. These attributes were subsequently categorized as intrinsic cues and extrinsic cues. Table 13.3 provides a summary of each product category and the mean scores on each attribute. Except for clothing, where styling was considered very important, the intrinsic cue, *product quality*, dominated all considerations. The extrinsic cue, *country of manufacture*, seems to have no major impact on selection of familiar products. In all product categories, except electronics and pharmaceuticals, it was considered the least important variable in the overall product attributes and in the list of extrinsic cues. The higher grand means for intrinsic product attributes suggest that in highly familiar product categories, South Koreans feel confident in their use of intrinsic cues rather than use of extrinsic cues, thus supporting Olson and Jacoby's (1972) findings. The only product category where equal weights occurred was in electronic products.

TABLE 13.3. Familiar Product Categories (Mean Scores of Product Attributes)

	Low Risk Products			High Risk Products		
	Clothing	Liquor	Sporting Goods	Electronics	Automobiles	Pharmaceuticals
Intrinsic Cues						
Quality	5.861	5.362	5.786	6.468	6.385	6.185
Styling	5.960	NA	4.632	4.905	5.789	NA
Prestige	4.131	4.410	4.211	4.570	4.328	4.431
Value	4.853	4.253	4.548	4.930	4.902	4.508
Grand Mean	5.20	4.675	4.79	5.22	5.351	5.04
Extrinsic Cues						
Price	5.26	4.338	4.955	5.21	5.48	3.915
Repair/Maintenance	3.792	NA	4.434	5.819	6.126	NA
Country of Manufacture	3.070	3.466	3.583	4.556	4.240	4.076
Availability	4.205	4.281	4.54	4.475	4.513	4.783
Warranty	5.025	NA	5.273	6.00	5.759	5.995
Grand Mean	4.27	4.03	4.56	5.21	5.22	4.69

Country of manufacture was also used as a single cue to measure purchase intentions. Respondents were asked how likely they were to purchase a product made in a specific country if that product were similar in price, quality, design, and styling. Responses were measured on a 1 (definitely would not purchase) to 7 (definitely would purchase) scale. The means of each product category is shown in Table 13.4 along with the percent of respondents who have experienced product items from each country.

For clothing, respondents indicated they were least likely to buy clothing with a Taiwanese label but more likely to buy Korean. Similar responses were reported for electronic goods, automobiles, alcoholic beverages, sporting goods, and pharmaceutical items. Although South Koreans view their products as having lower quality than U.S. and Japanese goods, and even though product quality is the most important attribute in product selection, they still prefer South Korean products. These data suggest a home country bias that is consistent with past research (Hallaq and Denton, 1987; Wang and Lamb, 1980, 1983; Gaedeke, 1973). This attitude, however, may also be a question of economics, since many of the respondents are not fully employed.

When Korea is removed, however, we find that there is a preference for Japanese electronic goods, and from the U.S., automobiles, alcoholic beverages, sporting goods, and pharmaceutical items. Interestingly, among this youth market, U.S. consumer goods are more popular than Japanese products. This popularity suggests that if South Korea were to appreciate its currency and continue to remove its trade barriers, the U.S. balance of trade deficit with this country might improve.

Another facet of this study was to determine whether those respondents more familiar with a country's products would be likely to purchase products from that country. Respondents were to check product items from each country that they had directly purchased or experienced. Each item total was subsequently placed in one of the six product categories, and the sum was used as one of the independent variables in a general linear model. Other independent variables included the countries and the six product categories. The dependent variable was the mean score for likelihood of purchase in each of the six product categories using the 7-point scale described

TABLE 13.4. Mean Scores on Likelihood of Purchase

Product Category	Country			
	Taiwan	Japan	USA	So. Korea
Clothing/Clothing Accessories	2.6	3.15	3.63	5.64
Electronic Goods & Equipment	2.6	4.92	4.50	4.69
Automobiles	2.27	4.05	4.75	5.05
Liquor, Wine, Beer	2.58	2.68	4.03	5.36
Sporting Goods Equipment	2.62	3.35	4.21	5.32
Medical/Pharmaceutical Supplies	2.78	3.32	4.76	4.98

Percent of Respondents Who Have Directly Experienced/Purchased
Goods that Have Been Manufactured by the Country Designated

	Taiwan	Japan	USA	So. Korea
Clothing	12.9%	32.8%	47.3%	99.0%
Clothing Accessories	13.9%	33.3%	26.4%	95.0%
Automobiles	0.5%	6.5%	10.9%	79.6%
Sporting Goods Equipment	0.6%	31.3%	31.8%	96.5%
Sporting Clothes & Footwear	5.5%	23.9%	34.3%	95.0%
Cigarettes	0.9%	24.4%	47.3%	72.1%
Furniture	0.5%	0.7%	8.5%	93.5%
Liquor	0.8%	15.4%	54.7%	83.6%
Wine, Beer	0.2%	7.5%	8.5%	92.5%
Computers	0.2%	15.9%	32.3%	71.1%
Cooking Utensils	11.4%	31.3%	34.3%	87.1%
Cameras	4.5%	77.6%	26.9%	78.1%
Electronics	0.6%	82.1%	48.8%	94.5%
Cosmetics	0.2%	23.4%	36.8%	92.0%

earlier. The results indicate that country of manufacture was a significant factor (p = .0001) in the model, but product categories were not significant (p = .45). In order to determine which of the four countries were significant, a subsequent general linear model using dummy variables was formed. This model was significant at p = .0001 and the amount of variance explained by the model resulted in an R-square value of .836. The Type III output, which does not consider hierarchial order of the variables, resulted in Table 13.5. The findings indicate that each of the importing countries does have a significant impact (p = .0001) on purchase intentions of products

TABLE 13.5. General Linear Model on Purchase Intentions

Dependent Variable: Likelihood of Purchase				
	D.F.	F-Value	P-Value	R-Square
Model	5	337.99	.0001*	.836
Error	19			
	24			
Source:				
Taiwan			.0001*	
Japan			.0001*	
United States			.0001*	
South Korea			.0097	
Familiar Products			.1869	

*Significant at p < .005

where individuals have directly experienced the product. Much of this influence may be attributable to the general stereotype images rather than the six product categories used in this study. As shown in Table 13.4, South Koreans are less likely to purchase Taiwanese products because of the general negative image of the products and the perceived similarity to South Korean products. On the other hand, U.S. and Japanese products are perceived to be of better quality, but expensive.

CONCLUSIONS

South Korea is emerging as an industrial nation that some suspect will challenge Japan in the next decade or two. Very few studies have been reported on this country's potentially lucrative market as its standard of living rises and it relaxes its restrictions on foreign imports.

With the possibility that the U.S. can be a potential exporter, an understanding of the attitudes of Korean consumers towards products made in various countries is quite relevant, to say the least. This has motivated the current study.

Results of South Korean attitudes support other country of origin studies reported by several researchers covering mostly traditional industrial nations at both the micro and macro levels, with one exception. Although Koreans demonstrate a bias for their own country's products, similar to findings on other countries, respondents seem aware and accepting of the fact that Korean products do not have the quality or reliability of those made by such countries as the U.S. and Japan. These results were consistent when using a variety of statistical techniques such as use of factor analysis, ANOVA, and a general linear model. Contrary to expectations, we found Korean respondents fairly familiar with and positive in their attitudes toward products made in the United States, which they consider to be more innovative than Japanese products and nearly as reliable.

Successful marketing plans make the best use of the resources available to the marketer. Certainly the overall positive image of U.S.-made products and the existing preference for U.S. consumer goods by South Koreans are advantages that should not be overlooked in designing entry-level marketing strategies.

REFERENCES

Barker, A. Tansu (1987). A Study of Attitudes Towards Products Made in Australia. *Journal of Global Marketing*, (Vol. 1: No. 1,2), 131-144.

Baumgartner G. and Jolibert, A. (1978). The Perception of Foreign Products in Europe. *Advances in Consumer Research*, 5.

Bilkey, W. and Nes, E. (1982). Country-of-Origin Effects on Product Evaluations. *Journal of International Business Studies*, (Spring/Summer), 89-99.

Bradley, M. F. (1981). National and Corporate Images. *Proceedings: European Academy for Advanced Research in Marketing*, 2, 1172-1189.

Brislin, R., Lonner, W. and Thorndike, R. (1973) *Cross Cultural Research Methods*. NY: John Wiley and Sons.

Cox, D. (1962). *Risk Taking and Information Handling in Consumer Behavior*. Cambridge, MA: Harvard University Press.

Darling, J. and Kraft, F. (1977). A Comparative Profile of Products and Associated Marketing Practices in Selected European and Non-European Countries. *European Journal of Marketing*, 11:2, 519-531.

Gaedeke, R. (1973). Consumer Attitudes Towards Products "Made In" Developing Countries. *Journal of Retailing*, 49, (Summer), 13-24.

Halfhill, D. (1980). Multinational Marketing Strategy: Implications of Attitudes Toward Country of Origin. *Management International Review*, 20:4, 26-30.

Hallaq, J. and Denton, M. (1987). Product Images of Industrial Countries: Perceptions of U.K. Consumers. *Academy of International Business Conference Proceedings*, New Orleans, LA, (November).

Hampton, Gerald M. (1979). Students as Subjects in International Business Studies. *Journal of International Business Studies*, (Fall), 94-95.

Hansen, F. (1976). Psychological Theories of Consumer Choice. *The Journal of Consumer Research*, 3, 117-142.

Hooley, G. J., Shipley, D., and Krieger, N. (1988). A Method for Modelling Consumer Perceptions of Country of Origin. *International Marketing Review*, 5:3, 67-76.

Jaffee, E. D. and Nebenzahl, I. D. (1984). Alternative Questionnaire Formats for Country Image Studies. *Journal of Marketing Research*, 21, 463-471.

Johansson, J. (1989). Determinants and Effects of the Use of "Made In" Labels. *International Marketing Review*, 6:1, 47-57.

Johansson, J. and Nebenzahl, I. (1986). Multinational Production: Effect on Brand Value. *Journal of International Business Studies*, (Fall), 101-126.

Johansson, J., Douglas, S., and Nonaka, I. (1985). Assessing the Impact of Country-of-Origin on Product Evaluations: A New Methodological Perspective. *Journal of Marketing Research*, 22 (November), 388-396.

Kaynak, E. and Cavusgil, S. (1983). Consumer Attitudes Towards Products of Foreign Origin: Do They Very Across Product Classes? *International Journal of Advertising*, 2, 147-57.

Khanna, S. R. (1986). Asian Companies and the Country Stereotype Paradox: An Empirical Study. *Columbia Journal of World Business*, 21:2, 29-38.

The Korean Herald. (1987). Cheaper Japanese Goods Hinder Switch to U.S., March 12, p. 4.

Lillis, Charles M. and Narayana, C. L. (1974). Analysis of "Made In" Product Images–An Exploratory Study. *Journal of International Business Studies*, (Spring), 119-127.

Malhotra, N. K. (1988). Some Observations on the State of the Art in Marketing Research, *Journal of the Academy of Marketing Science*, 16 (Spring), 4-24.

Morello, G. (1984). The "Made In" Issue: A Comparative Research on the Image of Domestic and Foreign Products. *European Research*, (June), 5-21.

Nagashima, A. (1970). A Comparison of U.S. and Japanese Attitudes Toward Foreign Products. *Journal of Marketing*, 34, (June), 68-74.

_____ (1977). A Comparative "Made In" Product Image Survey Among Japanese Businessmen. *Journal of Marketing*, 41, (July), 95-100.

Newsweek. (1988). The Pacific Century, February 22, 78-81.

Niffenberger, P., White, J., and Marmet, G. (1980). How British Retail Managers View French and American Products. *European Journal of Marketing*, 14(8), 493-498.

Olson, J. and Jacoby, J. (1972). Cue Utilization in the Quality Perception Process. In *Proceedings of the Third Annual Conference of the Association for Consumer Research*, edited by M. Venkatesan, 167-179.

Reierson, C. (1967). Attitude Changes Toward Foreign Products. *Journal of Marketing Research*, 4, (November), 385-387.

Schooler, R. D. and Wildt, A. R. (1968). Elasticity of Product Bias. *Journal of Marketing Research*, 5, (February), 78-81.

Simos, E. and Triantis, J. (1989). International Economic Outlook. *The Journal of Business Forecasting*, (Spring), 32-35.

Szybillo, G. J. and Jacoby, J. (1974). Intrinsic Versus Extrinsic Cues as Determinants of Perceived Product Quality. *Journal of Applied Psychology*, 55, 87-91.

U.S. Department of Commerce. International Trade Administration. (March 1988: FED 88-34). *Foreign Economic Trends and Their Implications for the United States*. Prepared by the American Embassy (Seoul, Korea).

Wall M. and Heslop, L. A. (1986). Consumer Attitudes Toward Canadian-Made Versus Imported Products. *Journal of Academy of Marketing Science*, 14:2, 27-36.

Wang, C. K. (1978). The Effect of Foreign Economic, Political and Cultural Environment on Consumers' Willingness to Buy Foreign Products. PhD dissertation, Texas A&M University.

Wang, C. K. and Lamb, C. W. (1980). Foreign Environmental Factors Influencing American Consumers Predispositions Toward European Products. *Journal of Academy of Marketing Science*, 8:4, 345-356.

Wang, C. K. and Lamb, C. W. (1983). The Impact of Selected Environmental Forces Upon Consumer Willingness to Buy Foreign Products. *Journal of Academy of Marketing Science*, 11:2, 71-84.

Zaichkowsky, J. and Sood, J. (1989). A Global Look at Consumer Involvement and Use of Products. *International Marketing Review*, 6:1, 20-34.

SECTION V.

MANAGERIAL IMPLICATIONS

Chapter 14

Implications of Standardization in Global Markets

A. Tansu Barker
Nizamettin Aydin

SUMMARY. The problems of implementation associated with standardization are presented following a discussion of the meaning of globalization. Standardization across different markets is untenable without consideration of the environmental specifics such as product-industry characteristics, the infrastructure, and the patterns of usage and purchase.

International firms must base strategic plans on an integrated global perspective, while the marketing mix should be grounded in the needs and the environment of the customer. Implementation requires paying careful attention to the organization at the headquarters and the subsidiaries.

INTRODUCTION

In the field of international business, the 1960s and the 1970s witnessed the emergence of multinational companies (MNC's) and problems associated with the transcending of national boundaries. The 1980s have been ruled by international competitiveness as a result of the spiralling debt of the Third World and the trade deficit of some of the industrialized countries. Efforts to increase competitiveness have been led and possibly transformed by the concept of "globalization." There has been constant reference to the growing interdependency of national economies, greater competition, and the need for economic cooperation to co-exist and live better. Consequently, the motivation to embark on a new set of strategies to maintain and improve one's competitive position has been very high. These activities and transformations have fueled the discussion on globalization in business, government, and academic circles.

The attention paid to the concept of globalization seems to hinge on two main reasons. The first is the opportunities promised by understanding and implementing globalization, and the rewards that can be reaped by becoming a global firm. The other is the threats posed by not becoming globally oriented and to have to compete in domestic markets with those companies that are global. Therefore, globalization has been portrayed as the necessary orientation to succeed both at home and internationally.

Deteriorating trade and balance of payments accounts, slowing rate of market growth, and loss of markets to foreign firms have forced many companies and countries to seek out opportunities beyond their own markets. Successful international companies use these concerns for promoting their cause by publicizing and highlighting their foreign operations and portraying themselves as "global" companies operating in a "global environment." Public policy makers also encourage discussions of globalization activities in the business, academic, and public domain to promote interest and involvement in international business.

The emergence of new competitors has altered the status quo permanently and some international firms have lost their dominant positions. Countries such as Japan, West Germany, and to a lesser degree Hong-Kong, Korea, and Singapore have emerged as economic powerhouses. All these developments have posed significant threats to the established companies as well as their home countries and forced them to engage in reactive and defensive strategies. Consequently, the parties that have been touched by the new international competition and the rules of the new economic order have started to discuss the new "global imperative."

The term "globalization" appears to have become a "catchall" concept that does not seem to be used within the same context by everyone. Each meaning is generally formulated in such a way that it contains the criteria used to identify problems and suggest solutions to improve future performance. Therefore, it is useful to look at the different meanings attributed to the term before discussing their merits. A review of the literature suggests that the term "globalization" is used in at least three different contexts. Some view it from a *holistic* perspective rather than as a collection of domestic markets. The second meaning is that of standardization versus adaptation. The third meaning of globalization refers to the environments of the firm, such as micro and macro levels, and includes only the macro variables within the domain of globalization.

The purpose of this study is to investigate only the first two meanings of globalization, which are more prevalent. The third sense in which globalization is used appears to be synonymous with "macro" (Lessem, 1988) and will not be dealt with any further. We then discuss the problems of implementation associated with the standardization versus adaptation argument as a tool in global strategy formulation.

GLOBALIZATION: A HOLISTIC VIEW

Jeannet and Hennessy (1988, p. 265) use the term "global strategy" as an application of a common set of strategic principles across most world markets. A company pursuing a global strategy should certainly analyze the world market as a whole rather than looking at markets on a country-by-country basis. The holistic approach advocates a broader and integrated consideration of worldwide factors from a system-analytic perspective in strategic decision making. As Kotler, Fahey, and Jatusripitak (1985, p. 125) point out, it is possible to define generic strategies for confrontation and market maintenance. Porter (1980) also advocates generic strategies for achieving competitive advantage. Analyzing the world as an integrated system is an *approach* to planning that is desirable in light of the realities and the interdependent nature of the international marketplace. The question that must still be answered is whether the holistic view allows the strategist to recommend only one worldwide strategy or is it possible to choose different strategies for different countries/regions after having analyzed the markets from a global perspective. On the other hand, an example of the holistic approach certainly is not a firm that embraces only one strategy without consideration of the global factors.

Porter (1980) defines a global industry as one in which the strategic positions of competitors in major geographic or national markets are fundamentally affected by their overall global position. Thus, the performance of any segment or subsidiary is closely related to the performance of other units in the rest of the world and must be viewed as a whole. Porter (1980, p. 276) also uses the term "globalness" to differentiate those companies that can view the world in such a manner from the multinationals. Multinationals are defined as companies having subsidiaries that are autonomous and where the competitive balance is struck on a country-by-country basis. In this context, multinational companies have a "multidomestic" orientation and "globalness" is the perspective of global businesses (Hout, Porter, and Rudden, 1982).

Garland and Farmer (1986, p. 19) define global orientation as the recognition that input and output markets are not confined to national boundaries and the economic climate is largely dependent on international economic forces. In this context, Kotler, Fahey, and Jatusripitak (1985, p. 173) argue that Japan has based its success on maintaining a global perspective by showing the ability to view the world as a potential market without losing flexibility. A firm does not have to have overseas operations in order to have a global perspective as long as it is recognized that input and output markets are not restricted to national boundaries.

GLOBALIZATION: STANDARDIZATION OF MARKETS

The proponents of standardization argue that the trends in international markets make it possible, even imperative, to provide the same types of goods and services in different overseas markets. The nature of the globalization debate suggests that it is useful to examine: (1) Precisely what is to be standardized? (2) Is standardization always desirable or required? (3) Is it possible or practical? and (4) What are the goals to be achieved? The notion that "If you do not know where you want to go, any road will take you there" seems to apply to the discussion of standardization. If cost reduction is the goal, for example, standardization might achieve this but at the expense of market share and total profits.

Jeannet and Hennessey (1988, p. 256) define standardization as the amount of similarity companies want to achieve across many markets with respect to their marketing strategies and marketing mix. According to Levitt (1983), standardization is to view the entire world (or major regions) as a single entity and to sell the same standardized product in the same way everywhere. This can be achieved because the whole world is converging toward a commonality as a result of the disappearance of national and regional preferences.

Although Levitt's interpretation of standardization is the most far-reaching, the issue of standardization has been studied by marketing scholars since the mid-1960s. Buzzell (1968) provided one of the pioneering analyses of standardization and the variables that should be considered. Likewise, Terpstra (1967) studied the impact of the formation of the European Common Market and found a certain degree of willingness on the part of corporations toward greater rationalization and harmonization.

Reasons for Standardization

Standardization certainly has tremendous appeal for its advocates. These can be grouped under (1) benefits stemming from economies of scale, and (2) the ease of market entry and operation.

Economies of scale can be realized in (1) research and development, (2) production, (3) marketing, and (4) management time and effort. The main benefit of economies of scale is cost reduction. If reflected in price, cost reductions will improve price competitiveness and, consequently, market share. Alternatively, cost reductions can be used to improve the profit margin.

Standardization can also provide greater ease of entry into new markets than an adaptation strategy. Quelch and Hoff (1986) claim that the driving factor in moving toward global marketing should be the "efficient worldwide use of good marketing ideas rather than scale economies from standardization." As well, standardization will make the task of planning and control easier. However, these benefits hinge fundamentally on the prerequisite that markets are indeed converging or are already homogeneous. The issue of convergence may be investigated by looking at consumer tastes and preferences, culture, legal and regulatory aspects, and the standard of living, as will be discussed in the next section.

Degree of Convergence

Just as the fundamental differences among markets were overstated in the past by resorting to a few selected examples, the degree and the speed of convergence presently alleged to be taking place is also exaggerated. Quite often the behavior of a minor segment is taken to be a reflection of the whole market. In an overwhelming number of markets, convergence will evolve slowly and it will be a long time before one can isolate fairly convergent markets. Expansion of the Asian food businesses in major metropolitan markets in the U.S. is hardly an indication of the transformation of the U.S. food industry. Likewise, establishment of McDonald's in France is not an indication of the demise of the French cuisine and restaurants. These examples only indicate the demand for a given product by consumers in a very specific market segment.

Tastes and Preferences

Levitt (1983) argued that "gone are accustomed differences in national or regional preferences." As an illustration, the cases of Coca-Cola, Pepsi-Cola, and cigarettes are provided. Even these extreme examples do not prove the disappearance of local tastes. In soft drinks, one can easily observe the differences in sugar content and the size and type of containers used. The success of the large MNC's against the local soft drinks is predominantly due to their sophisticated marketing activities. The case of cigarettes can be used to illustrate market divergence. While American firms are making inroads into mostly developing countries, cigarette smoking is decreasing in North America. In many countries, the policy of the state monopolies is not to encourage smoking through intensive marketing activities. Consequently, the variety, packaging, and promotional activities are kept to a minimum. Hence, foreign cigarette manufacturers readily capture a certain share of the local market mostly because of the supply-side imbalance that has been created by government policies and not as a result of wholesale convergence of the preferences of the local consumers.

In every country, there are some consumers who prefer and are willing to buy imported products either because they have lived abroad or because of social class association. For these consumers, anything less than imported or Western products might be unacceptable. However, the existence of small and well-to-do segments that are very receptive to standardization is hardly proof of convergence of tastes by the majority of the consumers in these markets. The authors have observed that when Turkey allowed importation of canned pet food and "Wonder" bread, the shelves were emptied quickly in the few stores that stocked these imports. However, most Turkish consumers consider Wonder bread an insult and continue to purchase freshly baked, unsliced loaves of bread at their neighborhood bakeries. One will have to wait for a long time to see the ownership of pets approach anything close to that of the U.S. due to cultural and economic factors. Therefore, canned pet food and imported bread will serve an insignificant portion of the Turkish market and certainly do not represent any amount of convergence with the U.S. market. Unlike Levitt, Clark (1989) argues that there is no such thing as a "global consumer" and that the choice of a specific product/brand in any situation is personal, singular, and influenced by different factors. His conclusion is that an understanding of the individual needs and values in each market is of particular importance to the success of international marketers. It is also a fundamental tenet of the marketing concept.

Standards of Living

Raising the standards of living by increasing the purchasing power of the masses has been a universal objective. However, due to the enormous income disparities between the developed countries and the others, a vast majority of the world population is not yet able to afford a great number of products and services. Therefore, they are not in a position to have an impact on the design or the marketing of many products. At their current levels of buying power, different marketing activities and products are required to accommodate their needs, wants, tastes, and preferences. This potential can only be met by providing them with the offerings that they need and can afford now. Otherwise, one has to wait until after these potential customers attain the minimum level of purchasing power and then purchase these products, which is the conventional concept of international product life cycle strategy.

The level of purchasing power, standards of living, and the hierarchy of needs are related. Even though the general category of the hierarchy of needs might be similar, the ranking of these needs in each category is hardly the same from country to country. Except for a select group of basic products to satisfy the most basic of human needs, these priorities and preferences are quite different. The differences in priorities make standardization quite difficult as the needs and even the meaning attached to goods is not the same across inter- and intra-national boundaries.

Legal and Regulatory Factors

Markets and marketing variables are strongly influenced by the consumers' behavior and government regulations. The impact of consumers' tastes, preferences, and purchasing power upon standardization have already been discussed above. Governmental regulations are the most significant attributes that distinguish international business from domestic business. While a variety of marketing tools are available to deal with or influence the individual's behavior, established government regulations are far more difficult to change. Fundamentally, independent nations are not yet ready to give up their sovereignty or control of business. Consequently, markets will be regulated differently especially in the areas of health, safety, environment, and technical standards.

In a democratic system, most of these regulations reflect the underlying consumer choices and preferences. Therefore, the existing regulatory differences are testimonials to the differences in consumers' choices, tastes, and preferences. Even economic integration efforts have not been all that successful in harmonizing these differences. The European Economic Community was formed primarily to do away with or harmonize the regulatory differences within the community. Thirty years later, the Community was still struggling to agree on a common definition of jam versus marmalade. More recently, the European Community's (EC) ban on hormone-treated meat products created a major trade conflict with the U.S. This ban is a regulatory action but it was adopted after strong and persistent public pressure. Therefore, government regulations are present not only to erect trade barriers but also to safeguard the public's common interest and the minimum acceptable level of its preference.

MARKETING MIX CONSIDERATIONS

One of the most important dimensions of the globalization concept is the standardization of the elements of the marketing mix. In this section, product, pricing, promotion, and channels of distribution decisions are analyzed to clarify some of the difficulties associated with the standardization versus adaptation issue.

Products

The most powerful argument in favor of product standardization is based on cost reductions due to substantial economies of scale in production. Levitt (1983) also posits that the needs and interests of consumers are becoming homogeneous all over the world. This will make implementation of standardization and achievement of economies of scale possible. Clark (1989) criticizes globalism for being concerned with manufacturing and products rather than consumers and brands. Douglas and Wind (1987) argue that production costs are often a minor component of total costs and, therefore, understanding the tastes and preferences of the consumers is far more important. Needless to say, at the very basic level of human needs, commonalities are far more prevalent. These basic needs can be satisfied by products that are similar at the core product level. What is of critical importance in order to penetrate, develop, and defend markets is to provide *augmented* products that not only meet these needs but create preference and brand loyalty in a given market segment. Without such penetration and brand loyalty, it is not possible to defend a segment against potential competitors without significant loss of one's own market share and profitability.

Boddewyn, Soehl, and Picard (1986) report that while standardization of consumer durables (which is generally greater than for consumer nondurables) in EC is up from 1973, industrialized goods manufacturers have standardized the most. However, even some of the industrial goods manufacturers were considering moving towards adaptation in the following five years. On the other hand, Masdag (1987) notes that selling food and beverages is most difficult as far as global strategy is concerned. Undoubtedly, lower tariffs, based on free trade negotiations, facilitate standardization. Consequently, the economic union in EC 1992 is seen as a facilitator of standardization by many people. Europe '92 removed the obstacles to free movement of people and financial resources above and beyond what used to exist. Hence, EC has removed mostly tariff regulations. However, the importance of non-tariff factors and structural differences must not be minimized. Some of the more important non-tariff barriers to standardization will, undoubtedly, be governmental regulations, health, safety, and other local standards. Structurally, the differences in the tastes of the consumers and infrastructure-related matters will impede standardization. As one executive put it, a common product in even two countries in Europe would often be impossible (*The New York Times*, 1985).

Hill and Still (1984) report that only one out of ten packaged goods destined for developing countries was sold without modification while on average 4.1 changes were made in terms of brand name, packaging, measurement units, labelling, contents, product features, and usage instructions. Different local usage characteristics as well as regulations often necessitate adaptation or modification of certain aspects of both consumer and industrial goods, although the latter are usually seen as being rather more standardized. While certain raw materials and component parts are indeed standardized, there are many cases where reliance on intuition may be misleading. For instance, the composition of many fertilizers must be modified to account for differences in the soil and climatic conditions (Gibson, 1986). Furthermore, in those countries where the government requires a certain level of local content, the availability and quality of the local inputs may preclude the achievement of a standardized world product. In short, customer preferences, usage, and local regulations as well as penetration and defensive marketing strategies necessitate modification and adaptation especially at the augmented product level.

Pricing

Standardization of prices could seek to achieve a uniform worldwide price or a uniform profit margin. Variations among countries in terms of level and distribution of income, intensity of competition, and the nature of demand make it very difficult to establish standard prices and at the same time achieve a desired level of sales. Based on various transportation, labor, and raw material costs, the cost of goods sold is likely to differ quite a bit from one market to another and even among the different regions in a target country. In addition to differences in demand elasticity among the markets, standardization of pricing must take into account factors such as the level of service required, the nature of warranties, discounts, terms of payment, and availability of credit. Clearly, the many target markets are far from being uniform along these dimensions and hinder a standard worldwide pricing policy.

Government restrictions, intensity of local and international competition, and exchange and interest rates are also determinants of price that present obstacles to standardization of pricing. Especially in industrial markets, the pervasive nature of negotiated prices and the multitude of discounts make uniform pricing impractical.

It is possible that a firm might want to maintain a uniform after-tax contribution in its worldwide markets. In this case, the various costs associated with transportation, storage, insurance, and varying tax rates would produce differences in the final price.

Sometimes a firm would want to concentrate its profits from several international operations in a particular country due to more favorable tax stipulations, investment and repatriation opportunities, risk of exposure, or a more stable exchange rate. Therefore, transfer pricing schemes might be used to funnel profits as well as charging different prices. Variable cost pricing and dumping are common examples of non-uniform pricing practices that can help certain objectives by employing differentiated pricing policies.

The closest that most international firms come to standardizing their prices is, possibly, to set prices to maintain a consistent image of value and quality within multi-product lines and relative to their competitors. Even then, lowering the price to penetrate a highly lucrative market is always a counter-strategy to be employed against an established competitor.

Standardization of prices across many international markets is not a realistic and viable strategy in the long run. It does not explicitly consider and take into account the differences in the economic environments, different cost structures, variations in the nature of competition, and the level of demand.

Channels of Distribution

Channel design and member selection are often constrained by availability in many overseas markets. Often it is not possible to go outside the existing channels, and the international company must work with the customary channels of distribution rather than trying to standardize them globally. The nature of the wholesalers, their ability to perform physical distribution functions, the adequacy of coverage, and the existing power structure may all dictate modifications and force the international firm to deviate from standardized channel strategies.

The existing infrastructure of the country in terms of storage, transportation, and materials handling are usually constraints that are not easy to control or change even by large global companies and necessitate adaptation. Loading and unloading facilities at the major harbors may preclude containerized shipping and cold storage facilities may be very limited or non-existent. Even protective packaging may be difficult to procure locally, and government regulations may prevent the company from importing the necessary materials.

Retail store availability in terms of store image, type of ownership, level of customer service, store types, product assortment, and even location are likely to require abandoning of certain standardized channel and retailing strategies. IKEA is not likely to be able to implement its strategy of building large stores and providing ample free parking in order to avoid paying high rent. Drawing customers outside of the busy shopping districts is simply not possible in those countries where car ownership is restricted to the rich segment. In fact, local tie-in arrangements, loyalty to old suppliers and customers, and government regulations hinder standardization. For example, in many European countries, beer and other alcoholic beverages are readily available at supermarkets and grocery stores, whereas in many cities in the U.S. and Canada, liquor is sold only at specially licensed retail outlets. Customers' habits might also influence the choice of the retail outlet and the type of product carried. In Turkey and in New Zealand, the customer does not think of a drugstore as a likely place to carry soft drinks, potato chips, or even postage stamps.

Promotion

Studies by Dunn (1976) and Takeuchi and Porter (1986) report that the percentage of companies using standard advertisements has decreased over the years. Others (Caffyn and Rogers, 1970; Hornik, 1980) conclude that overseas advertising is perceived to be less effective than local advertising. Mueller (1987) found that relatively few international campaigns have adopted the fully standardized approach and it was more common to use standardized campaigns between culturally and economically similar countries. As well, campaign standardization was significantly more common for TV advertisements than for print advertisements. Highly standardized campaigns were also found to contain significantly fewer information cues than specialized ones. Furthermore, a survey of 100 advertisers in the U.S. (*Marketing News*, 1987) found that 79% developed distinctly different media plans in each country and 40% believed that universal advertising that rises above cultural differences can be created only on "rare occasions." A separate study conducted in the EC countries reported similar results. Most respondents disagreed that traditional advertising is likely to disappear in the next ten years (*Marketing News*, 1987). Nevertheless, promotion, especially advertising, continues to be a likely element of the marketing mix to be standardized besides the product itself.

The barriers to standardization of advertising campaigns include discrepancies in the values and the cues that influence people. These distinctions stem from the differences in culture and language. Equally important are the differences in availability and quality of various media and the restrictions placed on them by governments. Restrictions on advertising may include content, message, duration, frequency, timing, and comparative advertising.

The way different roles are seen, the perceptions associated with them, the impact of language and culture, differences in symbols, and the general level of literacy are all factors that render standardized advertising difficult. There can be cost savings if the same commercial that costs thousands of dollars to produce can be dubbed and used all over the world. However, many people find foreign commercials rather difficult to identify with, regardless of the cost savings to the sponsoring organization. This is mainly because these commercials depict foreign-looking characters, in an unfamiliar environment, surrounded by a glimpse of a way of life that they are not accustomed to. On the other hand, it might be possible to have the advertising theme and the appeal standardized as long as the "copy" appeals to the specific target at which it is aimed.

In the area of salesforce management, the importance of language, familiarity with the cultural environment and the social niceties of the specific country, and knowledge of the customers and how they use the offering make standardization virtually impossible. Therefore, it is difficult to employ a common salesforce across all but the most exceptionally common national borders. In fact, even the utilization of salesforce management tools, techniques, and concepts such as the balance between commissions and straight salary or singing songs together to motivate the salespeople must be done with extreme care. Salespeople from other cultural backgrounds are likely to respond differently to these techniques due to cultural and socialization differences.

Sales promotion tools such as samples, coupons, and point-of-purchase (POP) displays all require the retailers, the wholesalers, and the consumers to possess certain characteristics. Coupons require the cooperation of the retailer in handling them. It is difficult to negotiate individually and set up POP displays with many independent retailers compared to large chains that have both the staff and adequate space for displays. In many LDC's the square footage of the store is so small that POPs or other displays simply are not practical or desirable by the owner. The logistics of managing the distribution and reimbursement of coupons with small retailers, some of whom might be in remote areas, is also problematic. Sampling that requires distribution by mail or door-to-door delivery and newspaper coupons or flyers presume the availability of a certain infrastructure.

Trade promotions may also be hampered by the presence of many small independents and a weak infrastructure. However, price-offs, free goods, and specialty advertising are more likely to be successful in a standardized campaign provided that certain language, safety, and legal requirements are met.

Business-to-business promotional tools such as trade shows, exhibits, and conventions are more likely to be standardized due to the more sophisticated nature of these customers. However, sales contests, games, and sweepstakes targeted to business customers or salespeople may be frowned upon in some cultures. Some customers may even scorn these contests based on their status and sense of prestige.

CONCLUSIONS

The claim that differences among markets are gone forever and the prediction of the demise of companies that do not adopt "globalization" is premature. Instead of helping international companies to compete better, standardization of the marketing mix may even mislead them. Convergence of markets quite often means other markets are becoming like the U.S. and the markets of Western Europe. The world simply is not comprised only of the driving forces that originate in the U.S., Europe, and Japan as described by the concept of "triad power." In fact, this impression may be quite detrimental to the international business community in the U.S., which is already suffering for not paying enough attention to the requirements of other markets.

Marketing decisions are influenced by all elements of the environment and particularly by its cultural component. While the core product and some elements of marketing might be standardized, other components of marketing are not amenable to standardization. Therefore, companies involved in international business would be well-advised to consider carefully the benefits of adaptation, especially in less-developed countries.

There is a trade-off between the extent of standardization and market share. Standardization (1) ignores niche marketing, (2) gives a false sense of security in defending its market against competitors, and (3) may result in missed opportunities in penetrating new markets by not differentiating the offering from the competitors.

The market convergence argument contains a certain degree of ethnocentrism and self-reference criteria. Evidence and examples provided to support this argument come from a few countries, mostly from the U.S. Marketers should be more sensitive and responsive to the local culture so that they may better meet the needs and the preferences of their international customers. Whenever convergent markets could be identified and when it is the objective of the firm to cater to the needs of similar markets, standardization might be practiced. However, it is very dangerous to attempt to generalize the standardization argument across different markets without verification of the environmental specifics. Certainly, most firms and many countries are feeling the pressure of global competition. There is also little doubt that advances in communication technology and transportation have created more convergent needs by narrowing the gap in the aspirations of more and more people than ever before. The reality is that sensitivity to the needs and preferences of the consumers and government regulations is necessary in order to be successful in international markets. The future success of globalization depends on careful application of the marketing concept. Naturally, firms should take advantage of synergies that are based on careful marketing research findings but resist the temptation of assuming similarities in different environments.

RECOMMENDATIONS AND IMPLEMENTATION

As Mintzberg (1989) eloquently stated, "There is no such thing as a prescription for everything because prescription applies within a context." The same is also true of "globalization." Certainly, across-the-board standardization is not possible (Killough, 1978; Jain, 1989). However, it is not an either-or situation, as there can be degrees of standardization (Quelch and Hoff, 1986) with national adjustments (Simmonds, 1985).

Standardization of marketing could occur in terms of the process or the program according to Sorenson and Wiechmann (1975). The process is the ways and means that are put into place to develop strategy and to implement it. Undoubtedly, it is possible for a firm to have a standard process to manage the development of its marketing programs. This could increase organizational efficiency by facilitating the flow of information among the various components of the system.

Having a standard process in place should enable the firm to have less difficulty in adopting a geocentric, or global, planning perspective. Firms that consider the position of their competitors in worldwide markets (Porter, 1980) and show the ability to view the entire world as a potential market (Kotler, Fahey, and Jatusripitak, 1985) have the necessary prerequisites for planning globally. In spite of this "globalness," the firm may or may not adopt the same strategy throughout the world. However, what is important is not the standardization of the strategy but the presence of a worldwide perspective. Most likely, the firm will require a confrontation strategy in some markets, whereas others will necessitate a defensive strategy. As Simmonds (1985) pointed out, geographical adjustment is the essence of global strategy. Furthermore, distinctive defensive strategies may have to be employed in different markets based on dissimilarities among the critical variables. Factors that influence strategy, such as the nature of the target market, market position, the product, and the customer, are considered in detail elsewhere (Jain, 1989; Rau and Preble, 1987; Yip, Loewe, and Yoshino, 1988).

Developing the appropriate elements of the marketing mix is the next step. Based on the discussion of the previous section, consideration of the variations in the environment and the customers does not necessarily lead to standardization of the four elements of the marketing mix.

Although the triad markets (The U.S., W. Europe, and Japan) might be ripe for globalization in some areas, the manager simply cannot assume standardization in any market. Certainly, product-industry characteristics (Douglas and Wind, 1987), the infrastructure, differences in the patterns of usage and purchase (Britt, 1974), and specifics of each unique environment must be carefully considered. Firms that tailor their programs specifically to their markets are likely to achieve a competitive advantage due to differentiation. While this approach might not minimize short-run costs, it is more likely to help (1) defend existing markets/segments or (2) penetrate new ones. Admittedly, it might be easier to standardize manufacturing than marketing.

Once the strategy and the program are in place, the challenge for a MNC is to get the organization to implement it (Davidson and Haspeslegh, 1982; Hamel and Prahalad, 1985; Quelch and Hoff, 1986; Fannin and Rodrigues, 1986; Yip, Loewe, and Yoshino, 1988; Raffee and Kreutzer, 1989). Much has been written about the organizational aspects of the headquarters vs. subsidiary relationship (Brandt and Hulburt, 1977; Bartlett and Ghoshal, 1986). It is beyond the scope of this chapter to elaborate on this problem except to emphasize the importance of having the support and the commitment of the subsidiary managers (Kashani, 1989). Suffice it to say that simultaneously requiring global integration and national responsiveness is most difficult (Chakravarthy and Perlmutter, 1985; Daniels, 1987).

In our view, having a unified strategic planning process is desirable. The actual strategies need not be identical but must be based on the same global perspective. The elements of the marketing mix (program) should be grounded in the needs and the environment of the customer in order to ensure long-term success. The implementation of the strategy and the program require paying careful attention to the organization (both the people and the structure) at the headquarters and the subsidiaries.

REFERENCES

Bartlett, G. A. and Ghoshal, S. (1986). Tap Your Subsidiaries for Global Reach. *Harvard Business Review*, Nov.-Dec., 64(4), 87-95.

Boddewyn, J. J., Soehl, R., and Picard, J. (1986). Standardization in International Marketing. *Business Horizons*, Nov.-Dec., 69-75.

Brandt, W. and Hulbert, J. M. (1977). Headquarters Guidance in Marketing Strategy in the Multinational Subsidiary. *Columbia Journal of World Business*, Winter, 7-13.

Britt, S. H. (1974). Standardizing Marketing for the International Market. *Columbia Journal of World Business*, Winter, 39-45.

Buzzell, R. D. (1968). Can You Standardize Multinational Marketing? *Harvard Business Review*, Nov.-Dec., 102-113.

Caffyn, J. and Rogers, N. (1970). British Reactions to TV Commercials. *Journal of Advertising Research*, June.

Chakravarthy, B. J. and Perlmutter, H. V. (1985). Strategic Planning for a Global Business. *Columbia Journal of World Business*, Summer, 20(2), 3-10.

Clark, H. F. (1989). Consumer and Corporate Value in Global Marketing. *International Journal of Advertising*, 8(1), 29-43.

Daniels, D. D. (1987). Bridging National and Global Marketing Strategies Through Regional Operations. *International Marketing Review*, Autumn, 4(3), 29-44.

Davidson, W. H. and Haspeslegh, P. (1982). Shaping a Global Product Organization. *Harvard Business Review*, July-August, 125-132.

Douglas, S. P. and Wind, Y. (1987). The Myth of Globalization. *Columbia Journal of World Business*, 22, Winter, 19-29.

Dunn, S. W. (1976). Effect of National Identity on Multinational Promotional Strategy in Europe. *Journal of Marketing*, 41, Oct., 50-57.

Fannin, W. R. and Rodrigues, A. F. (1986). National or Global?--Control vs. Flexibility. *Long Range Planning*, October, 19(5), 84-89.

Garland, J. and Farmer, R. N. (1986). *International Dimensions of Business Policy and Strategy*, Boston: Kent Publishing.

Gibson, W. D. (1986). Pinning Down a Global Marketing Strategy. *Chemical Week*, 139(14), October, 30-33.

Hamel, G. and Prahalad, C. (1985). Do You Really Have a Global Strategy? *Harvard Business Review*, July-Aug., 139-148.

Hill, J. S. and Still, R. R. (1984). Adapting Products to LDC Tastes. *Harvard Business Review*, March-April, 62, 91-101.

Hornik, J. (1980). Comparative Evaluations of International vs. National Advertising Strategies. *Columbia Journal of World Business*, Spring, 15(1), 36-45.

Hout, T., Porter, M., and Rudden, E. (1982). How Global Companies Win Out. *Harvard Business Review*, 60, Sept.-Oct., 98-105.

Jain, S. C. (1989). Standardization of International Marketing Strategy. *Journal of Marketing*, January, 53, 70-79.

Jeannet, J. P. and Hennessey, H. D. (1988). *International Marketing Management*, Boston: Houghton Mifflin.

Kashani, K. (1989). Beware the Pitfalls of Global Marketing. *Harvard Business Review*, Sept.-Oct., (5), 91-98.

Killough, J. (1978). Improved Payoffs from Transnational Advertising. *Harvard Business Review*, July-Aug., 102-110.

Kotler, P., Fahey, L., and Jatusripitak, S. (1985). *The New Competition*, NJ: Prentice Hall.

Lessem, R. (1988). *Global Management Principles*, UK: Prentice Hall, p. 8.

Levitt, T. (1983). The Globalization of Markets. *Harvard Business Review*, May-June, 92-102.

Marketing News (1987). Differences, Confusion Slow Global Marketing Bandwagon. 4 October, p. 1.

Masdag, V. H. (1987). Winging It in Foreign Markets. *Harvard Business Review*, Jan.-Feb., 65(1), 71-75.

Mintzberg, H. (1989). Keynote Speech presented at the ASAC Annual Meeting, June, Montreal, Canada.

Mueller, B. (1987). Multinational Advertising: An Examination of Standardization and Specialization in Commercial Messages, Unpublished PhD Dissertation, U. of Washington, 231 pp.

The New York Times (1985). Global Marketing Debated. Advertising Column, November 13.

Porter, M. (1980). *Competitive Strategy: Techniques for Analyzing Industries and Competitors*, NY: The Free Press.

Quelch, A. J. and Hoff, E. J. (1986). Customizing Global Marketing. *Harvard Business Review*, May-June, 59-68.

Raffee, H. and Kreutzer, R. (1989). Organizational Dimensions of Global Marketing. *European Journal of Marketing*, 23(5), 43-57.

Rau, A. and Preble, J. (1987). Standardization of Marketing by Multinationals. *International Marketing Review*, Autumn, 4(3), 18-28.

Simmonds, K. (1985). Global Strategy: Achieving the Geocentric Ideal. *International Marketing Review*, Spring, 8-15.

Sorenson, R. Z. and Wiechmann, U. E. (1975). How Multinationals View Marketing Standardization. *Harvard Business Review*, May-June, 53, 38, 167.

Takeuchi, H. and Porter, M. E. (1986). Three Roles of International Marketing in Global Strategy. In *Competition in Global Industries*, edited by Porter, 111-146.

Terpstra, V. (1967). *Marketing in the Common Market*, NY: Praeger.

Yip, G. S., Loewe, P. M., and Yoshino, M. Y. (1988). How to Take Your Company to the Global Market. *Columbia Journal of World Business*, 23(4), 37-48.

Chapter 15

A Values Comparison of Future Managers from West Germany and the United States

John Paul Fraedrich
Neil C. Herndon, Jr.
O. C. Ferrell

SUMMARY. This chapter reports on a study that examined differences in and similarities between certain values held by future West German and United States managers and considers what differences those values might make in the business environment of the 1990s. Specifically, the values tested were linked to a review of current literature concerning German unification and their potential influences on future business dealings.

Much of the research on business values has focused on the morals, ethics, and behavior of business people within the context of a single country (Becker and Fritzsche, 1987). These values, traits, or ethics, when combined within a country, constitute in part its culture. Different cultural and social traditions can lead to differing attitudes and behavior for managers within different national contexts (Sethi, 1987; Gecas, 1981). But little has been done to examine intercountry differences between managers and how these value differences might impact on decision making.

An extensive review of the literature found only one cross-cultural comparison of value-laden business behavior. Becker and Fritzsche (1987) compared samples of American, French, and German managers using vignettes concerned with ethical problems. While their work did not examine underlying attitude or value structures, it did consider the ways in which the managers said they would handle problems with ethical dimensions and it did find differences and similarities among the samples.

The purpose of this study is to test differences in and similarities of certain underlying values that are associated with the decision process and examine their consequences on future business dealings between and within West German (i.e., Federal Republic of Germany) and U.S. firms, using a sample of business students in each country who are likely to be future managers. In addition, potential influences on future West German managers and their decisions in the West German and European business arena are discussed. To clarify the values chosen for study, each is briefly explained and the research instrument presented. Next, the research methods are explained and the analysis of the data presented. Finally, the results are discussed and some potential research areas are noted. We begin with a brief discussion of the concept of values.

VALUES

Values are ". . . a conception, explicit or implicit, of what an individual or a group regards as desirable, and in terms of which he or they select, from among alternative available modes, the means and ends of action" (Guth and Tagiuri, 1965, p. 125). Vinson and Munson (1976) note a distinction between means and ends which they label, after Rokeach (1968a, 1968b), "instrumental" and "terminal" values. "Instrumental values relate to modes of conduct and represent a single belief which is personally and socially preferable in all situations with respect to all objects" and "Terminal values are a single belief that some end-state of existence is personally and socially worth striving for" (Vinson and Munson, 1976; p. 313). Values tend to underlie and guide behavior and be enduring (Rokeach, 1968a; Vinson and Munson, 1976).

From social psychology, Kaplan (1986) calls values ". . . symbolic expressions of more or less desirable experiential states' (p. 61). He conceptualizes values alternatively as continuous dimensions, as discrete and mutually exclusive categories, and in terms of their presence or absence. He orders them hierarchically, but notes that the applicability and priority of a value varies according to social context.

McMurry (1963) says that while it is generally understood that values are very different across individuals and across cultures, ". . . their influence on people's thinking, acting, and behavior tends to be seriously underestimated" (p. 131). Rokeach (1968a) calls a value ". . . an imperative to action . . ." (p. 16). Epstein (1987) calls these differences in value preferences "value pluralism" (p. 104).

Kahle, Poulos, and Sukhdial (1988) note that values are developed by people from both their heritage and their life experience and influence ". . . a wide variety of human behaviors . . ." (p. 35). They go on to suggest that an understanding of how values are changing can provide insight into how these changes might impact both individuals and the society that they inhabit.

Therefore, if one examines values presently held by individuals, these relatively enduring constructs that underlie and guide a variety of behaviors could provide some insights into the future behavior of individuals in a number of settings. Many managers enter business from a collegiate school of business. For example, the latest available data states that 46% of all U.S. students earning a bachelor's degree in business or management were working in business one year later (U.S. Department of Education, 1989). Therefore, it seems reasonable to examine future trends in business by considering some current values of business students, many of whom will become managers.

We also suggest from the discussion of values above, that these traits appear to be somewhat stable. Therefore, these current values may become increasingly more influential in the business setting as business students advance in rank and replace present managers over time. Consequently, this approach using business students may be a powerful tool for examining future business trends from a value-based perspective.

The values selected for this study are: authoritarianism, need-determined expression versus value-determined restraint, equalitarianism, and individualism. Although other values could have been used, these four measure important implicit decision criteria for people in business and have been widely used in the literature (Robinson and Shaver, 1985). Each value is defined (see Table 15.1) and then examined longitudinally, which forms the basis of the research hypotheses that follow.

TABLE 15.1. Definition of Constructs

Factor I	Agreement with Value Statements in Favor of Acceptance of Authority: concerned with authoritarianism, or adherence and obedience to authority.
Factor II	Agreement with Value Statements in Favor of Need-determined Expression versus Value-determined Restraint: concerned with hedonism versus the extent to which personal behavior is constrained by moral values.
Factor III	Agreement with Value Statements Favoring Equalitarianism: concerned with the equality of human rights.
Factor IV	Agreement with Value Statements Favoring Individualism: concerned with how people define themselves within their own belief/goal system which tends to involve departures from the norm.

AUTHORITARIANISM

A value that business managers discuss frequently is authoritarianism. Authoritarianism is defined as "an attitude characterized by the belief that there should be adherence and obedience to authority" and is applicable to both those in and/or subservient to authority (Reber, 1985, p. 70). Authority over others can only be obtained by the "consent of those on whom it may be exercised," and even then there are limits to that consent (Machan, 1983, p. 509). Furthermore, people allow others to govern them so they can live in an organized community in which their natural rights are respected. Therefore, they must consent to the obedience of certain powers that are established to protect and preserve those natural rights (Jacobson, 1974).

The concept of authority was exemplified in a post-war Germany whose goal was to reestablish, protect, and maintain German lifestyle and culture. Even though many Germans were not in agreement with the military occupation or their new government, they realized that adherence to these forces was a major factor in accomplishing their goal of redevelopment.

Germany's history is filled with struggles to protect its individuality by use of authority. Hence, the German people may have been subjected to a stronger need for and adherence toward authority. This view is generally supported by Friedrich (1990), Prager (1990), and

Babbie (1973). Babbie (1973) notes that these social regularities tend to persist when they make sense for the people of that time.

In a 1970s comparison between American business students and business persons born before 1945, it was found that American business students had a more negative view towards authority than those from before 1945 (Jacobson, 1974). This may indicate that since today's youth have not experienced any true direct threat to their nation's welfare as their parents or grandparents did, the need for a strong governing authority is not essential. This movement away from authoritarianism may also be happening within future business managers of West Germany as well.

This leads to the hypothesis (H_1) that future West German managers will be more accepting of authority than future U.S. managers. (This hypothesis and those that follow are listed in Table 15.2.) Hypothesis One is a reflection of the attitudes within cultures; however, recent anecdotal evidence suggests the opposite. For example, a refusal by West German employees of United Parcel Service (UPS) to adopt the UPS work culture in obedience to management direction ". . . nearly sank the operation" (Labich, 1988, p. 60). Further, Volkswagen management is facing ". . serious questions about its ability to oversee its own employees and to control their access to corporate funds" (Ingersoll, 1987, p. 61) after a fraud by its foreign exchange dealers cost Volkswagen about $260 million (Templeman, 1988b; Pluenneke, 1987d). Finally Bertelsmann, the West German media giant, ". . . has developed a decentralized structure that often depends heavily on the initiative of non-German managers" (Pluenneke, 1987c, p. 73), which suggests a less authoritarian corporate culture. These examples may indicate a shift in West German business values away from authoritarianism, which would be contrary to history.

NEED-DETERMINED EXPRESSION AND VALUE-DETERMINED RESTRAINT

Need-determined expression relates to a philosophy about life that is situation or act specific. This value type espouses a transitory, hedonistic lifestyle that is centered around the present instead of the

TABLE 15.2. Statement of Hypotheses

Factor I-H_1	Future WG managers will be more accepting of authority than future US managers. (**Authoritarianism**)
Factor II-H_2	Future WG and US managers will be more value-determined than need-determined. (**Need-determined Expression**)
Factor III-H_3	Future WG managers will be less equalitarian than future US managers. (**Equalitarianism**)
Factor IV-H_4	Future WG managers will be less individualistic than future US managers. (**Individualism**)

past or future. In contrast, value-determined restraint is more static with a moral foundation based on the discipline of one's desires. Bales and Couch (1969) note that "Hedonism" would be a good title for this value area if there were not the implication of passive rather than active pleasure implicit in the term. Simpson (1987) defines the concept as "the extent you are constraining your behavior based on moral values." Existence is defined more in terms of lasting relationships based on general moral rules. To the degree that U.S. society is guided by the Protestant work ethic with its emphasis on self-discipline, hard work, and future rewards (Velasquez, 1988; DeGeorge, 1990), one would expect U.S. business students to be more value-determined than need-determined in their actions.

A study conducted during the Occupation period by the Americans provides some understanding about the "motivations, drives, and interests" of the German people. One aspect of these surveys studied the views of German youth and adults on individual responsibility. Through such questions as "If a boy accompanied his friends in a theft, even though he did not agree with the action, should he be found guilty of the crime?" it was found that Germans believed one is responsible for one's actions, no matter what one's moral beliefs may be at the time (Merritt and Merritt, 1970). Therefore, one would also expect West Germans to be more value-determined than need-determined in their actions.

This leads to the hypothesis (H_2) that future West German and U.S. managers will be more value-determined than need-determined. (No research was found that predicts whether the West German or U.S. sample will show the greater degree of being value-determined.) However, anecdotal evidence suggests that at a time when the West German economy was in a recession and firms were finding profits squeezed, West German labor unions demanded higher wages and shorter hours than their Japanese and U.S. counterparts, despite the further damage these actions could have had on an already softening economy (Schares, 1988a; Pluenneke, 1987a; Miller, 1987; Templeman, 1987; Glasgall, 1987). In addition, Volkswagen management claimed its ". . . labor contracts are keeping the company from being competitive" (Templeman, 1988a, p. 45). These recent examples paint a picture of West German society as more need-determined than their traditional value-determined stereotype.

EQUALITARIANISM

Equalitarianism can be defined as the extent to which people agree with the equality of human rights in political, economical, and societal domains. Equalitarianism involves the law of equality, which is the idea that all parts of a population are seen as a part of the whole to the extent that all the parts are similar (Wolman, 1973). Bales and Couch (1969) note that this variable is uncorrelated with authoritarianism, and that it is an analytically independent variable.

One indicator of a culture's egalitarian attitudes is its reactions toward different racial and ethnic peoples. Even though America was founded on the principle of equality for all, it has had a long history of inequalities (Seeman, 1981). However, studies conducted between 1963 and 1977 found that white Americans have become "more accepting of virtually every aspect of racial integration" (Condran, 1979, p. 463). Condran (1979) found that the racial "liberals" were young, well-educated, and, in general, not from the South. The younger generation was more liberal because its members had been raised and socialized in a more open and "liberal" society. Greater education provided them with a broader intellectual experience and the opportunity to associate with members of a more general socioeconomic status. Non-southerners were more liberal because they tended to experience a "differential racial socialization" and more pressure through social control over racial attitudes (Condran, 1979, p. 463-464).

Although no empirical evidence was found, one could assume that since America was founded on the idea of democratic equality, its citizens generally would show higher acceptance of such an ideal. However, this is not meant to characterize Americans as completely accepting of other ethnic groups. By comparison, while empirical work about the extent of West German equalitarianism is also lacking, anecdotally, lower equalitarianism seems to continue to some degree to the present (Chua-Eoan, 1990; Meyer, 1990). One can therefore hypothesize (H3) that future West German managers will be less equalitarian than future U.S. managers.

Some current anecdotal literature does point to the idea that West Germans appear to be less equalitarian than their parents. For example, a consortium that includes West Germany that is designing a new NATO fighter to replace the U.S. F-16 now in use appears to be using U.S. export rules to inhibit, if not completely prevent, bidding by U.S. companies (Kapstein, 1987). Further, some critics suggest that major splits are occurring in West German business society along management and labor lines; where once there was harmony, there now appears to be a divided and unequal business society (Pluenneke, 1987b). West German business people also seem to fear dependence on U.S. technology (Schares, 1988b; Peterson, 1988).

INDIVIDUALISM

Individualism relates to "how people define themselves within their framework of beliefs, goals and values" (Waterman, 1984, p. 29). Bales and Couch (1969) report that individualism is independent of the other values presented. They also note that agreement with individualism has no determinate relationship with agreement with authority, but that agreement with individualism and agreement with equalitarianism are compatible. People that score high on individualism are usually those who perceive themselves as apart from the norm. They are categorized as those who set the standards. Leadership types usually have high individualistic traits. Reference group theory suggests that this nonconformist value trait translates into higher levels of conflict when nonconformist individuals disagree with a group's expressed beliefs (Singer, 1981).

One would expect a country so concerned with personal liberty as is the United States to foster more individualism in its managers than highly regulated countries such as West Germany. Therefore, one can hypothesize (H_4) that future West German managers will be less individualistic than future U.S. managers.

Anecdotally, however, Labich (1988) notes that UPS had great difficulty in getting West German employees to work overtime. UPS was concerned that their German employees would not give up leisure time to meet company needs. Also, Toys 'R' Us is anticipating that West Germans are becoming more individualistic in that it is spending $90 million to build 15 stores in Britain, France, and West Germany, even though most toys are sold in small toy shops in Europe (Tully, 1989). It seems that West Germans will have to exhibit considerably more nonconformist behavior in avoiding the usual and customary distribution channels than would be expected if Toys 'R' Us is to generate the sales volume necessary for success (Maremont, 1987).

These four values are important in considering the overall business and work environments of both countries, and in understanding how value differences might lead to decisions with certain national value characteristics. Previous research or historical data and anecdotal evidence appear to be in conflict with one another as to the direction some of these values are moving. This study attempts to clarify the direction these values are headed relative to their respective cultures (see Table 15.3).

RESEARCH DESIGN

A value profile (VP) scale developed by Bales and Couch (1969) was given to a non-random sample of 406 undergraduate business students in West Germany and 208 undergraduate business students at a southwestern U.S. university. The value profile was evaluated by Robinson and Shaver (1985) to be a general purpose inventory of values for interpersonal relations research and so was chosen for this study. The items were developed by Bales and Couch from consideration of several books and from recording discussions of groups with a goal of representing many value areas. This item selection is neither systematic nor random. Items from the original population of statements were reduced to the present 40 items by

TABLE 15.3. Summary of Study Results

		West German Future Managers	United States Future Managers
Factor I	Historically Expect:	more accepting of authority than US	less accepting of authority than WG
	Recent Anecdotal Evidence:	less accepting of authority than before	
	Study Results:	less accepting of authority than US (H_1 rejected)	
Factor II	Historically Expect:	more value-determined than need-determined	more value-determined than need-determined
	Recent Anecdotal Evidence:	less value-determined (i.e., more need-determined) than before	
	Study Results:	no significant difference (H_2 rejected)	
Factor III	Historically Expect:	less equalitarian than US	more equalitarian than WG
	Recent Anecdotal Evidence:	less equalitarian than parents	
	Study Results:	more equalitarian than US (H_3 rejected)	
Factor IV	Historically Expect:	less individualistic than US	more individualistic than WG
	Recent Anecdotal Evidence:	more individualistic than before	
	Study Results:	more individualistic than US (H_4 rejected)	

Bales and Couch based on non-discrimination among subjects at the item level (Robinson and Shaver, 1985).

The original sample for the development of the value profile included Harvard University undergraduates who answered a newspaper advertisement, Harvard faculty and graduate students, Radcliffe and Bennington College undergraduates, and some officer candidates from Maxwell Air Force Base (Bales and Couch, 1969). No validity measures were reported and average inter-item correlations were in the .40s for Factor I, and in the high teens for the other three Factors. In addition, no test-retest data were reported (Robinson and Shaver, 1985). Robinson and Shaver (1985) call the value profile useful because of its extremely comprehensive nature. Despite the lack of information about its validity, they note a large domain of possible value positions.

The research questionnaire was self-administered in a classroom setting. Self-administration is thought to reduce social desirability bias as compared to face-to-face interviewing (Dillman, 1978). The West German business students received the research questionnaire after it had been translated into German by staff members at the sample German university who spoke English but whose native language was German. The questionnaire was back-translated by U.S. researchers who spoke German but whose native language was English to ensure the correctness of the translation. The United States business students received the research questionnaire in its original (English) version. The original statements used by Bales and Couch for the Value Profile in 1969 were updated in some minor ways to reflect a more modern language usage, but was not judged by the researchers to significantly change any meanings.

The use of business students instead of actual managers was chosen for several reasons. First, as detailed above, this article deals with future trends within international business in terms of the values that may enter the business environment in the future. In this sense, the use of current managers does not entirely represent the future perspective as well as business students may. Second, by using a convenience sample of relatively homogeneous subjects as opposed to a more heterogeneous sample of managers who may differ in a variety of ways despite having similar titles, the statistical error term is reduced, thus increasing the probability of finding true differences in the comparisons (Lynch, 1982). Finally, by not using a random sample of managers, the findings are enhanced in that external validity is enlarged (Calder, Phillips, and Tybout, 1981, 1982) since some unidentified background factors may be excluded that might otherwise change the desired effects. The results were analyzed using SAS software and inferences were made based on standard statistical procedures.

The research questionnaire contained 40 statements, 10 of which were designed to measure each of four Factors on a Likert-type scale. The statements were arranged so that the first statement of each Factor was statement one through four in order on the questionnaire. The second statement of each Factor was statement five through eight on the questionnaire, and so on until all 40 statements had been placed on the questionnaire.

The subjects were instructed to indicate their immediate, honest impressions anonymously using a scale of 1 to 6:

1 = strongly agree
2 = agree
3 = slightly agree
4 = slightly disagree
5 = disagree
6 = strongly disagree.

Concern about social desirability bias, which Dillman (1978) notes is the result of answering sensitive questions according to group beliefs rather than true individual beliefs, resulted in subjects not being told the nature of the variables being tested. They were only told that the questionnaire contained value statements for business students. They were not permitted to discuss their responses prior to the completion of the research questionnaire. Both of these measures were intended to help reduce any potential social desirability bias in the responses, as was the self-administration of the research instrument noted above.

The responses for each statement were totaled and divided by the number of responses for that statement to obtain a statement mean. A "no-response" was entered as a zero and the divisor reduced by one for each no-response. In addition, three statements of Factor II–eight, nine, and ten–were designed to be reverse scored. Mean Factor responses were determined by summing the ten statement means for each Factor and dividing by ten. The t-test was used as a conservative measure of significance at a .95 confidence level even though more than 30 elements were available for analysis.

The study design does have several limitations. Despite back-translation of the test instrument, there is still a possibility that the words conveying such a complex construct as "value" have slightly different culturally-derived connotations in German than they do in English (or vice-versa). Further, the test instrument has not been proved reliable across cultures and it was designed using a broader population than undergraduate business students. Although we have not been able to measure these possible impacts within our study design, it does not appear that our results are significantly flawed.

RESULTS

Factor I results (Table 15.4) suggest that West Germans (WG) show a lesser acceptance of authority than the U.S. with a mean factor response of 4.805 (WG) versus 3.164 (US). All ten statements show a significant difference at a .95 level of significance using t-tests. Therefore, H_1 is rejected.

Factor II (Table 15.5) is less conclusive than Factor I with mean factor responses of 3.432 (WG) and 3.507 (US). The results do not indicate a clear tendency toward need-determined expression versus value-determined restraint. Of five statements that showed significance at the .95 level, three had higher agreement by US business students and two had higher agreement by the WG business students. Therefore, H_2 is rejected, which empirically suggests that there is still no basis to predict direction for this factor.

Factor III results (Table 15.6) show a greater feel for equalitarianism among WG business students with a mean factor response of 2.759 (WG) versus 3.441 (US). Eight of the ten statements were significant at the .95 level. Therefore, H_3 is rejected.

Factor IV results (Table 15.7) show that WG business students value individualism more than US business students with mean factor responses of 3.092 (WG) versus 3.552 (US). Nine of the ten statements for this Factor were significant at the .95 level. Therefore, H_4 is rejected.

DISCUSSION

From the analysis of these four factors one could conclude that future West German managers may be more individualistic, more equalitarian, and more independent of authoritative power sources

TABLE 15.4. FACTOR I–Agreement with Value Statements in Favor of Acceptance of Authority

	$\bar{X}_{WG}$	$\bar{X}_{US}$	Prob > 1 + 1 WG	US	$H_0: \mu_I = \mu_2$
1) Obedience and respect for authority are the most important virtues children should learn.	4.8049	2.6093	.0001	.0001	P < .001
2) There is hardly anything lower than a person who does not feel a great love, gratitude, and respect for his parents.	4.2321	3.3964	.0001	.0001	P < .001
3) What young people need most is strict discipline, rugged determination, and the will to work and fight for family and country.	5.3284	3.1075	.0001	.0001	P < .001
4) You have to respect authority and when you stop respecting authority, your situation isn't worth much.	4.5935	3.2151	.0001	.0001	P < .001
5) Patriotism and loyalty are the first and the most important requirements of a good citizen.	4.9015	2.6475	.0001	.0001	P < .001
6) Younger people sometimes have rebellious ideas, but as they grow up they ought to get over them and settle down.	4.1017	3.1183	.0001	.0292	P < .001
7) A child should not be allowed to talk back to his parents, because he will lose respect for them.	5.3394	3.3728	.0001	.0001	P < .001
8) The facts on crime and sexual immorality show that we will have to crack down harder on people if we are going to save our moral standards.	5.1481	3.0396	.0001	.0001	P < .001
9) Disobeying an order is one thing that you cannot excuse. If one can get away with disobedience, why can't everybody.	5.0369	3.6123	.0001	.0001	P < .001
10) A well-raised child is one who doesn't have to be told twice to do something.	4.5605	3.5071	.0001	.0001	P < .001
FACTOR I	4.8054	3.1642	.0001	.0001	P < .001

Key: WG = West German   1 - 3.50 = Favor acceptance of authority
          US = United States   3.51 - 6.0 = Do not favor acceptance of authority

TABLE 15.5. FACTOR II–Agreement with Value Statements in Favor of Need-determined Expression versus Value-determined Restraint

	$\bar{X}_{WG}$	$\bar{X}_{US}$	Prob > 1 + 1		$H_o: \mu_1 = \mu_2$
			WG	US	
1) Since there are no values which can be eternal, the only real values are those which meet the needs of a given moment.	4.1749	4.4928	.0001	.0001	P < .001
2) Nothing is static, nothing is everlasting, at any moment one must be ready to meet the change in environment by a necessary change in one's moral views.	2.9181	4.0791	.4027	.6106	P > .5
3) Let us eat, drink, and be merry, for tomorrow we die.	4.1716	3.8889	.0001	.0001	P < .001
4) The solution to almost any human problem should be based on the situation at the time, not on some general moral rules.	3.3916	3.6187	.0001	.0001	P < .001
5) Life is something to be enjoyed to the fullest, seriously enjoyed with relish and enthusiasm.	2.4173	1.7214	.001	.001	P < .001
6) Life is more a festival than a workshop or a school for moral discipline.	3.6165	3.6304	.0001	.0001	P < .001
7) The past is no more, the future may never be, the present is all that we can be certain of.	3.3867	3.5791	.001	.001	P < .001
8) Not to attain happiness, but to be worthy of it, is the purpose of our existence. (Reverse scored)	3.1754	3.6738	2.3267	9.076	.005 < P < .01
9) No time is better spent than that devoted to thinking about the ultimate purpose of our existence. (Reverse scored)	2.9677	3.8889	.4412	1.212	.2 < P < .5
10) In love tenderness is more important than passion. (Reverse scored)	4.0943	2.5629	.0001	.0001	P < .001
FACTOR II	3.4323	3.5066			.05 < P < .10

Key: WG = West German   1 - 3.50 = more need-determined
      US = United States   3.51 - 6.0 = more value-determined

TABLE 15.6. FACTOR III–Agreement with Value Statements Favoring Equalitarianism

	$\bar{X}_{WG}$	$\bar{X}_{US}$	Prob > 1 + 1 WG	Prob > 1 + 1 US	$H_0: \mu_1 = \mu_2$
1) Everyone should have an equal chance and an equal say.	1.6527	2.039	.001	.0001	P < .001
2) There should be equality for everyone because we are all human beings.	1.8617	2.1577	.001	.001	P < .001
3) A group of equals will work a lot better than a group with a rigid hierarchy.	2.9975	3.2607	.001	.001	P < .001
4) Each one should get what he needs–the things we have belong to all of us.	3.8936	3.8993	.001	.001	P < .001
5) No matter what the circumstances, one should never arbitrarily tell people what they have to do.	2.7896	3.9534	.001	.001	P < .001
6) It is the duty of every good citizen to correct anti-minority remarks made in his presence.	3.2519	3.7662	.001	.001	P < .001
7) Poverty could be almost entirely done away with if we made certain basic changes in our social and economic system.	3.4335	4.0932	.001	.001	P < .001
8) There has been too much talk and not enough real action in doing away with racial discrimination.	1.8988	3.3799	.001	.001	P < .001
9) In any group it is more important to keep a friendly atmosphere than to be efficient.	3.2469	3.9029	.001	.001	P < .001
10) In a small group there should be no real leaders because everyone should have an equal say.	2.5531	3.9283	.001	.001	P < .001
FACTOR III	2.7589	3.4406			P < .001

Key: WG = West German   1 - 3.50 = Favors equalitarianism
       US = United States   3.51 - 6.0 = Does not favor equalitarianism

than their U.S. counterparts. This suggests West German competitors who value "doing their own thing," who are freed from obeying the rules of the game in lockstep fashion, persons more likely to approach the business world in an egoistic, rather than nationalistic, manner. It also suggests a new freedom to compete in innovative

TABLE 15.7. FACTOR IV–Agreement with Value Statements Favoring Individualism

	$\overline{X}_{WG}$	$\overline{X}_{US}$	Prob > 1 + 1 WG	US	$H_o: \mu_1 = \mu_2$
1) To be superior, a man must stand alone.	2.6832	4.5786	.001	.001	P < .001
2) In life an individual should for the most part "go it alone," assuring himself of privacy, having much time to himself, attempting to control his own life.	2.1721	4.0393	.001	.001	P < .001
3) It is the man who stands alone who excites our admiration.	3.6675	3.4676	.001	.001	P < .001
4) The rich internal world of ideals, of sensitive feelings, of self-knowledge, is man's true home.	3.5941	2.6512	.001	.001	P < .001
5) One must avoid dependence upon persons or things, the center of life should be found within oneself.	2.7351	3.5663	.001	.001	P < .001
6) The most rewarding object of study any man can find is his own inner life.	3.1216	2.9532	.0001	.0001	.05 < P < .10
7) To be a man, one must not be a conformist.	4.1159	3.8957	.001	.001	P < .001
8) Contemplation is the highest form of human activity.	2.7432	3.5576	.001	.001	P < .001
9) The individualist is the man who is most likely to discover the best road to a new future.	3.5633	3.1143	.001	.001	P < .001
10) A man can learn better by striking out boldly on his own than he can by following the advice of others.	2.5262	3.6942	.001	.001	P < .001
FACTOR IV	3.0922	3.5521			P < .001

Key: WG = West German   1 - 3.50 = Favors individualism
     US = United States   3.51 - 6.0 = Does not favor individualism

ways on the world stage, at a time when an economic merger of East and West Germany will probably leave future West German managers in charge of many East German (i.e., German Democratic Republic) corporate activities (Friedrich, 1990; Templeman, 1990a,b; Tully, 1990c) and perhaps as much as 22% of Western Europe's economy (Javetski, 1990).

This new critical mass may suggest that non-German political or business forces may not be able to impose their will on these future West German managers (Javetski, 1990). This new independence may imply that West German managers may do what is best for their firm or their country regardless of potential harm to the larger world or European Community; the potential coalignment of both personal egoistic and national interests suggests a formidable business competitor.

This increased independence of future West German managers from authoritative power sources when compared to future U.S. managers appears to extend to the military as well. Recently, West German air force pilots refused to execute simulated nuclear bomb attacks, in effect committing mutiny (Mid-Atlantic Research Associates, 1990). Since retiring military officers often enter senior business and political positions, this independence and its potent effects may well enter the business arena through this route as well.

A sociological explanation of this new independence is that it may actually be a rational response (Babbie, 1973) to a long-term trend of improved living standards, more time off, and years of deferring or delaying some needs while rebuilding a nation shattered by World War II (Rademaekers, 1990). As West Germans seek to protect their gains, there would seem to be fewer reasons to give up certain freedoms in order to obtain incrementally less valuable benefits. Because of historical evidence and our findings, we would expect future West German managers to be very protective of market share and similar gains for their businesses, but to do so in innovative ways, less respectful of traditional business practices and less respectful of business superiors. This suggests a more open decision-making style characterized by freer discussions with senior managers and less regimented thinking.

Future West German managers who appear to place more value on their individualism than their U.S. counterparts may also be more likely to have trouble conforming to different cultures, even different organizational cultures. This may become a problem, especially when the European community is seeing large amounts of cross-border investments (Tully, 1990a) and more global managers (Tully, 1990b). However, this finding may be negated by the fact that these future West German managers appear more equalitarian than their U.S. counterparts. Because the growth of executive recruitment in West Germany for cross-border managers is increasing (executive recruitment was illegal in West Germany until the late 1970s) (Tully, 1990b), this increase in equalitarianism could make future West German managers more attractive to international businesses. To the degree that cross-border experience is a prerequisite to future personal business success, this trait may increase opportunities for future West German managers.

Although more individualistic, recent anecdotal evidence suggests that German managers may still have a strong sense of nationalism. For example, German nationalism may have been a factor in a cooperative effort by Deutsche Bank, the Nixdorf family, and Siemens to keep the $3.3 billion Nixdorf Computer firm in West German hands and away from both the French and Italians (Reichlin, 1990). This purchase should allow the West German computer firm to survive an expected shakeout among European computer manufacturers, thus shifting potential losses to companies outside of West Germany (Reichlin, 1990). Further, Jackson (1990) reports that West German managers are signing exclusive contracts to supply merchandise to East German managers, which effectively forecloses a portion of that growing market to other international suppliers. While blocking non-German competitors appears rational from a business perspective and ethical from an egoist moral framework, there appears to have been no utilitarian consideration in these examples of "the greatest good for the greatest number" in any international sense, which suggests an aggressively competitive approach to international business.

CONCLUSIONS

This study examined differences in and similarities between certain values held by West German and United States business students who have a high propensity to become managers, and then considered what differences those values might make in the business environment. It found that there may be a trend toward a future West German management culture that may be less accepting of authority, more tolerant of other cultures, and more individualistic than their U.S. counterpart.

For authoritarianism, our findings suggest that recent anecdotal evidence concerning West German managers is correct. Future West German managers appear to be less accepting of authority than their U.S. counterparts.

Concerning the need-determined expression versus value-determined restraint factor, the empirical findings suggest no significant differences between the samples. The means indicate that both groups tend to be need-determined. This may imply that both groups are not likely to wait for outcomes, results, or long-term payoffs. However, this observation is tentative at best, because managers have many more than the four value factors studied here embedded in their make-up.

The analysis of the equalitarian factor suggests that contrary to historical and anecdotal evidence, empirically, future West German managers may be more sensitive to other people and cultures. However, this result does not conclusively prove that nationalism as a value trait does not also enter into the values equation.

Finally, our research shows that contrary to historical data, future West German managers are becoming more individualistic relative to future U.S. managers. Recent anecdotal evidence has also shown support for this finding.

Based on this work, we expect future West German managers to compete in innovative ways essentially independent of non-German political or business forces. We expect these future managers to be very protective of market share and similar gains; they will be formidable competitors worthy of international respect. And, we expect to see more West German managers of non-German firms, especially in the European arena.

Given the nature of this study, several areas seem appropriate for further research. A longitudinal study based on these same measures could give researchers a more reliable indicator of strength and direction for the changes that were found. Research on instrument validation across cultures is another area that needs attention.

Macro studies about how value trends are moving in specific West German industries and their differential impact across West German, European, and U.S. markets should also be considered. On a more micro level, an examination of purchasing and sales personnel–the two ends of the production stream where boundary-spanning personnel are concentrated–as well as financial officers, could yield valuable trend information about these interfaces with other businesses, nations, and customers.

In conclusion, we do not attach any value judgment to these trends. Nor do we believe that these are the only values that are significant for managers. What this research does show is that values are changing and that both managers and researchers need to understand their impact. From that perspective, this study can be used as a benchmark for managers and researchers on both continents.

REFERENCES

Babbie, Earl R. (1973), *Survey Research Methods*, 27, Belmont, CA: Wadsworth Publishing Company, Inc.

Bales, Robert F. and Arthur S. Couch (1969), "The Value Profile: A Factor Analytic Study of Value Statements," *Sociological Inquiry*, 39 (Winter), 3-17.

Becker, Helmut and David J. Fritzsche (1987), "A Comparison of the Ethical Behavior of American, French, and German Managers," *Columbia Journal of World Business*, Winter, 87-95.

Calder, Bobby J., Lynn W. Phillips, and Alice M. Tybout (1981), "Designing Research for Application," *Journal of Consumer Research*, 8 (September), 197-207.

Calder, Bobby J., Lynn W. Phillips, and Alice M. Tybout (1982), "The Concept of External Validity," *Journal of Consumer Research*, 9 (December), 240-244.

Chua-Eoan, Howard G. (1990), "Ambivalence amid Plenty," *Time*, July 9, 74-75.

Condran, J. (1979), "Change in White Attitudes Towards Blacks: 1963-1977," *Public Opinion Quarterly*, 48 (Winter), 463-464.

DeGeorge, Richard T. (1990), *Business Ethics*, 3rd ed., 10-11, NY: Macmillan Publishing Company.

Dillman, Don A. (1978), *Mail and Telephone Surveys: The Total Design Method*, 62-63, NY: John Wiley & Sons, Inc.

Epstein, Edwin M. (1987), "The Corporate Social Policy Process: Beyond Business Ethics, Corporate Social Responsibility, and Corporate Social Responsiveness," *California Management Review*, 29 (Spring), 99-114.

Friedrich, Otto (1990), "Toward Unity," *Time*, July 9, 66-71.

Gecas, Viktor (1981), "Contexts of Socialization," in *Social Psychology: Sociological Perspectives*, edited by Morris Rosenberg and Ralph H. Turner, 165-199, NY: Basic Books, Inc.

Glasgall, William (1987), "What Will It Take to Budge Germany?" *Business Week*, November 23, 48-52.

Guth, William D. and Renato Tagiuri (1965), "Personal Values and Corporate Strategy," *Harvard Business Review*, 43 (September-October), 123-132.

Ingersoll, Robert (1987), "Can Volkswagen Pull Itself Out of the Mud?" *Business Week*, June 22, 60-61.

Jackson, James O. (1990), "Speeding Over the Bumps," *Time*, July 30, 30-31.

Jacobson, G. (1974), "Examination of Change in Authoritarianism Values, and Cognitive Complexity with Business Implications," *Dissertations Abstract International*, 34 (May), 6808.

Javetski, Bill (1990), "One Germany," *Business Week*, April 2, 46-49.

Kahle, Lynn R., Basil Poulos, and Ajay Sukhdial (1988), "Changes in Social Values in the United States During the Past Decade," *Journal of Advertising Research*, 28 (February-March), 35-41.

Kaplan, Howard B. (1986), *Social Psycholology of Self-Referent Behavior*, 61-77, NY: Plenum Press.

Kapstein, Jonathan (1987), "NATO Pushes the 'Eject' Button on U.S. Contractors," *Business Week*, February 2, 50.

Labich, Kenneth (1988), "Big Changes at Big Brown," *Fortune*, January 18, 56-64.

Lynch, John G., Jr. (1982), "On the External Validity of Experiments in Consumer Research," *Journal of Consumer Research*, 9 (December), 225-239.

Machan, Tibor (1983), "Individualism and the Political Authority," *The Monist*, 66 (October), 509, 512, 514.

Maremont, Mark (1987), "Toys 'R' Us Goes Overseas–and Finds that Toys 'R' Them, too," *Business Week*, January 26, 71-72.

McMurry, Robert N. (1963), "Conflicts in Human Values," *Harvard Business Review*, 41 (May-June), 130-145.

Merritt, A. and R. Merritt (eds.) (1970), *Public Opinion in Occupied Germany, 1945-1949*, Urbana, IL: University of Illinois Press, Foreword.

Meyer, Michael (1990), "The Myth of German Unity," *Newsweek*, July 9, 37.

Mid-Atlantic Research Associates (1990), "West German Pilots Undertake 'Mutiny,' " *Insight*, July 9, 38.

Miller, Frederic A. (1987), "Why a Stubborn Germany Won't Fire Up Its Economy, *Business Week*, April 27, 48-49.

Peterson, Thane (1988), "The Americans are Hitting High-Tech Homers in Europe, *Business Week*, April 11, 72.

Pluenneke, John E. (1987a), "Weakened Labor Is Still Talking Tough," *Business Week*, January 12, 60.

Pluenneke, John E. (1987b), "The Strange Appeal of Helmut Kohl," *Business Week*, January 26, 48-49.

Pluenneke, John E. (1987c), "Bertelsmann's U.S. Invasion May Be Just Beginning," *Business Week*, August 10, 72-73.

Pluenneke, John E. (1987d), "A Currency Scandal Adds to VW's Woes," *Business Week*, March 23, 54-56.

Prager, Karsten (1990), "Down Memory Lane," *Time*, July 9, 72-73.

Rademaekers, William (1990), "The Oh So Good Life," *Time*, July 9, 80-82.

Reber, Arthur S. (1985), *Dictionary of Psychology*, 70, NY: Viking Publications.

Reichlin, Igor (1990), "Why Siemens Wrote Such a Big Check," *Business Week*, January 22, 42.

Robinson, John P. and Philip R. Shaver (1985), *Measures of Social Psychological Attitudes*, 2nd ed., 528, Survey Research Institute, Institute for Social Research, University of Michigan, Ann Arbor, Michigan.

Rokeach, Milton J. (1968a), "A Theory of Organization and Change Within Value-Attitude Systems," *Journal of Social Issues*, 24 (January), 13-33.

Rokeach, Milton J. (1968b), "The Role of Values in Public Opinion Research," *Public Opinion Quarterly*, 32 (Winter), 547-559.

Schares, Gail (1988a), "Are Labor Leaders Asking for the Moon?" *Business Week*, September 19, 50.

Schares, Gail (1988b), "Can Siemens Buy Itself High Times in High Tech?" *Business Week*, February 22, 49.

Seeman, Melvin (1981), "Intergroup Relations," in *Social Psychology: Sociological Perspectives*, edited by, Morris Rosenberg and Ralph H. Turner, 378-410, NY: Basic Books, Inc.

Sethi, S. Prakash (1987), "A Conceptual Framework for Environmental Analysis of Social Issues and Evaluation of Business Response Patterns," in *Business and Society: Dimensions of Conflict and Cooperation*, edited by S. Prakash Sethi and Cecilia M. Falbe, 39-52, Lexington, MA: D.C. Heath and Company.

Simpson, Jeffrey A. (1987), Assistant Professor of Psychology, Texas A&M University, personal communication, February 16.

Singer, Eleanor (1981), "Reference Groups and Social Evaluations," in *Social Psychology: Sociological Perspectives*, edited by Morris Rosenberg and Ralph H. Turner, 66-93, NY: Basic Books, Inc.

Templeman, John (1987), "Europe Can't Move Any Faster than Germany," *Business Week*, April 6, 50-51.

Templeman, John (1988a), "What's Bugging Volkswagen," *Business Week*, June 13, 45.

Templeman, John (1988b), "Why Bonn Just Can't Let Go," *Business Week*, April 4, 48.

Templeman, John (1990a), "Going for Broke: The Daring Plan to Rebuild the East," *Business Week*, April 2, 50-52, 54.

Templeman, John (1990b), "German Unity: A Threat to Europe 1992?" *Business Week*, January 22, 40-41.

Tully, Shawn (1989), "The Coming Boom in Europe," *Fortune*, April 10, 108-114.

Tully, Shawn (1990a), "What Eastern Europe Offers," *Fortune*, March 12, 52-55.

Tully, Shawn (1990b), "The Hunt for the Global Manager," *Fortune*, May 21, 140-144.

Tully, Shawn (1990c), "Doing Business in One Germany," *Fortune*, July 2, 80-83.

U.S. Department of Education, National Center for Education Statistics (1989), "Survey of Graduates, 1987," in *Outcomes of Education*, 373.

Velasquez, Manuel G. (1988), *Business Ethics*, 2nd ed., 105, Englewood Cliffs, NJ: Prentice Hall.

Vinson, Donald E. and J. Michael Munson (1976), "Personal Values: An Approach to Market Segmentation," in *Marketing: 1776-1976 and Beyond*, edited by Kenneth L. Bernhardt, 313-317, Chicago, IL: American Marketing Association.

Waterman, Alan S. (1984), *The Psychology of Individualism*, 29-35, NY: Praeger Press.

Wolman, Benjamin (ed.) (1973), *Dictionary of Behavioral Sciences*, 125, NY: Van Nostrand Reinhold.

Index